Curriculum Development in Language Teaching

CAMBRIDGE LANGUAGE EDUCATION
Series Editor: Jack C. Richards

This series draws on the best available research, theory, and educational practice to help clarify issues and resolve problems in language teaching, language teacher education, and related areas. Books in the series focus on a wide range of issues and are written in a style that is accessible to classroom teachers, teachers-in-training, and teacher educators.

In this series:

Curriculum Development in Language Teaching

Jack C. Richards

Southeast Asian Ministers of Education Organization

Regional Language Centre, Singapore

CAMBRIDGE
UNIVERSITY PRESS

CAMBRIDGE
UNIVERSITY PRESS

32 Avenue of the Americas, New York, NY 10013–2473, USA

Cambridge University Press is part of the University of Cambridge.

It furthers the University's mission by disseminating knowledge in the pursuit of education, learning and research at the highest international levels of excellence.

www.cambridge.org
Information on this title: www.cambridge.org/9780521804912

First published 2001
18th printing 2014

Printed in the United States of America

A catalog record for this book is available from the British Library.

Library of Congress Cataloging in Publication data
Richards, Jack C.
Curriculum development in language teaching / Jack C. Richards.
p. cm.
ISBN 978-0-521-80491-2
I. Language and languages—Study and teaching. 2. Curriculum planning. I. Title.
P53.295.R53 2001
418'.0071—dc21

ISBN 978-0-521-80060-0 hardback
ISBN 978-0-521-80491-2 paperback

Credits appear on page xiv.

Contents

Series editor's preface

The activities of language teaching have often been viewed from a very narrow perspective. This is evident from the fascination with teaching methods that has characterized the history of language teaching until relatively recently. Methods have often been regarded as the most important factor in determining the success of a language program, and advances in language teaching have sometimes been seen as being dependent on the adoption of the latest method. A perspective often missing from the method-based view of teaching is that of how methods interact with other factors in the teaching-learning process. Who are the learners and the teachers? What expectations do they have for the program? What learning and teaching styles do they bring to the program? For what purposes is the language needed? What goals does the program have, and how are these goals expressed? In what settings will teaching take place, and what organizational structure is in place to support and maintain good teaching? What resources will be used, and what are their roles? What is the role of textbooks and other materials? What measures will be used to determine the success of the program? Choice of teaching method cannot therefore be made unless a great deal is known about the context for the language program and the interactions between the different elements involved. It is this perspective that characterizes a curriculum-based approach to language teaching.

This book presents an approach to the teaching-learning process that sees successful language as being dependent upon the activities of curriculum development, that is, the use of a variety of planning and implementation processes involved in developing or renewing a language program. These processes include determining learners' needs, analysis of the context for the program and consideration of the impact of contextual factors, the planning of learning outcomes, the organization of a course or set of teaching materials, the selection and preparation of teaching materials, provision for and maintenance of effective teaching, and evaluation of the program. These elements constitute a set of interrelated elements, and their nature and function form the focus of this book. The book seeks to survey key issues and practices within language curriculum development in order to provide the basis for more effective planning and decision making in language program development, implementation, and review. I hope that teachers and other language teaching professionals will find that this book helps them better understand and use the skills involved in developing effective language programs.

Jack C. Richards

Preface

Like many language teaching professionals, I entered the field of language teaching as a classroom teacher, anticipating that as I accumulated experience and professional knowledge, I would become a better teacher. As many others have discovered, however, I soon came to realize that being an effective teacher meant much more than becoming a more skillful and knowledgeable classroom practitioner. It meant learning how to develop and adapt materials, to plan and evaluate courses, to adapt teaching to students' needs, and to function within an institutional setting. It became clear that effective teaching was dependent on understanding the context for teaching, the needs of teachers and learners, the careful planning of courses and materials, as well as the monitoring of teaching and learning. In short, it was necessary to try to understand teaching as a part of an interrelated set of factors and processes that are often referred to as curriculum development.

This book seeks to describe and examine the processes of curriculum development in language teaching in order to acquaint language teachers and teachers-in-training with fundamental issues and practices in language curriculum development. Curriculum development is an essentially practical activity since it seeks to improve the quality of language teaching through the use of systematic planning, development, and review practices in all aspects of a language program. The book tries to provide as many examples as possible of how some of the practical problems in language program development have been addressed by practitioners in many parts of the world. At the same time, the practices employed in developing and renewing language programs themselves reflect ongoing theories and developments in language teaching pedagogy, second language acquisition theory, educational theory, and related fields; hence the book also seeks to highlight important theoretical issues that can have a significant impact on language curriculum practices.

The book is planned for use in in-service courses and workshops as well as to provide a sourcebook for teachers, program administrators, and other language teaching professionals. The book as a whole examines the key processes in curriculum development, including needs analysis, planning goals and outcomes, course planning, teaching, materials development, and evaluation. In the earlier chapters, I have provided a historical perspective on how the field of curriculum development in language teaching has evolved, since I believe it is important for language teaching professionals to have some sense of the history of the issues that have shaped the development of language teaching. The subsequent chapters seek to survey key issues related to curriculum development issues and processes, illustrating different points of view and providing detailed practical examples by way of illustration. Discussion questions at the end of each chapter provide opportunities for further reflection and application of some of the issues discussed.

The book reflects my own 30 years of experience as a teacher, teacher educator, program director, and materials writer in many different parts of the world. Any expertise I can claim to have in curriculum development is a result of learning through the practical experience of developing curriculum and materials and directing language programs. My initial explorations in language curriculum development took me from New Zealand, where I received my initial teacher training, to Quebec, where I completed my doctoral research in syllabus design with W. F. Mackey in the 1970s. Subsequently, I have spent periods of time in universities and teacher training centers in Indonesia, Singapore, Hong Kong, Hawaii, and New Zealand, working in all aspects of language teaching from curriculum and materials development, to teaching, to program administration. I have also served as a consultant to a number of curriculum projects and institutions in different parts of the world. A recent 10-year annual consultancy with the Ministry of Education of the Sultanate of Oman also provided an invaluable opportunity to provide input to curriculum and materials development projects at a national level. At the same time, experience as a writer of commercial language teaching materials with a worldwide market has provided opportunities to work regularly with teachers and teacher trainers in more than twenty countries, an experience that has given additional perspectives on problems involved in developing and using teaching materials. In recent years I have been in the pleasant position of being able to divide my time between classroom teaching, teacher training, and writing, from the congenial environment provided by the Regional Language Center in Singapore, whose unique library resources and materials collection proved invaluable during the preparation of this book.

Earlier versions of this book have been used in postgraduate and in-service courses at the University of Arizona in the United States; the University of Auckland, New Zealand; the National Institute of Education, Singapore; the Regional Language Center, Singapore; and the SEAMEO Regional

Training Center, Ho Chi Minh City, Vietnam. I am grateful for the comments and suggestions received from teachers and students at these institutions. I am also grateful for detailed comments on the manuscript from Dr. Jun Liu, University of Arizona, Dr. Ted Rodgers, University of Hawaii, Geoffrey Crewes, CEO of the Indonesian-Australian Language Foundation, Jakarta, Indonesia, and several anonymous reviewers.

Jack C. Richards

Credits

Page 17: Appendix 1 Entries from *A General Service List of English Words*. Reproduced by permission of the University of London, Institute of Education. **Pages 20 and 21:** Appendix 3 Part of an early English grammatical syllabus. Reproduced by permission of Oxford University Press. From *Teaching Structural Words and Sentence Patterns* by A. S. Hornby © Oxford University Press 1959. **Pages 45 and 46:** Appendix 1 Example of scientific writing. Reprinted by permission of Pearson Education Limited. **Pages 141 and 142:** Appendix 3 ESOL standards for grades 4–8. From TESOL. (1997). *ESL Standards for Pre-K–12 Students* (p. 71). Alexandria, VA: Author. Copyright © 1997 by Teachers of English to Speakers of Other Languages, Inc. Reprinted with permission. **Pages 174 and 175:** Appendix 2 Description of performance levels; writing. Reprinted from *ESP Journal*, vol. 11, B. Paltridge, EAP placement testing: An integrated approach, pages 243–268, copyright 1992, with permission from Elsevier Science. **Pages 187 to 194:** A unit from *Passages 1*. Page 187 (*top row, left to right*) © David Hanover/Tony Stone Images; © Pete Saloutos/The Stock Market; © Mikki Ansin/Liaison Agency; (*bottom row, left to right*) © Mike Malyszko/FGP International; © Robert E. Daemmrich/Tony Stone Images; © Christophe Lepetit/Liaison Agency. Page 188 © Mug Shots/The Stock Market. Page 189 (*top*) © Ariel Skelley/The Stock Market; (*bottom*) © David Young Wolff/Tony Stone Images. Source (*top*): From *Eccentrics* by David Weeks and Jamie James, Copyright © 1995 by David Weeks. Reprinted by permission of Villard Books, a Division of Random House Inc. Page 191: (*bottom left*) Photo courtesy of 3M Company; Post-it is a registered trademark of 3M; (*all others*) © Richard Bachmann. Page 192: © Rick Rusing/Leo de Wys. Page 194: (*left to right*) Courtesy of Sony Electronics Inc. **Pages 231 to 232:** Appendix 3 Assessment criteria for teaching practice. Reproduced by permission of the University of Cambridge Local Examinations Syndicate.

1 The origins of language curriculum development

The focus of this book is the processes involved in developing, implementing, and evaluating language programs. By a language program I refer to any organized course of language instruction. Second and foreign language teaching is one of the world's largest educational enterprises and millions of children and adults worldwide devote large amounts of time and effort to the task of mastering a new language. Teachers too invest a great deal of their energies into planning language courses, preparing teaching materials, and teaching their classes. What educational principles are these activities based on? What values do these principles reflect? Whose interests do they serve? And can our practices be improved through reviewing the principles we operate from and critically examining the practices that result from them? The goal of this book is to provide some of the tools for this process of review and reflection through surveying approaches to language curriculum development and examining ways of addressing the issues that arise in developing and evaluating language programs and language teaching materials. Language curriculum development deals with the following questions, which provide the framework for this book:

- What procedures can be used to determine the content of a language program?
- What are learners' needs?
- How can learners' needs be determined?
- What contextual factors need to be considered in planning a language program?
- What is the nature of aims and objectives in teaching and how can these be developed?
- What factors are involved in planning the syllabus and the units of organization in a course?
- How can good teaching be provided in a program?
- What issues are involved in selecting, adapting, and designing instructional materials?
- How can one measure the effectiveness of a language program?

1

Language curriculum development is an aspect of a broader field of educational activity known as curriculum development or curriculum studies. Curriculum development focuses on determining what knowledge, skills, and values students learn in schools, what experiences should be provided to bring about intended learning outcomes, and how teaching and learning in schools or educational systems can be planned, measured, and evaluated. Language curriculum development refers to the field of applied linguistics that addresses these issues. It describes an interrelated set of processes that focuses on designing, revising, implementing, and evaluating language programs.

Historical background

The history of curriculum development in language teaching starts with the notion of syllabus design. Syllabus design is one aspect of curriculum development but is not identical with it. A syllabus is a specification of the content of a course of instruction and lists what will be taught and tested. Thus the syllabus for a speaking course might specify the kinds of oral skills that will be taught and practiced during the course, the functions, topics, or other aspects of conversation that will be taught, and the order in which they will appear in the course. Syllabus design is the process of developing a syllabus. Current approaches to syllabus design will be discussed in Chapter 6. Curriculum development is a more comprehensive process than syllabus design. It includes the processes that are used to determine the needs of a group of learners, to develop aims or objectives for a program to address those needs, to determine an appropriate syllabus, course structure, teaching methods, and materials, and to carry out an evaluation of the language program that results from these processes. Curriculum development in language teaching as we know it today really began in the 1960s, though issues of syllabus design emerged as a major factor in language teaching much earlier. In this chapter we will look at the approaches to syllabus design that emerged in the first part of the twentieth century and that laid the foundations for more broadly based curriculum approaches that are used in language teaching today.

If we look back at the history of language teaching throughout the twentieth century, much of the impetus for changes in approaches to language teaching came about from changes in teaching methods. The method concept in teaching – the notion of a systematic set of teaching practices based on a particular theory of language and language learning – is a powerful one and the quest for better methods has been a preoccupation of many teachers and applied linguists since the beginning of the twentieth century. Many methods have come and gone in the last 100 years in pursuit of the "best method," as the following chronology illustrates, with dates suggesting periods of greatest dominance:

Grammar Translation Method (1800–1900)
Direct Method (1890–1930)
Structural Method (1930–1960)
Reading Method (1920–1950)
Audiolingual Method (1950–1970)
Situational Method (1950–1970)
Communicative Approach (1970–present)

Mackey (1965, 151) commented that although there has been a preference for particular methods at different times, methods often continue in some form long after they have fallen out of favor; this observation is still true today, with grammar translation still alive and well in some parts of the world. Common to each method is the belief that the teaching practices it supports provide a more effective and theoretically sound basis for teaching than the methods that preceded it. The characteristics of many of the methods listed above have been described elsewhere and need not concern us further here (e.g., Richards and Rodgers 1986). But it is important to recognize that although methods are specifications for the processes of instruction in language teaching – that is, questions of *how* – they also make assumptions about *what* needs to be taught, that is, the content of instruction. For example, the oral-based method known as the Direct Method, which developed in opposition to the Grammar Translation Method in the late nineteenth century, prescribes not only the way a language should be taught, with an emphasis on the exclusive use of the target language, intensive question-and-answer teaching techniques, and demonstration and dramatization to communicate meanings of words; it also prescribes the vocabulary and grammar to be taught and the order in which it should be presented. The Direct Method hence assumes a particular type of syllabus. However, as new methods emerged to replace the Grammar Translation Method, the initial concern was not with syllabus questions but with approaches to teaching and methodological principles that could be used to support an oral-based target-language–driven methodology. Harold Palmer, the prominent British applied linguist who laid the foundations for the Structural Method in the 1920s, summarized the principles of language teaching methodology at that time as follows:

1. Initial preparation – orienting the students towards language learning
2. Habit-forming – establishing correct habits

3. Accuracy – avoiding inaccurate language
4. Gradation – each stage prepares the student for the next
5. Proportion – each aspect of language given emphasis
6. Concreteness – movement from the concrete to the abstract
7. Interest – arousing the student's interest at all times
8. Order of progression – hearing before speaking, and both before writing
9. Multiple line of approach – many different ways used to teach the language

(Palmer [1922] 1968, 38–39)

Once a consensus had emerged concerning the principles underlying an oral-based methodology, applied linguists then turned their attention to issues of the content and syllabus design underlying the Structural Method. Initial steps in this direction centered on approaches to determining the vocabulary and grammatical content of a language course. This led to procedures that were known as *selection* and *gradation*.

In any language program a limited amount of time is available for teaching. One of the first problems to be solved is deciding what should be selected from the total corpus of the language and incorporated in textbooks and teaching materials. This came to be known as the problem of *selection*. Mackey (1965, 161) comments: "Selection is an inherent characteristic of all methods. Since it is impossible to teach the whole of a language, all methods must in some way or other, whether intentionally or not, select the part of it they intend to teach." The field of selection in language teaching deals with the choice of appropriate units of the language for teaching purposes and with the development of techniques and procedures by which the language can be reduced to that which is most useful to the learner (Mackey 1965). All teaching, of course, demands a choice of what will be taught from the total field of the subject, and the teaching of a language at any level and under any circumstances requires the selection of certain features of the language and the intentional or unintentional exclusion of others. Two aspects of selection received primary attention in the first few decades of the twentieth century: *vocabulary selection* and *grammar selection*. Approaches to these two aspects of selection laid the foundations for syllabus design in language teaching.

Vocabulary selection

Vocabulary is one of the most obvious components of language and one of the first things applied linguists turned their attention to. What words should be taught in a second language? This depends on the objectives of the course and the amount of time available for teaching. Educated native speakers are thought to have a recognition vocabulary of some 17,000 words, but this is a much larger number of words than can be taught in a language course. Not all the words that native speakers know are necessarily useful for second language learners who have only a limited time available for learning. Should they set out to learn 500, 1,000, or 5,000 words? And if so, which ones? This is the issue of vocabulary selection in language teaching. Is selection something that should be left entirely to the intuitions of textbook writers and course planners or are there principles that can be used to produce a more objective and rational approach? Leaving selection issues to the intuitions of textbook writers can lead to very unreliable results. For example, Li and Richards (1995) examined five introductory textbooks used for teaching Cantonese (the language spoken in Hong Kong) in order to determine what words the textbook compilers considered essential for foreigners to learn and the extent to which textbook writers agreed on what constitutes the basic vocabulary of Cantonese as a second language. Each of the books was designed for a similar type of student and assumed no background knowledge of the language. Each set out to teach basic communicative skills, though the methodology of each book varied. It was found that the five books introduced a total of approximately 1,800 different words, although not all of these words occurred in each of the five texts. The distribution of words in the five books is as follows:

Words occurring in one of the texts	1,141 words	= 63.4%
Words occurring in two of the texts	313 words	= 17.4%
Words occurring in three of the texts	155 words	= 8.6%
Words occurring in four of the texts	114 words	= 6.3%
Words occurring in all of the texts	77 words	= 4.3%

(Li and Richards 1995)

From these figures it can be seen that a substantial percentage of the corpus (63.4 percent) consists of words that occurred in only one of the five texts. These words could not therefore be considered to belong to the essential vocabulary of Cantonese for second language learners and would not be worth learning. Many are probably items that are specific to the topic of a dialogue or situation that was used to practice a particular grammatical item or structure. The same could be said of words occurring in only two of the texts, which constituted a further 17.4 percent of the corpus. Only words that occurred in three or more of the texts could reasonably be described as being important vocabulary, because three or more of the textbook writers included them in their textbooks. This list contains 346 words or some 20 percent of the corpus. The conclusion that can be drawn is that a student study-ing from any of the books in this study would spend a large amount of time trying to understand and use vocabulary that is probably of little importance. It was to avoid this kind of problem with regard to English that applied lin-guists in the first few decades of the twentieth century turned to the issue of vocabulary selection.

The goals of early approaches to selection are described in the foreword to West (1953):

> A language is so complex that selection from it is always one of the first and most difficult problems of anyone who wishes to teach it systematically. It has come to be more and more generally realized that random selection is a wasteful approach, and that only a complete system capable of continuous enlargement can form a satisfactory objective for the first stage in any attempt to grasp as much as possible of the entire language as may ultimately be necessary. Roughly a language system may be considered as consisting of words entering into grammatical constructions spoken with conventional stress and intonation. To find the minimum number of words that could operate together in constructions capable of entering into the greatest variety of contexts has therefore been the chief aim of those trying to simplify English for the learner. Various criteria have been employed in choosing the words, but the dominant activity throughout the period among all those concerned with systematic teaching of English has been vocabulary selection. (Jeffery, in West 1953, v)

Some of the earliest approaches to vocabulary selection involved counting large collections of texts to determine the frequency with which words oc-curred, since it would seem obvious that words of highest frequency should be taught first. But what kinds of material should be analyzed? Obviously, a frequency count based on children's books might identify a different set of words than an analysis of words used in *Time Magazine*. The earliest fre-quency counts undertaken for language teaching were based on analysis of popular reading materials and resulted in a *word frequency list*. (This was in the days before tape recorders made possible the analysis of words used in the spoken language and before computers could be used to analyze the words used in printed sources.) Word frequency research revealed some in-teresting facts about vocabulary usage. For example, it was discovered that a small class of words (around 3,000) accounted for up to 85 percent of the words used in everyday texts but that it would take an extra 6,000 words to increase this by 1 percent. It was also found that about half the words in a text occur only once. However, recognizing 85 percent of the words in a text is not the same as understanding 85 percent of the text. One or two words per line will still not be understood, and these are often the key words in the text since they reflect the topic of the text and the new information in it. Van

Els, Bongaerts, Extra, Van Os, and Janssen-van Dieten (1984, 206) also point out:

Text comprehension is not just a function of the proportion of familiar words, but depends on a number of other factors as well, such as the subject matter of the text, the way in which the writer approaches the subject, and the extent to which the reader is already familiar with the subject.

Word frequencies are important in planning word lists for language teaching. But frequency is not necessarily the same thing as usefulness because the frequency of words depends on the types of language samples that are analyzed. The most frequent words occurring in samples of sports writing will not be the same as those occurring in fiction. In order to ensure that the frequency of occurrence of words in a corpus corresponds to their relative importance for language learners, the texts or language samples chosen as the basis for the corpus must be relevant to the needs of target learners and words must be frequent in a wide range of different language samples. This indicates a word's *range* or *dispersion* in a corpus. Words with the highest frequency and the widest range are considered to be the most useful ones for the purposes of language teaching. The following figures illustrate the difference between frequency and range in a 1 million-word corpus (cited in McCarthy 1990, 84–85). For every word, the first column gives the frequency of the word in the corpus, the second column describes the number of text types the word occurred in (e.g., sports writing, film reviews, newspaper editorials) out of a total of 15. The third column tells the number of individual text samples a word occurred in: the maximum number is 500 samples, each of which is 200 words long.

sections	49	8	36
farmers	49	8	24
worship	49	8	22
earnings	49	7	15
huge	48	11	39
address	48	11	36
conscious	47	14	34
protest	47	13	33
dependent	47	07	30
comfort	46	14	39
exciting	46	13	37

It was soon realized, however, that frequency and range were not sufficient as a basis for developing word lists, because words with high frequency and wide range in written texts are not necessarily the most teachable words in an introductory language course. Words such as *book, pen, desk, dictionary,* for example, are not frequent words yet might be needed early on in a language course. Other criteria were therefore also used in determining word lists. These included:

Teachability: In a course taught following the Direct Method or a method such as Total Physical Response, concrete vocabulary is taught early on because it can easily be illustrated through pictures or by demonstration.

Similarity: Some items may be selected because they are similar to words in the native language. For example, English and French have many cognates such as *table, page,* and *nation,* and this may justify their inclusion in a word list for French-speaking learners.

Availability: Some words may not be frequent but are readily "available" in the sense that they come quickly to mind when certain topics are thought of. For example, *classroom* calls to mind *desk, chair, teacher,* and *pupil,* and these words might therefore be worth teaching early in a course.

Coverage: Words that cover or include the meaning of other words may also be useful. For example, *seat* might be taught because it includes the meanings of *stool, bench,* and *chair.*

Defining power: Some words could be selected because they are useful in defining other words, even though they are not among the most frequent words in the language. For example, *container* might be useful because it can help define *bucket, jar,* and *carton.*

The procedures of vocabulary selection lead to the compilation of a *basic vocabulary* (or what is now called a *lexical syllabus*), that is, a target vocabulary for a language course usually grouped or graded into levels, such as the first 500 words, the second 500 words, and so on. Word frequency research has been an active area of language research since the 1920s and continues to be so because of the ease with which word frequencies and patterns of word distribution can be identified using computers. One of the most important lexical syllabuses in language teaching was Michael West's *A General Service List of English Words* (1953), which contains a list of some 2,000 "*general service* words considered suitable as the basis for learning English as a foreign language" (vii). The list also presents information on the frequencies of different meanings of each word based on a semantic frequency count (see Appendix 1). The *General Service List* incorporated the findings of a major study on vocabulary selection by the then experts in the field: The *Interim Report on Vocabulary Selection,* published in 1936 (Faucett, Palmer, West, and Thorndike 1936). One objective of this report was the simplification of teaching, as opposed to the simplification of the English language. It was based on the findings of almost all of the research done up to the 1930s and also utilized the empirical studies made by some prominent applied linguists in the decade prior to its publication. The *General Service List* was for many years a standard reference in making decisions about what words to use in course books, graded readers, and other teaching materials. Hindmarsh (1980) is another important vocabulary list and contains 4,500 words grouped into 7 levels (see Appendix 2).

Grammar selection and gradation

The need for a systematic approach to selecting grammar for teaching purposes was also a priority for applied linguists from the 1920s. The number of syntactic structures in a language is large, as is seen from the contents of any grammar book, and a number of attempts have been made to develop basic structure lists for language teaching (e.g., Fries 1952; Hornby 1954; Alexander, Allen, Close, and O'Neill 1975).

The need for grammatical selection is seen in the following examples from Wilkins (1976, 59), which are some of the structures that can be used for the speech act of "asking permission."

Can/may I use your telephone, please?
Please let me use your telephone.
Is it all right to use your telephone?
If it's all right with you, I'll use your telephone.
Am I allowed to use your telephone?
Do you mind if I use your telephone?
Do you mind me using your telephone?
Would you mind if I used your telephone?
You don't mind if I use your telephone (do you)?
I wonder if you have any objection to me using your telephone?
Would you permit me to use your telephone?
Would you be so kind as to allow me to use your telephone?
Would it be possible for me to use your telephone?
Do you think you could let me use your telephone?

How can one determine which of these structures would be useful to teach? Traditionally the grammar items included in a course were determined by the teaching method in use and there was consequently a great deal of variation in what items were taught and when.

The majority of courses started with finites of *be* and statements of identification ('This is a pen', etc.). Courses that gave prominence to reading presented the Simple Tenses (essential for narrative) early, but those that claimed to use a

'Direct-Oral Method' presented the Progressive (or Continuous) Tense first and postponed the Simple tenses. (Hornby 1959, viv)

The same is sometimes true today particularly for the less commonly taught languages. For example, in the study of the content of introductory text-books for teaching Cantonese referred to earlier (Li and Richards 1995), the grammatical structures included in the five books were analyzed. The five books were found to introduce a total of 221 different grammatical items, though they varied greatly in the number of grammatical items introduced, which no doubt influences learners' perceptions of the ease or difficulty of each book. The number of different grammatical items in each book is as follows:

Textbook A	100
Textbook B	148
Textbook C	74
Textbook D	91
Textbook E	84

However, not all of the same grammatical items occurred in each of the five texts. The distribution of grammatical items was as follows:

Total grammatical items in the five texts		221
Items occurring in one of the texts	= 92	41.6%
Items occurring in two of the texts	= 54	24.4%
Items occurring in three of the texts	= 36	16.3%
Items occurring in four of the texts	= 17	7.7%
Items occurring in five of the texts	= 22	10%

(Li and Richards 1995)

As was found with vocabulary distribution in the five course books, a substantial portion of the grammatical items occurred in only one of the texts (41.6 percent) suggesting that the authors of the texts have very different intuitions about which grammatical items learners of Cantonese need to know.

In regard to the teaching of English, from the 1930s applied linguists began applying principles of selection to the design of grammatical syllabuses. But in the case of grammar, selection is closely linked to the issue of *gradation*. Gradation is concerned with the grouping and sequencing of teaching items in a syllabus. A grammatical syllabus specifies both the set of grammatical structures to be taught and the order in which they should be taught. Palmer, a pioneer in work on vocabulary and grammar selection, explains the principle of gradation in this way ([1922], 1968, 68):

The grammatical material must be graded. Certain moods and tenses are more useful than others; let us therefore concentrate on the useful ones first. In a language possessing a number of cases, we will not learn off the whole set of prepositions, their uses and requirements, but we will select them in accordance with their degree of importance. As for lists of rules and exceptions, if we learn them at all we will learn them in strict order of necessity. In most languages we shall probably find certain fundamental laws of grammar and syntax upon which the whole structure of the language depends; if our course is to comprise the conscious study of the mechanism of a given language, then, in accordance with the principle of gradation, let us first learn these essentials and leave the details to a later stage.

But whereas those working on vocabulary selection arrived at their word lists through empirical means starting with word frequency lists, grammatical syllabuses have generally been developed from different principles based not on the frequency of occurrence of grammatical items in texts but on intuitive criteria of simplicity and learnability. The goal has been to develop a list of structures, graded into a logical progression, which would provide an accessible and gradual introduction to the grammar of English. The approach used has been analytic. The following principles have been used or suggested as a basis for developing grammatical syllabuses.

Simplicity and centrality: This recommends choosing structures that are simple and more central to the basic structure of the language than those that are complex and peripheral. By these criteria the following would occur in an introductory-level English course:

The train arrived. (Subject Verb)
She is a journalist. (Subject Verb Complement)
The children are in the bedroom. (Subject Verb Adverb)
We ate the fruit. (Subject Verb Object)
I put the book in the bag. (Subject Verb Object Adverb)

The following would be excluded by the same criteria:

Having neither money nor time, we decided buying a ticket to the opera was out of the question.
For her to speak to us like that was something we had never anticipated.

Frequency: Frequency of occurrence has also been proposed in developing grammatical syllabuses, but relatively little progress was made in this area for some time because of the difficulty of deciding on appropriate grammatical units to count and the difficulty of coding grammatical structures for analysis. It is only recently that computer corpuses have enabled the distribution of structures in real language to be examined. Not surprisingly, there are often significant differences between the lists of grammatical structures developed intuitively by applied linguists and the information revealed in analyses of corpuses of real language. McCarthy and Carter (1995), for example, report on data taken from a corpus of conversational language and identify a number of features of spoken grammar, not typically included in standard teaching syllabuses: For example:

Subject and verb ellipsis, such as "Don't know" instead of "I don't know."
Topic highlighting, such as "That house on the corner, is that where you live?"
Tails, such as the following phrases at the end of sentences: "you know," "don't they?"
Reporting verbs, such as "I was saying," "They were telling me."

Learnability: It has sometimes been argued that grammatical syllabuses should take into account the order in which grammatical items are acquired in second language learning. For example, Dulay and Burt (1973, 1974) proposed the following order of development of grammatical items, based on data elicited during interviews with second language learners at different proficiency levels:

1. nouns	11. *wh*-questions
2. verbs	12. present continuous
3. adjectives	13. directions
4. verb *be*	14. possessive adjectives
5. possessive pronouns	15. comparatives
6. personal pronouns	16. offers
7. adverbs of time	17. simple future
8. requests	18. simple past
9. simple present	19. infinitives/gerunds
10. futures	20. first conditional

Although the validity of this acquisition sequence has been questioned (e.g., Nunan 1992, 138), the idea that grammatical structures are acquired in a natural order and that this order should inform teaching has been proposed by a number of applied linguists (e.g., Pienemann 1989). However little reliable information on acquisition sequences has been produced that could be of practical benefit in planning a grammar syllabus.

In addition to decisions about which grammatical items to include in a syllabus, the sequencing or gradation of grammatical items has to be determined. The need to sequence course content in a systematic way is by no means a recent concern. The seventeenth-century scholar Comenius (summarized by Mackey 1965, 205) argued:

The beginning should be slow and accurate, rightly understood and immediately tested. Unless the first layer is firm, nothing should be built on it; for the whole structure will be developed from the foundations. All parts should be bound together so that one flows out of the other, and later units include earlier ones. Whatever precedes forms a step to what follows and the last step should be traceable to the first by a clear chain of connection.

The following approaches to gradation are possible:

Linguistic distance: Lado (1957) proposed that structures that are similar to those in the native language should be taught first. "Those elements that are similar to [the learner's] native language will be simple for him and those elements that are different will be difficult" (Lado 1957, 2). This assumption underlay the approach to language comparison known as *contrastive analysis.*

Intrinsic difficulty: This principle argues that simple structures should be taught before complex ones and is the commonest criterion used to justify the sequence of grammatical items in a syllabus.

Communicative need: Some structures will be needed early on and cannot be postponed, despite their difficulty, such as the simple past in English, since it is difficult to avoid making reference to past events for very long in a course.

Frequency: The frequency of occurrence of structures and grammatical items in the target language may also affect the order in which they appear in a syllabus, although as we noted, little information of this sort is available to syllabus planners. Frequency may also compete with other criteria. The present continuous is not one of the most frequent verb forms in English, yet it is often introduced early in a language course because it is relatively easy to demonstrate and practice in a classroom context.

In addition to these factors, in designing a course one is also faced with a choice between two approaches to the sequencing of items in the course, namely, a *linear* or a *cyclical* or *spiral* gradation. With a linear gradation, the items are introduced one at a time and practiced intensively before the next items appears. With a cyclical gradation, items are reintroduced throughout the course.

In a course in which the material is ordered cyclically the individual items are not presented and discussed exhaustively, as in strictly linear gradation, but only essential aspects of the item in question are presented initially. These items then keep recurring in the course, and every time new aspects will be introduced which will be related to and integrated with what has already been learned. (Van Els et al. 1984, 228)

Although few would doubt the advantages of cyclical over linear gradation, in practice such recycling is usually left to the teacher because cyclical gradation would often result in textbooks that were excessively long.

In the 1940s, beginners' courses in English began to appear in which principles of vocabulary and grammatical control were evident and in which grammatical structures were organized into graded sequences. The methods in use at the time placed a major emphasis on the learning of "structures." The U.S. linguist Fries outlined the major structures he thought foreign students needed to learn in his books *Teaching and Learning English as a Foreign Language* (1946) and *The Structure of English* (1952) and these formed the grammar component for courses and materials developed at the influential English Language Institute of the University of Michigan. The Michigan materials with their focus on the core grammatical structures of English soon came to influence all materials developed in the United States for teaching ESL students and became the dominant methodology in the United States for more than 20 years (Darian 1972). In Britain Hornby built on the prewar efforts of Palmer on the grading of sentence patterns and developed a comprehensive grammatical syllabus (together with a structural approach to teaching English) in his books *Guide to Patterns and Usage in English* (1954) and *The Teaching of Structural Words and Sentence Patterns* (1959). These set out the basic grammatical structures needed in English-language syllabuses and courses at different levels. The resulting pedagogical grammar of English (or variations on it) formed the basis for the grammatical syllabus of most teaching materials produced at that time (see Appendix 3). Since then other language teaching specialists have refined and further developed grammatical syllabus specifications as a basis for course design and materials development (e.g., Alexander et al. 1975).

Although both lexical and grammatical syllabuses have provided important guidelines for the development of language teaching textbooks and materials since the first such syllabuses appeared in the 1920s, it is grammar syllabuses that have been regarded as the core of a language course or program. Wilkins notes (1976, 7):

The use of a grammatical syllabus can be regarded as the conventional approach to language teaching since the majority of syllabuses and published courses have as their core an ordered list of grammatical structures. The vocabulary content is secondary in importance and certainly rarely provides the basic structure of a course. The view is widely held that until the major part of the grammatical system has been learned, the vocabulary load should be held down to what is

pedagogically necessary and to what is desirable for the sake of ensuring
adequate variety in the content of learning.

Assumptions underlying early approaches to syllabus design

We can now examine the assumptions behind the approaches to syllabus design that emerged in the first part of the twentieth century and in the process
reveal the limitations that subsequent directions in syllabus design sought
to address.

The basic units of language are vocabulary and grammar

Those working in the traditions discussed in this chapter approached the
teaching of English largely through its vocabulary and grammar. Although
the role of speaking and pronunciation were not ignored during the actual
teaching of the language, the priority in planning was vocabulary and grammar and these were seen as the main building blocks of language development. Once some system and order could be introduced into these areas
through careful syllabus planning and specification it was believed that language teaching could be put on a more rational and sound basis.

Learners everywhere have the same needs

The focus in language teaching was on "general" English, hence the title of
West's word list. It was believed that the core vocabulary of the *General
Service List* together with a grammatical syllabus of the type Hornby elab-
orated would serve as the basis for almost all language courses.

Learners' needs are identified exclusively in terms of language needs

No matter who the learners are or the circumstances of their learning, it is
assumed that mastery of English will solve their problems. The goal of English teaching is to teach them English – not to teach them how to solve their
problems through English.

The process of learning a language is largely determined by the textbook

The primary input learners received to the language learning process was
the textbook, hence the importance of the principles of selection and gra-

dation as ways of controlling the content of the textbook and facilitating language learning.

The context of teaching is English as a foreign language

Most of the early work by Palmer, West, and Hornby on the development of lexical and grammatical syllabuses was done in contexts where English was a foreign language, that is, where students studied English as a formal subject in school but had no immediate need for it outside of the classroom. The classroom and the textbook provided the primary input to the language learning process, hence the goal of syllabus developers was to simplify and rationalize this input as far as possible through the processes of selection and gradation.

Changes in the status of English around the world and in the purposes for which English was studied from the 1940s on led to the next phase in the development of language curriculum development. These changes and the approaches to language curriculum development that resulted from them are the focus of Chapter 2.

Discussion questions and activities

1. This book is about planning and implementing language courses and materials. What are three aspects of these processes that are of greatest interest to you? List these in the form of questions and compare with others.
2. What is the difference between syllabus design and curriculum development?
3. How are syllabuses developed in language programs you are familiar with?
4. What are the characteristics of a language teaching method? In what ways do methods raise issues related to curriculum development?
5. How relevant are the issues of selection and gradation to language teaching today? What factors influence current views of selection and gradation?
6. Examine a low-level language teaching text. What factors influence the selection and gradation of grammatical items in the text?
7. Are the concepts of selection and gradation compatible with the use of authentic texts or sources in language teaching?
8. How useful are word lists such as those illustrated in Appendixes 1 and 2 today?

Appendix 1   Entries from *A General Service List of English Words*

The list (from West 1953) identifies a core 2,000-word vocabulary and also the frequency of different meanings of each word.

FLOWER	605e			
flower, n.		(1a)	*(part of a plant)*	
			Pick flowers	
		(1b)	*(a flowering plant)*	
			Flowers and vegetables	86%
		Phrase:		
			In flower *(= in bloom)*	1%
		(2)	*(figurative)*	
			The flower of *(= best specimens)*	4%
			In the flower of his youth *(= best part)*	1%
flower-/			Flower-garden, *etc.*	0.7%
flower, v.			The roses are flowering	4%

FLY	805e			
fly, v.		(1)	*(travel through the air)*	
			Birds fly; aeroplanes fly	
			Fly an aeroplane, a kite	39%
		Special use:		
			Fly a flag	3.5%
		(2)	*(go quickly)*	
			Time flies	
			He flew to the rescue	14%
		(3)	*(Phrases implying sudden rapid motion)*	14%
			Fly to arms; fly at; fly in the face of	4.8%
			Fly into a rage; [fly out at]	1.3%
			Sent it flying; the door flew open	1.6%
flying, adj.			Flying-boat, -fish, -jump; flying column	14%
			[*= flee, 6.3%. The word* Flee, fled, 202e *is not included in the Report, but* fled *is rather necessary for narrative*]	

fly, n.			*(flying insect, especially housefly)*	11%

FOLD	196e			
fold, v.			Fold a piece of paper	
			Fold up one's clothes	
			Fold it up in paper	
			Fold one's arms	43%

Appendix 2 Entries from *Cambridge English Lexicon*

A 4,500-word vocabulary list grouped into 7 levels (Hindmarsh 1980).

1 baby
  1 *n.* a young child
  6 *n.* youngest: *which of you is the baby?*
  7 *adj.* not fully developed: *baby marrows*
4 baby-sitter *n.*
1 back
  1 *adv.* towards the rear: *head winds drove them back*
  1 *n.* part of the body or of an object, opposite of front: *the back of his head*
  2 *adv.* to a former state: *back to life*
  2 *adv.* in return: *to have the money back*
  3 *adv.* of time: *back in the Middle Ages*
  4 *adv.* in retaliation: *answer back; hit back*
  4 *v.* reverse: *he backed the car away*
  6 *v.* gamble on: *back a cause*
5 back out of *v.* withdraw
  1 badly
  1 *adv.* roughly, untidily: *badly made*
  2 *adv.* much: *badly in need of repair*
  5 *adv.* very much: *she wants it badly*
  6 *adv.* poor: *badly off*
5 badge *n.* sign of occupation, office, membership
1 bag
  1 *n.* container for carrying solid things
  7 *n.* lots of: *bags of money*
  7 *v.* get by hunting: *bag some duck*
3 baggage *n.* luggage
2 bake
  2 *v.* cook

  3 *v.* harden: *these pots were baked in our kiln*
  7 *v.* warm one's body: *baking in the sun at the resort*
2 baker *n.*
3 balance
  3 *v.* cause to be steady: *balance a ruler on one finger*
  5 *n.* instrument for weighing
  6 *v.* equate: *balance the accounts*
  6 *n.* state of equilibrium: *balance of power*
  7 *n.* outstanding amount: *hand in the balance*
5 balcony
  5 *n.* platform on exterior of building
  7 *n.* raised level of seating in theatre
4 bald *adj.* without hair on head
1 ball
  4 *n.* round object: *cricket ball; meatball; a ball of wool*
  6 *n.* dance: *May Ball*
5 ballet *n.*
2 balloon *n.* bag or envelope filled with air
4 ballpoint *n.*
1 banana *n.*
3 band
  3 *n.* group of persons, generally musicians
  4 *n.* connecting piece: *rubber bands*
  6 *v.* join together
  6 *n.* strip: *a band of colour*
5 bandage *n.*
5 back up *v.* support
5 backbone
  5 *n.* spine
  7 *n.* main strength: *backbone of the crew*

4 background
    4 *n.* part of a view
    7 *n.* setting: *the background to the report*
5 backwards
    5 *adv.* away from front: *go back-wards*
    5 *adv.* reverse order: *say the letters backwards*
5 backyard *n.*
1 bad
    1 *adj.* useless: *a bad worker*
    1 *adj.* unpleasant, incorrect: *bad manners*
    1 *adj.* immoral: *a bad man, bad behaviour*
    2 *adj.* painful: *I've got a bad head*
    4 *adj.* rotten: *go bad*
5 bang
    5 *n.* sudden loud noise
    6 *n.* a violent blow
    6 *v.* strike: *bang in that nail with a hammer*
2 bank
    2 *n.* establishment for handling money
    5 *n.* a ridge: *bank of earth*
    6 *v.* place securely: *to bank one's money*
3 Bank Holiday *n.*
5 banker *n.*
5 bankrupt *adj.*
2 bar
    2 *n.* a drinking place
    4 *n.* a rod of wood or metal: *a bar of gold*
    5 *v.* obstruct: *to bar the door*
    5 *n.* obstacle: *a bar across the road*
    7 *n.* place in court: *prisoner at the bar*
4 barber *n.*
3 bare
    3 *adj.* naked: *bare skin; bare head*
    6 *adj.* mere: *kill with your bare hands*
    6 *adj.* very slight: *a bare majority*
    7 *v.* make naked: *bare one's head*
3 bargain
    3 *v.* negotiate by argument: *you have to bargain in a Persian bazaar*
    5 *n.* thing bought cheaply
    5 *n.* agreement: *strike a bargain*
3 bark
    3 *v.* cry (dogs, foxes)
    3 *n.* cry so made
    6 *v.* shout sharply: *he barked his orders*
5 barman *n.*
4 barrel
    4 *n.* round container: *a barrel of beer*
    7 *n.* tube: *barrel of a rifle*
4 base
    4 *n.* foundation: *base of a pillar*
    5 *v.* establish on foundation: *base the argument*
    6 *n.* headquarters, main office: *go back to base for supplies*
    7 *adj.* dishonourable: *acting from base motives*
4 basement *n.*

Appendix 3   Part of an early English grammatical syllabus (from Hornby 1959)

This	is	John (Mary) Mr. (Mrs., Miss)	Brown (Green, White).
		a	stone (cow, horse, desk, book).
		an	apple (egg, inkpot, umbrella).
That		my (your)	bag (desk, pen, head, mouth).

These	are			stones (cows, trees, desks, books, eggs, umbrellas).
Those		my (your)		books (pens, pencils).
This	is	my	left	hand (eye, ear).
That	is	your	right	

What is What's	this? that?
What are	these? those?

It is It's	a my your	book. pen. pencil.
They are They're	(–) my your	books. pens. pencils.

Is	this that		a pen or a pencil? a bag or a box? my book or your book?
Are	these those		pens or pencils? bags or boxes? my books or your books?

Is	this that	a	cow? bird? horse?	Yes, it's	a	cow. bird. horse.
	it	my your	book? box?	No, it isn't	my your	book. box.
Are	these those		cows? birds? horses?	Yes, they're		cows. birds. horses.
	they	my your	books? boxes?	No, they aren't	my your	books. boxes.

References

Alexander, L. G., W. Stannard Allen, R. A. Close, and R. J. O'Neill. 1975. *English grammatical structure.* London: Longman.

Darian, S. 1972. *English as a foreign language: History, development, and methods of teaching.* Norman: University of Oklahoma Press.

Dulay, H., and M. Burt. 1973. Should we teach children syntax? *Language Learning* 23: 245–258.

Dulay, H., and M. Burt. 1974. Natural sequences in child second language acquisition. *Language Learning,* 24: 37–53.

Faucett, L., H. Palmer, M. West, and E. L. Thorndike. 1936. *Interim report on vocabulary selection.* London: P. S. King.

Fries, C. 1946. *Teaching and learning English as a foreign language.* Ann Arbor: University of Michigan Press.

Fries, C. 1952. *The structure of English.* New York: Harcourt Brace.

Hindmarsh, R. 1980. *Cambridge English lexicon.* Cambridge: Cambridge University Press.

Hornby, A. S. 1954. *Guide to patterns and usage in English.* Oxford: Oxford University Press.

Hornby, A. S. 1959. *The teaching of structural words and sentence patterns.* Oxford: Oxford University Press.

Lado, R. 1957. *Linguistics across cultures.* Ann Arbor: University of Michigan Press.

Li, D., and J. C. Richards. 1995. *Cantonese as a second language: A study of learner needs and Cantonese course books.* Research Monograph 2, English Department, City University of Hong Kong.

Mackey, W. F. 1965. *Language teaching analysis.* London: Longman.

McCarthy, M. 1990. *Vocabulary.* Oxford: Oxford University Press.

McCarthy, M., and R. Carter. 1995. Spoken grammar: What is it and how can we teach it? *ELT Journal* 49(3): 207–218.

Nunan, D, 1992. *Research methods in language teaching.* Cambridge: Cambridge University Press.

Palmer, H. E. 1968 [1922]. *The principles of language study.* Oxford: Oxford University Press.

Pienemann, M. 1989. Is language teachable? *Applied Linguistics* 6: 186–214.

Richards, J. C., and T. Rodgers. 1986. *Approaches and methods in language teaching.* New York: Cambridge University Press.

Van Els, T., T. Bongaerts, G. Extra, C. Van Os, and A. Janssen-van Dieten. 1984. *Applied linguistics and the learning and teaching of foreign languages.* London: Arnold.

West, M. 1953. *A general service list of English words.* London: Longman.

Wilkins, D. 1976. *Notional syllabuses.* Oxford: Oxford University Press.

2 *From syllabus design to curriculum development*

The approach to syllabus design outlined in Chapter 1 was largely sufficient to support language teaching up to the 1950s. This consisted of a focus on general English using materials graded for their vocabulary level and linguistic difficulty. English was taught through its structure and vocabulary. Darian (1972, 94), commenting on the influential Michigan materials produced at the University of Michigan, complains:

There is little in the way of "contextual material." Sentences chosen for exercises are perfectly normal utterances, but they seldom have any relation to one another. . . . In addition, almost all responses are complexly controlled, and there is little provision for students to generate any utterances different from the controlled responses being practiced.

Other approaches to language teaching were also available at this time, such as travel and commercial English books that were organized around topics, situations, and phrases as well as some that focused on technical English or the English used in specific occupations. But the latter type of book or language course was incidental to the main trend in language teaching, which focused on the teaching of general English, or, as it has sometimes been referred to, English for No Specific Purpose.

The quest for new methods

The teaching of English as a second or foreign language became an increasingly important activity after World War II. Immigrants, refugees, and foreign students generated a huge demand for English courses in the United Kingdom, Canada, the United States, and Australia. The role of English as a language of international communication had expanded rapidly by the 1950s. There was much greater mobility of peoples as a result of growth in air travel and international tourism. English was increasingly important in international trade and commerce. The role of English was supported by the growth of radio, film, and television. White (1988, 9) comments:

Whereas in medieval times English was the language of an island nation and French was the language of a continental one, in the twentieth century English has become the language of the world thanks to the linguistic legacy of the British Empire, the emergence of the USA as an English-speaking superpower and the fortuitous association of English with the industrial and technological developments of the nineteenth and twentieth centuries.

All of these developments supported the need for a practical command of English for people in many parts of the world rather than an academic mastery of the language as one might acquire in a typical school course.

The initial response of the English-language teaching profession was to explore new directions in methodology. It was assumed that in order to meet the changing needs of language learners, more up-to-date teaching methods were needed that reflected the latest understandings of the nature of language and of language learning. Linguistics was a source of theories about the organization and structure of language and these were eagerly applied in the cause of new "scientifically based" teaching methods. The 1950s and 1960s in language teaching were hence times of methodological excitement. In Britain, applied linguists developed a methodology that drew on the oral approach that had been developed in the twenties and thirties linked to a carefully graded grammatical and lexical syllabus. The methodology had the following characteristics:

- A structural syllabus with graded vocabulary levels
- Meaningful presentation of structures in contexts through the use of situations to contextualize new teaching points
- A sequence of classroom activities that went from Presentation, to controlled Practice, to freer Production (the P P P method)

This became known as the *situational approach* or the *structural-situational approach* or *Situational Language Teaching* and was the mainstream teaching method in British language teaching circles from the 1950s. A well-known course-book series based on this method is Robert O'Neill's Kernel series (Longman 1978). In countries and territories such as Singapore, under colonial administration "the curriculum of English-medium schools in the early 1950s followed the tradition of English teaching in British schools, with the integration of language and literature" (Ho 1994, 222). The same applied in other colonies such as Malaysia, India, and Hong Kong.

There was no provision for language work specially designed to help the non-native learner, and school grammars like those of the prolific J. C. Nesfield, which were originally written to get British youngsters through the Oxford and

Cambridge Local Examinations, were imported in large numbers to the colonies.
. . . From the early days until the mid-1960s . . . English was taught in these
schools as a discrete subject aimed at providing students with a reading
knowledge of English through the study of English grammar and selected texts
and applying such grammatical principles and whatever vocabulary was required
to the comprehension of texts often with the help of a bilingual dictionary. (Ho
1994, 222–226)

Later this was replaced by a "TESL/TEFL" approach based on a structural
syllabus and a situational drill-based methodology. The structural-situational approach was also used in Australia as the basis for English teaching
programs for immigrants from the 1950s (Ozolins 1993). In the United
States in the 1960s, language teaching was also under the sway of a powerful method – the *Audiolingual Method.* Stern (1974, 63) describes the period from 1958 to 1964 as the "Golden Age of Audiolingualism." This drew
on the work of American structural linguistics, which provided the basis for
a grammatical syllabus and a teaching approach that drew heavily on the
theory of behaviorism. Language learning was thought to depend on habits
that could be established by repetition. The linguist Bloomfield (1942, 12)
had earlier stated a principle that became a core tenet of audiolingualism:
"Language learning is overlearning: anything less is of no use." Teaching
techniques made use of repetition of dialogues and pattern practice as a basis for automatization followed by exercises that involved transferring
learned patterns to new situations. Rivers (1964) stated the assumptions of
audiolingualism as:

- Habits are strengthened by reinforcement.
- Foreign language habits are formed most effectively by giving the right
  response, not by making mistakes.
- Language is behavior and behavior can be learned only by inducing the
  student to behave.

Lado's *Lado English Series* (Lado 1978) is based on this approach. A similar method was developed in Europe and became known as the *Audiovisual
Method* because of its use of visual means for presenting and practicing new
language items.

The fascination with methods and the quest for the best method remained
a preoccupation of language teaching for the next 20 years. Lange observes
(1990, 253):

Foreign language [teaching] . . . has a basic orientation to methods of teaching.
Unfortunately the latest bandwagon "methodologies" come into prominence
without much study or understanding, particularly those that are easiest to

immediately apply in the classroom or those that are supported by a particular "guru." Although concern for method is certainly not a new issue, the current attraction to "method" stems from the late 1950s, when foreign language teachers were falsely led to believe that there was a method to remedy the "language learning and teaching problem."

Changing needs for foreign languages in Europe

But a missing element in the enthusiasm for new methods was a consideration of the extent to which teaching methods addressed learners' needs. Jupp and Hodlin raised this issue in 1975:

The upsurge in English language teaching [since the mid-1950s] was accompanied by the introduction of new methods and materials in the classroom, particularly during the 1960s. These changes were often radical and can be called a language teaching revolution. But this revolution has taken little account of the situation or motivation of the learners; on the contrary it has been about *how* people learn and *what* language is. . . . Consideration of *why* people learn a second language or evaluation of results has been more or less missing. (8)

One response to this concern was a reevaluation of language teaching policy in many European countries in the 1970s with a view to determine such things as which foreign languages should be taught in the school system, at what year languages should be introduced into the curriculum, and with what intensity (e.g., two, four, or six class periods a week). The status of the teaching of classical languages was also being reviewed.

In 1969, the Council of Europe (a regional organization of European countries designed to promote cultural and educational cooperation), in order to promote the more effective learning of foreign languages within the community, decided that:

- If full understanding is to be achieved among the countries of Europe, the language barriers between them must be removed;
- Linguistic diversity is part of the European cultural heritage and that it should, through the study of modern languages, provide a source of intellectual enrichment rather than an obstacle to unity;
- Only if the study of modern European languages becomes general will full mutual understanding and cooperation be possible in Europe. (Council of Europe 1969, 8)

In order to respond to these concerns it became apparent that policies could only be based on information about societies' needs. Van Els, T. Bongaerts, G. Extra, C. Van Os, and A. Janssen-van Dieten (1984, 159) pose the questions that were considered at this time:

- Does the community consider it important that all its members know a foreign language, or is this considered necessary only for certain professional domains?
- How many languages, and which languages, are felt to be necessary?
- How great is the demand for each individual language? Does everyone need the same skills, or the same level of command per skill?
- Is there a stable needs pattern?

Although individual countries responded to these issues in different ways, one important response was initiated by the Council of Europe, which proposed that a "unit-credit system" be used as a framework for developing language teaching programs for adults. This was defined as follows:

An educational system in which the syllabus, curriculum or body or material (knowledge and skills) to be studied, learned or acquired, is broken down into a number of quantum units of work, each with its own precise definition of the terminal behavior to be achieved by the learner, all of the units being accompanied by a carefully constructed system of credit ratings. (Kingsbury 1971, 11)

A level of proficiency described as the *Threshold Level* was described that was "the lowest level of general foreign language ability to be recognized in the unit-credit system" (Van Ek and Alexander 1975, 7). It was during this period that Communicative Language Teaching (CLT) emerged as a new direction for language teaching, and it attracted widespread interest and enthusiasm as a way of moving language teaching beyond an obsession with the latest teaching methods and to a reexamination of basic assumptions about the goals, nature, and processes of language teaching. (CLT is discussed further later in this chapter.) At this point it is important to note that rather than considering the way forward in language teaching as dependent on changes in teaching methods, what was now being considered was the whole context of teaching and learning and the need to consider societal and learner needs as the starting point in a reevaluation of language teaching. Once needs were identified, learning targets could be described, as, for example, with the unit-credit system and threshold level proposed by the Council of Europe.

English for specific purposes

The concern to make language courses more relevant to learners' needs also led during this period to the emergence of the Languages for Specific Purposes (LSP) movement, known in English-language teaching circles as ESP (English for Specific Purposes). The ESP approach to language teaching began as a response to a number of practical concerns:

• the need to prepare growing numbers of non-English background students for study at American and British universities from the 1950s
• the need to prepare materials to teach students who had already mastered general English, but now needed English for use in employment, such as non-English background doctors, nurses, engineers, and scientists
• the need for materials for people needing English for business purposes
• the need to teach immigrants the language needed to deal with job situations

In contrast to students learning English for general purposes for whom mastery of the language for its own sake or in order to pass a general examination is the primary goal, the ESP student is usually studying English in order to carry out a particular role, such as that of foreign student in an English-medium university, flight attendant, mechanic, or doctor. Jupp and Hodlin (1975, 10) describe the traditional pre-ESP response to this situation in the 1950s citing the example of a country that needs to teach foreign languages to key personnel dealing with trade or foreign business. Trainees are released for four hours daily for a year. Two language laboratories are equipped with materials and the trainees follow a state-of-the-art audiovisual course in "spoken colloquial English" "based on selection and gradation by structural criteria with some additional 'situational' language." However, the course

takes no account of functional communicative needs or the learner's own immediate situation. The English setting is largely a matter of an English family and some English surroundings; there is certainly no attempt to teach the English 'rules of use' in terms of situations and relationships. The concept of 'spoken colloquial English' is one largely based upon a structural description of written English and without reference to functional uses and to roles. (Jupp and Hodlin 1975, 11)

The same was true of the language courses and materials developed at the University of Michigan in the United States in the early 1950s and which served as the basis for courses for foreign students entering American universities. The materials largely address language patterns and vocabulary

(Darian 1972). Increasingly from this time and throughout the 1960s it was realized that for learners in situations such as these, what was needed was not more and more lessons in "advanced English" or "colloquial English," whatever that was, but training in the kinds of English learners would use or encounter in their specific occupations and situations. This seemed to be largely a matter of determining what the linguistic features were of such situations. The 1960s therefore saw a number of books applying the principles of selection and gradation to the English of science, business, medicine, engineering, or manufacturing, the same principles that had been used until then in designing general English courses. It was assumed that there were specialized varieties of English, such as "scientific English," "business English," or "technical English." The characteristics of these specialized Englishes could be identified through word frequency counts and discourse analysis:

> The generally accepted view around 1970 was essentially a linguistic one: there were different varieties of English, the distinctive features of which could be described and taught through the use of appropriately selected texts, and carefully devised practice exercises. (Howatt 1984, 222)

This approach was reflected in such widely used books of the period as Ewer and Latorre's *Course in Basic Scientific English* (1969) and Swales's *Writing Scientific English* (1971). Ewer and Latorre is based on a frequency count of three million words of scientific English covering ten areas of science and technology and sets out to teach

> the basic language of scientific English. This basic language is made up of sentence patterns, structural (functional) words and non-structural vocabulary which are common to all scientific disciplines and form the essential framework upon which the special vocabulary of each discipline is superimposed. (Ewer and Latorre 1969, ix)

The analysis revealed a number of features of scientific English that differed from general English and that were typically underrepresented in ESL/EFL course books, namely:

-ing forms replacing a relative
infinitive as substitute for longer phrases
words similar in form but with different meanings for the same function
most prefixes and suffixes
most structural and qualifying words and phrases
compound nouns
passives
conditionals
anomalous finites

cause-and-result constructions
words similar in form but with different functions
past participle usage
two-part verbs

(Ewer and Hughes-Davies 1971, 65–70)

Appendix 1 contains an example of scientific writing from an early ESP course that exemplifies some of these characteristics. Praninskas (1972) investigated the core vocabulary of academic reading materials. She carried out a word frequency count of ten university-level textbooks used in first-year courses at the American University of Beirut focusing on frequently occurring words that were not covered in the *General Service List* (see Appendix 2).

Throughout the 1970s the ESP approach in language teaching drew on *register analysis* and *discourse analysis* to determine the linguistic characteristics of different disciplines such as medicine, engineering, or science. A register is a variety of language determined according to its use:

Types of linguistic situation differ from one another, broadly speaking, in three respects: first, as regards to what is actually taking place; secondly, as regards what part the language is playing; and thirdly, as regards who is taking part. These three variables, taken together, determine the range within which meanings are selected and the forms which are used for their expression. In other words, they determine the 'register'. (Halliday 1978, 31)

Register analysis studies the language of such fields as journalism, medicine, or law for distinctive patterns of occurrence of vocabulary, verb forms, noun phrases, and tense usage. For example as preparation for designing business communications courses, Chiu (1975) analyzed the language used in administrative correspondence and boardroom discussions in Canada and found, not surprisingly, that certain verbs, such as *attach, enclose, appreciate, refer, forward, request, advice,* and *thank,* had a much higher frequency of occurrence in her corpus than in corpuses of general English. She also found distinctive uses of verb forms and verb phrases. Martin (1976, cited in Jordan 1997, 53) describes the register of academic vocabulary and groups it into three categories:

a) *the research process:* the vocabulary is primarily verbs and nouns and is "presented in a context which discusses the five steps of research: formulating, investigating, analyzing, drawing conclusions and reporting results."

b) *the vocabulary of analysis:* it includes high-frequency and two-word verbs needed "in order to present information in an organized sequence," for example, *consist of, group result from, derive, base on, be noted for.*

Verbs of analysis are grouped in a number of semantic sets, for example, *consist of, be composed of, contain, be made up of.*

c) *The vocabulary of evaluation:* it includes adjectives and adverbs that occur in reviews, critiques, and some reports, for example, *exhaustive, controversial, coherent, indispensable, comprehensive, distinctive, pervasive, substantive: objective-subjective, implicit-explicit, inductive-deductive, significant-insignificant.*

Discourse analysis. Register analysis focused primarily at the level of the word and the sentence and sought to identify the registers that characterized different uses of language, such as business letters, academic textbooks, and technical writing. In order to identify the linguistic structure of longer samples of speech or text, an approach called discourse analysis was introduced in the 1970s. It is based on the analysis of units of organization within texts (e.g., narratives, instructions, reports, business letters) or speech events and examines patterns of rhetorical organization such as definition, identification, and comparison. Jordan (1997, 229) describes the scope of discourse analysis:

It examines the communicative contexts that affect language use, for example, in social transactions, the relationship between the discourse and the speakers and listeners. It looks at how, for example, the choice of verb tenses or other grammatical features affect the structure of the discourse. The analysis also looks at the relationship between utterances, for example, aspects of cohesion, and the discourse markers or cohesive devices that are employed.

Identifying patterns of text organization was a focus of this approach. For example, a common discourse structure found in many scientific papers is the *problem-solution* structure. Hoey (1979, 1983) describes this as follows:

1. Introduction
   a) Direct the reader's attention to the subject or the problem.
   b) Explain your experience with the subject – the reason why you can write with authority.
   c) Establish bridges with the reader by pointing out shared beliefs, attitudes, and experiences.
2. Background
   a) Explain the nature of the problem, its history, and causes.
   b) Explain its relevance to the reader's problems, desires, and interests – the reasons why the problem is important to the reader.

3. Argument
   a) State the major premise. Include any information necessary to make it clear and acceptable.
   b) State the minor premise, again including necessary information.
   c) State your conclusion.
   d) Show your position is better by pointing out defects in the premise or inferences of alternative positions. Explain why the alternatives cannot solve the problem; or if they can, why your solution solves it better.
4. Conclusion
   a) Explain the implications of your argument.
   b) Summarize your argument: the problem (2a), your conclusion (3c), and the reasons for accepting it (3a and 3b).

Both the concepts of register and discourse type were the basis for the first generation of ESP courses in the 1970s, such as the *English in Focus* series (Allen and Widdowson 1974).

Although one of the main directions of the ESP approach through the 1960s and 1970s was the development of language courses and materials that taught the registers and discourse features of science, business, or medicine, the focus in ESP on the purposes for which learners need a language prompted the development of approaches to *needs analysis,* one of the basic processes of curriculum and syllabus design. Needs analysis will be the focus of Chapter 3, but it will be useful here to review how needs analysis is related to ESP.

Needs analysis in ESP

An important principle of ESP approaches to language teaching is that the purposes for which a learner needs a language rather than a syllabus reflecting the structure of general English should be used in planning an English course. Rather than developing a course around an analysis of the language, an ESP approach starts instead with an analysis of the learner's needs. Schutz and Derwing (1981, 30) point out that this was a new concern with ESP: "most language planners in the past have bypassed a logically necessary first step: they have presumed to set about going somewhere without first determining whether or not their planned destination was reasonable or proper." Different types of students have different language needs and what they are taught should be restricted to what they need. These needs are fairly specific; they can be identified and they should determine the content of any course. Strevens (1977) pointed out that several levels of restriction are involved.

The content of [ESP] courses are thereby determined, in some or all of the following ways: (i) *restriction:* only those "basic skills" (understanding speech, speaking, reading, writing) are included which are required by the learner's purposes; (ii) *selection:* only those items of vocabulary, patterns of grammar, functions of language are included which are required by the learner's purposes; (iii) *themes and topics:* only those themes, topics, situations, universes of discourse, etc. are included which are required by the learner's purposes; (iv) *communicative needs:* only those communicative needs . . . are included which are required for the learner's purposes.

In ESP learner's needs are often described in terms of performance, that is, in terms of what the learner will be able to do with the language at the end of a course of study. Whereas in a general English course the goal is usually an overall mastery of the language that can be tested on a global language test, the goal of an ESP course is to prepare the learners to carry out a specific task or set of tasks. Robinson (1980, 11) comments:

The student of ESP is usually studying to *perform a role.* The measure of success for students learning English for hotel waiters, or the English for food technology, is whether they can perform convincingly as hotel waiters in English or whether they can act appropriately as food technologists in English (and pass exams in food technology, rather than exams in English).

In order to determine the learner's needs as the starting point for developing ESP programs, a number of approaches were suggested. Richterich and Chanceril (1978), working within the Council of Europe framework, proposed that learners, teachers, and employers could all be involved in determining learners' needs. Information could be collected about the resources of the teaching institution, objectives, the methods of assessment used, and needs analysis should be an ongoing process throughout a course. Information would also be needed about the different kinds of activities the learner would be using the language for (e.g., telephoning, interviewing), the language functions involved (e.g., explaining, requesting, complaining), the situations (e.g., face-to-face, in a work group), and which of the four language skills would be needed. Procedures suggested for conducting needs analysis included questionnaires, surveys, and interviews.

   Munby (1978), in an influential book of the time, describes a systematic approach to needs analysis in ESP course design and focuses on two dimensions of needs analysis: the procedures used to specify the target-level communicative competence of the student, and procedures for turning the information so gathered into an ESP syllabus. The Munby model describes the kind of information needed to develop a profile of the learner's communicative needs and is summarized by Schutz and Derwing (1981, 32) as follows:

Profile of Communicative Needs

1. Personal	Culturally significant information about the individual, such as language background
2. Purpose	Occupational or educational objective for which the target language is required
3. Setting	Physical and psychosocial setting in which the target language is required
4. Interactional variables	Such as the role relationships to be involved in the target language use
5. Medium, mode, and channel	Communicative means
6. Dialects	Information on dialects to be utilized
7. Target level	Level of competence required in the target language
8. Anticipated communicative events	Micro- and macro-activities
9. Key	The specific manner in which communication is actually carried out

An example will illustrate how the model could be applied in carrying out a needs profile. If one were profiling the needs of restaurant staff such as waiters and waitresses, the following information might be revealed through applying the Munby model:

1. Personal	Who the employees are, their age, nationalities, sex, educational background, work experience
2. Purpose	The kinds of outcomes expected, such as the types of communicative skills the clients need to develop
3. Setting	The type of restaurant in which the employees work and the kinds of customers who use the restaurant
4. Interactional variables	The role relationships, such as waiter/waitress to customer, waiter/waitress to restaurant manager, waiter/waitress to kitchen staff

5. Medium, mode, and channel	Whether spoken or written; face to face
6. Dialects	Whether both formal and casual styles
7. Target level	Whether basic, intermediate, or advanced level
8. Anticipated communicative events	For example, greetings, taking requests, clarifying information, describing menu items
9. Key	For example, unhurriedly, quietly, politely

The needs profile is then translated into a statement of the list of specific language skills the students will need based on the skills taxonomy Munby provides. This consists of some 300 subskills grouped into 54 categories. For example, in relation to the "macroskill" of reading, Munby lists the following skills:

• Understanding relations between parts of a text through lexical cohesion devices of:
repetition
synonymity
hyponymity
antithesis
apposition
lexical set/collocation
pro-forms/general words

• Understanding relations between parts of a text through grammatical cohesion devices of:
reference (anaphoric and cataphoric)
comparison
substitution
ellipsis
time and place relaters
logical connectors

The skills taxonomy appears to be little more than a compilation of then-current opinion about the components of the different language skills. When it was published, the Munby model was welcomed as a systematic and objective set of processes for arriving at a specification of student needs and selecting language to match them. However, those who attempted to use the model soon discovered that it depended on subjective and often arbitrary judgments and decisions at almost every level. After completing a two-day training session in the use of the Munby model during which they produced profiles of imaginary students, a group of British Council specialists reported "there was no evidence that groups would have been better off using live informants" (cited in Robinson 1980, 30).

Communicative language teaching

The emergence of ESP with its emphasis on needs analysis as a starting point in language program design was an important factor in the development of current approaches to language curriculum development. A second influence was the communicative approach to language teaching that emerged in the late 1960s and 1970s as a replacement for the structural-situational and audiolingual methods. Communicative Language Teaching (CLT) is a broad approach to teaching that resulted from a focus on communication as the organizing principle for teaching rather than a focus on mastery of the grammatical system of the language. The 1970s was a period when everyone was "going communicative," although precisely what was meant by that varied considerably. CLT was not so much a change in method as a set of changes in assumptions about the nature of language, the nature of goals, objectives, and the syllabus in language teaching, and a search for an appropriate methodology in the light of these changes.

CLT was a response to changes in the field of linguistics in the 1970s, as well as a response to the need for new approaches to language teaching in Europe as a result of initiative, by groups such as the Council of Europe. Linguistics moved away from a focus on grammar as the core component of language abilities to a consideration of how language is used by speakers in different contexts of communication. The capacity to use language appropriately in communication based on the setting, the roles of the participants, and the nature of the transaction was referred to as *communicative competence*. Applied linguists sought to apply this notion to language teaching. Whereas a grammatical syllabus is based on the notion of *grammatical competence* – the knowledge people have of a language that underlies their capacities to produce and recognize sentences in the language – a different type of syllabus would be needed to teach communicative competence. What would such a syllabus look like? An important book in 1976 by Wilkins (who was one of the members of a committee set up by the Council of Europe that formulated the *Threshold Level*) sought to answer this question. Wilkins described the traditional type of grammar-based syllabus as a *synthetic approach*. A synthetic approach is contrasted with an *analytic approach*, which is one where there is no attempt at this careful linguistic control of the learning environment. Components of language are not seen as building blocks which have to be progressively accumulated. Much greater variety of linguistic structure is permitted from the beginning and the learner's task is to approximate his behavior more and more closely to the global language. . . . Analytic approaches are behavioral (though not behaviorist). They are organized in terms of the purposes for which people are learning languages and the kinds of language performance that are necessary to meet those purposes. (Wilkins 1976, 2, 13)

Wilkins proposed a *notional syllabus* as a new type of syllabus that meets these criteria. A notional syllabus would contain three kinds of categories of meaning: *semantico-grammatical meaning, modal meaning,* and *communicative function.* Semantico-grammatical meaning describes the meaning underlying grammatical contrasts and concepts such as:

time
    a) point of time
    b) duration
    c) time relations
    d) frequency
    e) sequence
quantity
    a) divided and undivided reference
    b) numerals
    c) operations

Wilkins suggested that modal meaning includes the following categories of meaning:

modality
scale of certainty
scale of commitment

Communicative function refers to the meanings communicated by what linguists referred to as *speech acts,* such as:

requests
complaints
apologies
compliments
suggestions

In fact, all Wilkins had done with the first two categories was to take traditional items of grammar and restate them in terms of concepts or notions.

This semantic sleight of hand did not turn out to be much of an advantage in syllabus design. The third category of communicative function, however, was seized on as a useful and practical way of thinking about a language syllabus. Applied linguists reacted eagerly to the idea of expressing a syllabus in terms of communicative units rather than grammatical ones and the literature of the late 1970s and 1980s contains a variety of proposals for communicative or functional syllabuses. Yalden (1987, 86–87) describes the goal of syllabus designers at that time:

This means that if we now wish to make up the deficit in earlier syllabus types, and ensure that our learners acquire the ability to communicate in a more appropriate and efficient way, we have to inject a larger number of components into the make-up of the syllabus. These components could be listed as follows:

1. as detailed a consideration as possible of the *purposes* for which the learners wish to acquire the target language;
2. some idea of the *setting* in which they will want to use the target language (physical aspects need to be considered, as well as social setting);
3. the socially defined *role* the learners will assume in the target language, as well as the role of their interlocutors;
4. the *communicative events* in which the learners will participate: everyday situations, vocational or professional situations, academic situations, and so on;
5. the *language functions* involved in those events, or what the learner will be able to do with or through the language;
6. the *notions* involved, or what the learner will need to be able to talk about;
7. the skills involved in the "knitting together" of discourse: *discourse and rhetorical skills;*
8. the *variety* or varieties of the target language that will be needed, and the levels in the spoken and written language which the learners will need to reach;
9. the *grammatical content* that will be needed;
10. the *lexical content* that will be needed.

This framework is essentially that of the *Threshold Level* (see Van Ek and Alexander 1975, 5). As various proposals for the implementation of a communicative approach to syllabus design were advanced and debated, applied linguists began to consider how syllabuses were arrived at in other fields of study and to apply procedures developed in the field of curriculum development.

Emergence of a curriculum approach
in language teaching

As we saw in Chapter 1, the term *curriculum studies* refers to a very broad field of inquiry that deals with what happens in schools and other educational institutions, the planning of instruction, and the study of how curriculum plans are implemented. A curriculum in a school context refers to the whole body of knowledge that children acquire in schools. Rodgers (1989, 26) comments:

Syllabi, which prescribe the content to be covered by a given course, form only a small part of the total school program. Curriculum is a far broader concept. Curriculum is all those activities in which children engage under the auspices of the school. This includes not only what pupils learn, but how they learn it, how teachers help them learn, using what supporting materials, styles and methods of assessment, and in what kind of facilities.

One of the most important statements on the nature and process of curriculum development was made by Tyler in 1949 in a book that brought about a revival in curriculum studies throughout the 1950s. His approach is summarized on the first page:

Four fundamental questions must be answered in developing any curriculum and plan of instruction. These are:

(1) What educational purposes should the school seek to attain?
(2) What educational experiences can be provided that are likely to attain these purposes?
(3) How can these educational experiences be effectively organized?
(4) How can we determine whether these purposes are being attained?

(Tyler 1950, 1)

This was sometimes reduced to an even simpler model:

Aims and objectives
↓
Content
↓
Organization
↓
Evaluation

As Lawton (1973) pointed out, this rather naive view of the curriculum process was not really intended by Tyler himself, whose book was a response to his observation that many teachers seemed unable to explain what the goals of their teaching were, except in the most general way. If asked to explain their objectives, they might say, "We are trying to produce well-educated and well-rounded students." Such a statement, however, does not help identify the kind of teaching that might contribute to this goal or the kind of learning that would result from it. Tyler argued that educational objectives should describe learner behavior (not teacher behavior) and should identify what changes have come about in learners as a result of teaching. Tyler's model or variations of it soon penetrated wide areas of educational thought and practice and curriculum and training manuals were soon full of models such as the following (Inglis 1975):

1. NEED   2. PLAN
   Aims   Objectives   Strategies   Tactics

3. IMPLEMENTATION   4. REVIEW
   Methods   Techniques   Evaluation   Consolidation

Critics of the Tyler model (of which there were many) raised a number of objections, some arguing that the notion of objectives represents a limited view of knowledge (see Chapter 5) and some criticizing the technical and rationalist approach of the model, which seemed better suited to business or industry than education. Others criticized the linear approach implied by the model, which leaves evaluation as the final stage rather than building it in at every stage. In its place they proposed a cyclical model.

Nicholls and Nicholls (1972, 4), for example, describe curriculum development as involving four stages;

(a) The careful examination, drawing on all available sources of knowledge and informed judgement, of the objectives of teaching, whether in particular subject courses or over the curriculum as a whole.
(b) The development and trial use in schools of those methods and materials which are judged most likely to achieve the objectives which teachers agreed upon.
(c) The assessment of the extent to which the development work has in fact achieved its objectives. This part of the process may be expected to provoke new thought about the objectives themselves.
(d) The final element is therefore feedback of all the experience gained, to provide a starting point for further study.

This view of curriculum development processes has been widely adopted in language teaching from the 1980s. It has been described as an *ends–means* model because it starts with a determination of the kinds of language skills the learner needs in order to accomplish specific roles and tasks and then sets out to teach the language needed to get there. In the field of curriculum studies the approach was sometimes reduced to a mechanistic set of procedures and rules known as a systems-design model. A system in this context is "an integrated plan of operation of all components (sub-systems) of a system, designed to solve a problem or meet a need" (Briggs 1977, 5). The systems model belongs to an approach to educational planning that sees curriculum development as a rational and somewhat technical process. Its practitioners believed that this was the key to the design of successful educational programs. In the 1980s, funding for large-scale curriculum projects in many parts of the world was often dependent on their being couched in this framework. Rodgers (1989, 27) observes:

The curricular systems-design model has been prescriptive and rule-driven. It describes a linear sequence of events comprising formulation of objectives, selection of content, task analysis, design of learning activities, definition of behavioral outcomes and evaluative measures for determining the achievement or non-achievement of these outcomes.

The Munby model has many of the same characteristics as a systems approach and was found to be cumbersome, unrealistic, and impractical in actual practice. However, since the 1980s the view that curriculum development processes are central elements in language program design has become more widely accepted in language teaching, though not in the narrow prescriptive form of the systems model. In many countries, language curriculum development units have been established in ministries of education since the 1980s with a mandate to review and develop national language teaching curriculum based on a curriculum development perspective. For example, Lim (1988, 2, cited in Ho 1994) comments on such an initiative in Singapore and notes that curriculum development now includes "needs analysis, goal setting, syllabus design, materials design, language programme design, teacher preparation, implementation of programmes in schools, monitoring, feedback and evaluation." The debates over teaching methods that were common in the 1970s have been replaced by a focus on the interlinked processes that compose curriculum development, of which methodology is simply one element.

"Curriculum development" is used in this book to refer to the range of planning and implementation processes involved in developing or renewing a curriculum. These processes focus on needs analysis, situational analysis, planning learning outcomes, course organization, selecting and preparing teaching materials, providing for effective teaching, and evaluation. These elements are viewed as forming a network of interacting systems. The notion of system suggests that change in one part of the system has effects on other parts of the system. For example, whether or not teachers are provided with textbooks to teach from, itself reflecting a policy decision, may affect the kinds of classroom discourse and learning input that teachers are able to provide. Similarly, the amount of attention students give to learning activities may reflect their judgment of the relevance of the kinds of learning experiences they encounter, which may depend on the adequacy of a needs analysis. In this book, no attempt is made to present the classic systems approach to curriculum development. Such an approach typically depicts teachers as on the receiving end of a process controlled and directed by others. The approach taken here seeks to place teachers and language teaching professionals at the center of the planning and decision-making process. While the products of these decision-making processes are easy to identify and analyze because they exist in the form of policy documents, syllabuses, tests, teaching materials, teaching programs, textbooks, and teaching and learning acts (Johnson 1989), the processes that lead to them are more difficult to identify and analyze because they often reflect the contributions of a variety of people with different roles and goals. Johnson (1989, 3) represents these different decision-making roles and products in the following diagram:

TABLE 1 Stages, decision-making roles and products in curriculum development (from Johnson 1989)

Developmental stages	Decision-making roles	Products
1. curriculum planning	policy makers	policy document
2. specification: ends means	needs analyst	syllabus
	methodologists	
3. programme implementation	materials writers	teaching materials
	teacher trainers	teacher-training programme
4. classroom implementation	teacher	teaching acts
	learner	learning acts

Clark (1987) emphasizes that these are often processes of renewal rather than development, since some sort of curriculum is already in place. Teachers and curriculum planners are engaged in ongoing processes of review and evaluation in order to bring about curriculum renewal and change. Clark identifies the following components of the process of curriculum renewal:

- the review of principles to guide the language teaching/learning process in the light of applied linguistic theory and classroom experience
- the reworking of syllabuses embodying aims, objectives, content, and a broad methodology
- the review of classroom teaching/learning strategies
- the choice, adaptation, and creation of resources embodying appropriate learning experiences
- the review of assessment designed to monitor, record, report, and provide feedback on learner progress
- the review of classroom schemes of work relating all of the above together
- the review and creation of strategies designed to assist teachers to evaluate classroom practices and to improve them
- the identification of areas for research to determine possible ways forward in any of the above areas
- the review or devising of in-service education designed to assist teachers to widen their conceptual and pragmatic base in particular areas, and to find solutions to their own classroom problems

(Clark 1987, xii–xiii)

The aim of the following chapters is to survey concepts, issues, and practices in each of these areas in order to better facilitate the kind of planning and decision making that is involved in developing better language programs.

Discussion questions and activities

1. Why were "new methods" criticized as a response to changing language teaching needs from the 1960s?
2. What is the rationale behind the ESP approach to language teaching? In what ways is this approach different from earlier approaches to language teaching?
3. How did the ESP movement contribute to the concept of needs analysis?
4. How can register analysis and discourse analysis contribute to ESP? Suggest situations where they might be particularly important.
5. Examine the sample of scientific English in Appendix 1 and the lists of features of scientific English from Ewer and Hughes-Davies given in this chapter. Which of these features are exemplified in the sample?

6. Examine the Munby profile of communicative needs in this chapter. How might this apply to determining the needs of flight attendants who require training in English (or learners in another situation you are familiar with)? Give examples of the kind of information that would be sought and suggest possible answers.

7. What is the difference between grammatical competence and communicative competence? How is this difference relevant to syllabus design?

8. What is meant by an ends–means model of curriculum development? What are the limitations of this approach?

9. Explain a "systems approach" to curriculum development. What criticisms have been made of this approach?

Appendix 1   Example of scientific writing (from Ewer and Latorre 1969)

Scientific method and the methods of science

It is sometimes said that there is no such thing as the so-called 'scientific method'; there are only the methods used in science. Nevertheless, it seems clear that there is often a special sequence of procedures which is involved in the establishment of the working principles of science. This sequence is as follows: (1) a problem is recognized, and as much information as appears to be relevant is collected; (2) a solution (i.e. a hypothesis) is proposed and the consequences arising out of this solution are deduced; (3) these deductions are tested by experiment, and as a result the hypothesis is accepted, modified or discarded.

As an illustration of this we can consider the discovery of air-pressure. Over two thousand years ago, men discovered a method of raising water from one level to another by means of the vacuum pump. When, however, this machine passed into general use in the fifteenth and sixteenth centuries, it was discovered that, no matter how perfect the pump was, it was not possible to raise water vertically more than about 35 feet. Why? Galileo, amongst others, recognized the problem, but failed to solve it.

The problem was then attacked by Torricelli. Analogizing from the recently-discovered phenomenon of water-pressure (hydrostatic pressure), he postulated that a deep 'sea of air' surrounded the earth; it was, he thought, the pressure of this sea of air which pushed on the surface of the water and caused it to rise in the vacuum tube of a pump. A hypothesis, then, was formed. The next step was to deduce the consequences of the hypothesis. Torricelli reasoned that this 'air pressure' would be unable to push a liquid heavier than water as high as 35 feet, and that a column of mercury, for example, which weighed about 14 times more than water, would rise to only a fourteenth of the height of water, i.e. approximately 2.5 feet. He then tested this deduction by means of the experiment we all know, and found that the mercury column measured the height predicted. The experiment therefore supported the hypothesis. A further inference was drawn by Pascal, who reasoned that if this 'sea of air' existed, its pressure at the bottom (i.e. sea-level) would be greater than its pressure further up, and that therefore the height of the mercury column would decrease in proportion to the height above sea-level. He then carried the mercury tube to the top of a mountain and observed that the column fell steadily as the height increased, while another mercury column at the bottom of the mountain remained steady (an example of another of the methods of science, the controlled experiment). This further proof not only established Torricelli's hypothesis more securely, but also demonstrated that, in some aspects, air behaved like water; this, of course, stimulated further enquiry.

Appendix 2   Words found often in academic reading materials

Words not found in the *General Service List* but that occur frequently in academic reading materials, with frequencies of occurrence in ten first-year university textbooks (from Praninskas 1972).

an indicator an indication	to indicate			98
an interpretation a misinterpretation a reinterpretation	to interpret	interpretive		52
an involvement	to involve			103
a method – methodology		methodolical methodological		144
		negative	negatively	68
		obvious	obviously	45
primitiveness		prime primary primitive primeval	primarily	135
a procedure – proceedings	to proceed			72
a publication a publisher	to publish to publicize			57
a range	to range			70
a region		regional interregional	regionally	91
a requirement	to require			149
a similarity		similar	similarly	133
a specification – specificity	to specify	specific specifiable	specifically	199
	to suffice	sufficient insufficient	sufficiently	56

References

Allen, P., and H. Widdowson (eds.). 1974. *English in focus*. Oxford: Oxford University Press.

Bloomfield, L. 1942. *Outline guide for the practical study of foreign languages*. Baltimore: Linguistic Society of America.

Briggs, L. (ed.). 1977. *Instructional design: Principles and applications*. Englewood Cliffs, NJ: Educational Technology Publications.

Chiu, R. 1972. Measuring register characteristics: A prerequisite for preparing advanced level TESOL programs. *TESOL Quarterly,* 6(2) (1972): 129–141.

Clark, J. 1987. *Curriculum renewal in school foreign language learning*. Oxford: Oxford University Press.

Council of Europe. 1969. *The work of the Council of Europe in the field of modern languages*. Strasbourg: Council of Europe.

Darian, S. 1972. *English as a foreign language: History, development, and methods of teaching*. Norman: University of Oklahoma Press.

Ewer, J. R., and G. Latorre. 1969. *A course in basic scientific English*. London: Longman.

Ewer, J. R., and G. Hughes-Davies. 1971. Further notes on developing an English programme for students of science and technology. *English Language Teaching* 26(1): 65–70.

Halliday, M. A. K. 1978. *Language as social semiotic*. London: Arnold.

Ho, W. K. 1994. The English language curriculum in perspective: Exogeneous influences and indigenization. In S. Gopinathan, A. Pakir, H. W. Kam, and V. Saravanan (eds.), *Language, society, and education in Singapore* (2d ed.). Singapore: Times Academic Press. 22–244.

Hoey, M. 1979. *Signaling in discourse: A functional analysis of a common discourse pattern in written and spoken English*. Birmingham: University of Birmingham, English Language Research Unit.

Hoey, M. 1983. *On the surface of discourse*. London: Allen and Unwin.

Inglis, F. 1975. Ideology and the curriculum: The value assumptions of system builders. In M. Golby, J. Greenwald, and R. West (eds.), *Curriculum design*. London: Croom Helm.

Howatt, A. P. R. 1984. *A history of English language teaching*. Oxford: Oxford University Press.

Johnson, R. K. 1989. *The second language curriculum*. New York: Cambridge University Press.

Jordan. R. 1997. *English for academic purposes*. Cambridge: Cambridge University Press.

Jupp, T. C., and S. Hodlin. 1975. *Industrial English*. London: Heinemann.

Kingsbury, R. 1971. A proposed model for critical discussion and study of a possible unit/credit system in modern language learning and teaching for adults in Europe. In Council of Europe, *Linguistic content, means of evaluation and their interaction in the teaching and learning of modern languages in adult education.* Council of Europe, Strasbourg: 10–16.

Lado, R. 1978. *Lado English series.* New York: Regents.

Lange, D. 1990. A blueprint for a teacher development program. In J. C. Richards and D. Nunan (eds.), *Second language teacher education.* New York: Cambridge University Press. 245–268.

Lawton, D. 1973. *Social change, educational theory and curriculum planning.* London: University of London Press.

Mackay R., and J. Palmer. (eds.). 1981. *Languages for specific purposes: Program design and evaluation.* Rowley, MA: Newbury House.

Morris, P. 1995. *The Hong Kong school curriculum.* Hong Kong: Hong Kong University Press.

Munby, J. 1978. *Communicative syllabus design.* Cambridge: Cambridge University Press.

Nicholls, A., and H. Nicholls. 1972. *Developing curriculum: A practical guide.* London: Allen and Unwin.

O'Neill, R. 1978. *Kernel one.* London: Longman.

Ozolins, U. 1993. *The politics of language in Australia.* Melbourne: Cambridge University Press.

Praninskas, J. 1972. *American University word list.* London: Longman.

Richards, J. C., and T. Rodgers. 1986. *Approaches and methods in language teaching.* New York: Cambridge University Press.

Richtertich, R., and J. L. Chancerel. 1978. *Identifying the needs of adults learning a foreign language.* Strasbourg: Council for Cultural Co-operation of the Council of Europe.

Rivers, W. 1964. *The psychologist and the foreign language learner.* Chicago: University of Chicago Press.

Robinson, P. 1980. *ESP (English for specific purposes).* Oxford: Pergamon.

Rodgers, T. 1989. Syllabus design, curriculum development and polity determination. In R. K. Johnson (ed.), *The second language curriculum.* New York: Cambridge University Press. 24–34.

Schutz, N., and B. Derwing. 1981. The problem of needs assessment in English for specific purposes: Some theoretical and practical considerations. In Mackay and Palmer (1981), 29–44.

Stern, H. 1974. Directions in language teaching theory and research. In J. Qvistgaard et al. (eds.). 1974. *Applied linguistics: Problems and solutions.* Heidelberg. 61–108.

Strevens, P. 1977. Special-purpose language learning: a perspective. Survey article. *Language Teaching and Linguistics Abstracts* 10(3): 145–163.

Swales, J. 1971. *Writing scientific English.* London: Nelson.

Tyler, R. 1949. *Basic principles of curriculum and instruction.* Chicago: University of Chicago Press.

Van Ek, J. L., and L. G. Alexander. 1975. *The threshold level in a European unit/credit system for modern language learning by adults.* Oxford: Pergamon.

Van Els, T., T. Bongaerts, G. Extra, C. Van Os, and A. Janssen-van Dieten. 1984. *Applied linguistics and the learning and teaching of foreign languages.* London: Arnold.

White, R. 1988. *The ELT curriculum.* Oxford: Blackwell.

Wilkins, D. A. 1976. *Notional syllabuses.* Oxford: Oxford University Press.

Yalden, J. 1987. *The communicative syllabus.* Englewood Cliffs, NJ: Prentice-Hall.

3 Needs analysis

One of the basic assumptions of curriculum development is that a sound educational program should be based on an analysis of learners' needs. Procedures used to collect information about learners' needs are known as needs analysis. Needs analysis as a distinct and necessary phase in planning educational programs emerged in the 1960s as part of the systems approach to curriculum development and was part of the prevalent philosophy of educational accountablity (Stufflebeam, McCormick, Brinkerhoff, and Nelson 1985). If providers of training programs wanted public or other sources of funding in order to provide different kinds of training programs, they were required to demonstrate that a proposed program was a response to a genuine need (Pratt 1980). Subsequently needs analysis developed into something of an industry. Berwick (1989, 51) comments:

The need for convincing precision in educational needs assessment was also reinforced during this period by the "behavioral objectives" movement in educational planning, particularly in North America, which insisted on specifying in measurable form all goals of importance within an educational system. The emphasis on precision and accountability clearly influenced the appearance of needs assessment as a form of educational technology and its diversification into a collection of educational research methodologies.

Needs analysis was introduced into language teaching through the ESP movement (see Chapter 2). From the 1960s, the demand for specialized language programs grew and applied linguists increasingly began to employ needs analysis procedures in language teaching. By the 1980s, in many parts of the world a "needs-based philosophy" emerged in language teaching, particularly in relation to ESP and vocationally oriented program design (Brindley 1984). In this chapter we will examine approaches to needs analysis and consider the purposes of needs analysis, the nature of needs, who needs analysis is intended for, who the target population is, who collects information, what procedures can be used, and how the information collected can be used. (Examples of two different needs analyses are given on pages 68–71.)

The purposes of needs analysis

Needs analysis in language teaching may be used for a number of different purposes, for example:

- to find out what language skills a learner needs in order to perform a particular role, such as sales manager, tour guide, or university student
- to help determine if an existing course adequately addresses the needs of potential students
- to determine which students from a group are most in need of training in particular language skills
- to identify a change of direction that people in a reference group feel is important
- to identify a gap between what students are able to do and what they need to be able to do
- to collect information about a particular problem learners are experiencing

In the case of K–12 ESL programs (e.g., for ESL students in public schools) Linse (1993) identifies the following purposes for needs analysis:

- to compile a demographic profile of all the languages and language groups represented by the students
- to assess their level of language acquisition in their native language and in English
- to determine their communicative abilities in English
- to determine their formal knowledge of English
- to find out how students use language on a daily basis
- to determine what English language skills are necessary to enable students to participate in all school and community activities in English
- to find out what prior experiences students have had with formal education
- to determine the attitudes of the students and their families toward formal schooling and education
- to find out what preliteracy and literacy skills the students possess
- to ascertain the students' level of cognitive development and acquisition of academic skills in their native language(s)
- to ascertain what cognitive and academic skills students have acquired in English
- to determine the cultural, political, and personal characteristics of students

The first step in conducting a needs analysis is therefore to decide exactly what its purpose or purposes are. For example, when a needs analysis of restaurant employees is conducted, the purposes might be:

- to determine current levels of language proficiency of employees
- to determine how many employees are in need of the language training
- to identify senior restaurant staff's perception of language problems employees have on the job
- to identify employees' perceptions of language difficulties they face on the job
- to ascertain the types of transactions employees typically perform in English
- to determine the language characteristics of those transactions
- to assess the extent to which employees' needs are met by currently available programs and textbooks

In many cases, learners' language needs may be relatively easy to determine, particularly if learners need to learn a language for very specific purposes, for example, employment in fields such as tourism, nursing, or the hotel industry. In this case the tasks employees typically carry out in English can be observed and the language needs of those tasks determined. The information obtained can then serve as a basis for planning a training program. In some cases, "needs" also includes students' rights. Linse comments:

It is the school's responsibility to take into account the cultural, political, and personal characteristics of students as the curriculum is developed in order to plan activities and objectives that are realistic and purposeful. It is not the responsibility of the school to act on political matters, but it is the school's responsibility to provide equal access to school opportunities and to validate the experiences of all students, regardless of their political and/or cultural backgrounds. (Linse, in Hudelson 1993, 46)

In other cases, learners' needs may not be so immediate – for example, students learning English as a secondary school subject in an EFL context. Here English may be a compulsory subject that is considered an important part of a child's general education. However, even though the students may not have any immediate perceptions of needs, curriculum planners will generally have consulted employers, parents, teachers, and others to find out what knowledge of English they expect high school graduates to achieve. In many countries, the introduction of English or another foreign language in elementary or secondary school is based on what curriculum planners consider best for students to study at school in the same way that math, history, and physical education are included in the school curriculum. Learners are not consulted as to whether they perceive a need for such knowledge. Their needs have been decided for them by those concerned with their long-term welfare. Needs analysis thus includes the study of perceived and present needs as well as potential and unrecognized needs.

Needs analysis may take place prior to, during, or after a language program. Much of the literature on needs analysis is based on the assumption that it is part of the planning that takes place as part of the development of a course. It assumes that time and resources are available to plan, collect, and analyze relevant information for a planned program of instruction. This "a priori" approach to needs analysis requires long-term planning and assumes adequate time and resources to devote to needs analysis. Example 1 (pages 68–70) is a needs analysis of this type.

In some cases, however, long-term planning is not an option. Little may be known in detail about a group of learners apart from the fact that a group of forty-five Mexican civil servants will be arriving in 3 weeks' time and want to work on their language skills. In these circumstances, needs analysis has to be carried out as part of the delivery of the course. Goals, content, and the teaching approach are shaped by information collected during the teaching of the course. Example 2 (pages 70–71) is a needs analysis of this kind.

At other times, the bulk of the information that constitutes the needs analysis may be collected after the course is finished. The information collected is then analyzed in order to obtain a more comprehensive view of the learners' needs as a basis for evaluating and revising the program (see Chapter 9).

What are needs?

The term *needs* is not as straightforward as it might appear, and hence the term is sometimes used to refer to wants, desires, demands, expectation, motivations, lacks, constraints, and requirements (Brindley 1984, 28). Needs are often described in terms of a linguistic deficiency, that is, as describing the difference between what a learner can presently do in a language and what he or she should be able to do. This suggests that needs have objective reality and are simply there waiting to be identified and analyzed. Porcher (1977, in Brindley 1984, 29) offers a different perspective: "Need is not a thing that exists and might be encountered ready-made on the street. It is a thing that is constructed, the center of conceptual networks and the product of a number of epistemological choices (which are not innocent themselves, of course)." What is identified as a need is dependent on judgment and reflects the interests and values of those making such a judgment. Teachers, learners, employers, parents, and other *stakeholders* (discussed in the next section) may thus all have different views as to what needs are. For example, in considering the needs of immigrants, representatives of the majority population may see the immigrants' needs as achieving cultural and linguistic assimilation as quickly as possible and hence may want a needs analysis to identify the language skills immigrants require in order to survive, and ultimately, assimilate into the dominant culture. The immigrants themselves, however, may see their goals as concerned with communication for survival and independence, particularly economic survival, but may have no wish to assimilate into the dominant culture (Burnett 1998). Auerbach (1995, 9) has pointed out that English language teaching has often been viewed as a "neutral transfer of skills, knowledge, or competencies" and that such an approach is based on the needs of social institutions, rather than language learners, and ignores questions of power:

Pedagogical choices about curriculum development, content, materials, classroom processes, and language use, although appearing to be informed by apolitical professional considerations, are in fact inherently ideological in nature, with significant implications for learners' socioeconomic roles. (Auerbach 1995, 9)

Needs are often described in terms of language needs, that is, as the language skills needed to survive in an English-dominant society. But as Auerbach (1995) and others have pointed out, in many cases, particularly that of immigrant minorities in English-dominant societies, such persons also have other kinds of needs. These relate to housing, health care, access to schooling for their children, access to community agencies and services, and ways of addressing exploitation and discrimination in the workplace. How can the curriculum give learners the linguistic and other resources they need to understand and access resources they have the right to make use of in the community and to articulate and defend their own rights and interests? Planning an ESL curriculum in this case not only involves identifying students' language needs, but seeks "to enable them to critically examine [the existing order] and become active in shaping their own roles in it" (Auerbach 1995, 15). This issue will be examined in more detail when we consider alternative curriculum models and their value, in Chapter 5.

The users of needs analysis

A needs analysis may be conducted for a variety of different users. For example, in conducting a needs analysis to help revise the secondary school English curriculum in a country, the end users include:

- curriculum officers in the ministry of education, who may wish to use the information to evaluate the adequacy of existing syllabus, curriculum, and materials

- teachers who will teach from the new curriculum
- learners, who will be taught from the curriculum
- writers, who are preparing new textbooks
- testing personnel, who are involved in developing end-of-school assessments
- staff of tertiary institutions, who are interested in knowing what the expected level will be of students exiting the schools and what problems they face

In the case of a needs analysis conducted by a private institute of language needs of trainee accountants in international accounting firms, the target users might be:

- trainers responsible for designing training programs and materials
- a funding body, such as the local professional society for accountants who are interested in seeing a concrete product as an outcome of their funding
- employers who are interested in improving the job performance of new staff

With small-scale needs analysis such as that carried out by a single teacher on his or her class, the audience might consist of the teacher, other teachers, and the program coordinator. In cases of large-scale needs analysis, there will be multiple audiences for the results of a needs analysis. Determining the likely audiences is an important first step in planning a needs analysis in order to ensure that the information they need is obtained and that the needs analysis will have the impact it is designed to have. Stufflebeam et al. (1985, 25) comment: "It is important to remember that not all key audiences are likely to be identified at the start of a study. Also, it is entirely possible that the relative importance of various audiences will change during the study."

Needs analysis can thus have a political dimension. It can be used to support a particular agenda, for example, by giving priority to one group to the exclusion of others within a population or in order to justify a decision that has already been made on economic or other grounds. For example, an employer might want to use information from a needs analysis to justify replacing certain staff rather than investing in providing for retraining. In any situation where needs analysis is being undertaken, there are thus different stakeholders, that is, those who have a particular interest or involvement in the issues or programs that are being examined, and it is important to try to get a sense of what their different agendas are. Connelly and Clandinin (1988, 124) define a stakeholder as "a person or group of persons with a right to comment on, and have input into, the curriculum process offered in schools." Different stakeholders will want different things from the curriculum. Connelly and Clandinin (1988, 131–132) suggest that when a group of persons are working on a curriculum committee or trying to solve a curriculum problem they should think of the planning process as a curriculum stakeholder situation and ask the following questions:

1. What is the purpose of the curriculum situation?
2. If there is a group, what is the makeup of the group?
3. Who set up the project?
4. How were the group's membership and purpose established?

From the answers to these questions, further questions follow:

1. How accountable am I to this stakeholder?
2. How much will this stakeholder be affected by my decision?
3. How much risk is there in ignoring this stakeholder?
4. How much right has this stakeholder to direct my action?

The target population

The target population in a needs analysis refers to the people about whom information will be collected. Typically, in language programs these will be language learners or potential language learners, but others are also often involved depending on whether they can provide information useful in meeting the purposes of the needs analysis. For example, in conducting a needs analysis to determine the focus of an English program in public secondary schools in an EFL context, the target population might include:

- policy makers
- ministry of education officials
- teachers
- students
- academics
- employers
- vocational training specialists
- parents
- influential individuals and pressure groups
- academic specialists
- community agencies

Within each target group, subcategories of respondents might be needed to provide different perspectives on needs. For example, in conducting a needs analysis of students studying foreign languages at a New Zealand university (Richards and Gravatt 1998), the following categories of students were included to help determine students' motivations for selecting a language course, dropping a language course, or choosing not to take a language course:

- students currently enrolled in a foreign language course
- students previously enrolled but no longer studying a language
- students who have never studied a foreign language

In determining the target population, an important issue is that of sampling. In some cases, the population is small enough for every learner to be included in the sample. In other cases, this approach is not feasible and so decisions must be made about the size of the sample to be included in a needs analysis. Sampling involves asking a portion of the potential population instead of the total population and seeks to create a sample that is representative of the total population. Elley (1984) points out that a number of factors influence the approach to sampling, such as the homogeneity of the population in terms of the kinds of skills, attitudes, or knowledge being sought or the need to study subgroups within the sample – for example, based on sex, language group, or other factors. Where the target population is large, specialized advice is often needed to determine what approach to sampling best suits the purpose of the study and the sources of information available.

Administering the needs analysis

Planning a needs analysis involves deciding who will administer the needs analysis and collect and analyze the results. Needs analyses vary in their scope and demands, from a survey of a whole school population in a country to a study of a group of thirty learners in a single institution. Sometimes a team of personnel is assembled specifically for the purpose of doing the analysis; at other times two or three interested teachers may be the only ones involved. For example, in a needs analysis of the language needs of non-English-background students studying at a New Zealand university (see Appendix 3), the following were involved:

- the research team made up of two academics and a research assistant
- colleagues in different departments who discussed the project and reviewed sample questionnaires
- students who piloted the questionnaire

- academic staff of the university who administered some of the question-naires
- secretarial support involved in preparing questionnaires and tabulating data

In some language programs, informal needs analysis is part of a teacher's ongoing responsibilities. Shaw and Dowsett (1986) describe this approach in the Australian Adult Migrant Education Program:

Informal needs assessment deals with the informal negotiations that take place between class teachers and students in the form of chats with either individual students, groups of students, or the whole class in order to select a focus for the class and create group cohesion by establishing a coincidence of learning needs. . . . Informal needs assessment is normally the main task of the classroom teacher during week one of the course. . . . [It] is a necessary component of information retrieval on students' learning needs and should be recorded. It can subsequently be used as an input for aims and objectives setting and for devising course outlines. (Shaw and Dowsett 1986, 47–49)

Information collected in this way may complement information collected through more formal means.

Procedures for conducting needs analysis

A variety of procedures can be used in conducting needs analysis and the kind of information obtained is often dependent on the type of procedure selected. Since any one source of information is likely to be incomplete or partial, a *triangular approach* (i.e., collecting information from two or more sources) is advisable. Many different sources of information should be sought. For example, when a needs analysis of the writing problems encountered by foreign students enrolled in American universities is conducted, information could be obtained from the following sources:

- samples of student writing
- test data on student performance
- reports by teachers on typical problems students face
- opinions of experts
- information from students via interviews and questionnaires
- analysis of textbooks teaching academic writing
- survey or related literature
- examples of writing programs from other institutions
- examples of writing assignments given to first-year university students

Procedures for collecting information during a needs analysis can be selected from among the following:

Questionnaires

Questionnaires are one of the most common instruments used. They are relatively easy to prepare, they can be used with large numbers of subjects, and
they obtain information that is relatively easy to tabulate and analyze. They
can also be used to elicit information about many different kinds of issues,
such as language use, communication difficulties, preferred learning styles,
preferred classroom activities, and attitudes and beliefs.

Questionnaires are either based on a set of structured items (in which the
respondent chooses from a limited number of responses) or unstructured (in
which open-ended questions are given that the respondent can answer as he
or she chooses). Structured items are much easier to analyze and are hence
normally preferred. Appendix 2 illustrates a questionnaire designed as a basis for planning courses in Cantonese for non-Chinese residents of Hong
Kong. It seeks information on the following:

- situations in which Cantonese could be used
- self-assessment of current proficiency level in Cantonese
- previous experience of Cantonese courses
- views on textbooks for learning Cantonese
- views on approaches to teaching Cantonese
- learning-style preferences
- views on Cantonese as a language

A disadvantage of questionnaires, however, is that the information obtained
may be fairly superficial or imprecise and will often need follow-up to gain
a fuller understanding of what respondents intend. It should also be recognized that there are many badly designed questionnaires in educational research, and it is advisable to become familiar with the principles of good
questionnaire design to ensure that the information obtained is reliable. Piloting of questionnaires is essential to identify ambiguities and other problems before the questionnaire is administered. Some issues involved in the
design of questionnaires are given in Appendix 1.

Self-ratings

These consist of scales that students or others use to rate their knowledge
or abilities. (Self-ratings might also be included as part of a questionnaire.)
For example, a student might rate how well he or she can handle a job in-

terview in English. The disadvantage of such an instrument is that it provides only impressionistic information and information that is not very precise.

Interviews

Interviews allow for a more in-depth exploration of issues than is possible with a questionnaire, though they take longer to administer and are only feasible for smaller groups. An interview may often be useful at the preliminary stage of designing a questionnaire, since it will help the designer get a sense of what topics and issues can be focused on in the questionnaire. A structured interview in which a set series of questions is used allows more consistency across responses to be obtained. Interviews can be conducted face-to-face or over the telephone.

Meetings

A meeting allows a large amount of information to be collected in a fairly short time. For example, a meeting of teachers on the topic "students' problems with listening comprehension" might generate a wide range of ideas. However, information obtained in this way may be impressionistic and subjective and reflect the ideas of more outspoken members of a group.

Observation

Observations of learners' behavior in a target situation is another way of assessing their needs. For example, observing clerks performing their jobs in a bank will enable the observer to arrive at certain conclusions about their language needs.

However, people often do not perform well when they are being observed, so this has to be taken into account. In addition, observation is a specialized skill. Knowing how to observe, what to look for, and how to make use of the information obtained generally requires specialized training.

Collecting learner language samples

Collecting data on how well learners perform on different language tasks (e.g., business letters, interviews, telephone calls) and documenting the typical problems they have is a useful and direct source of information about learners' language needs. Language samples may be collected through the following means:

- *written or oral tasks:* Examples of students written or oral work are collected.
- *simulations or role plays:* Students are given simulations to carry out and their performance is observed or recorded.
- *achievement tests:* Students are tested for their abilities in different domains of language use.
- *performance tests:* Students are tested on job-related or task-related behaviors, such as "how well a job interview can be carried out in English."

Task analysis

This refers to analysis of the kinds of tasks the learners will have to carry out in English in a future occupational or educational setting and assessment of the linguistic characteristics and demands of the tasks. For example, a hotel employee might have to perform the following tasks in English:

- greet hotel guests
- inquire about their accommodation needs
- inform them of accommodation available at the hotel
- help them make a suitable choice of accommodation
- handle check-in procedures

Berwick (1989, 57) observes: "The emphasis of target situation analysis is on the nature and effect of target language communications in particular situations (in offices, on assembly lines, in meeting rooms, in content-area classrooms, for example). Expert analysis of communication establishes standards against which current performance can be gauged." Once target tasks have been identified, their linguistic characteristics are determined as a basis for designing a language course or training materials.

Case studies

With a case study, a single student or a selected group of students is followed through a relevant work or educational experience in order to determine the characteristics of that situation. For example, a newly arrived immigrant might be studied for three months, during which time the student keeps a log of his or her daily language experiences in English, the situations in which the language is used, and the problems he or she encounters. Although it is generally not possible to generalize from a case study, it provides a very rich source of information that may complement information obtained from other sources.

Analysis of available information

In any situation where a needs analysis is needed, a large amount of relevant information is generally available in various sources. These include:

- books
- journal articles
- reports and surveys
- records and files

An analysis of available information is normally the first step in a needs analysis because there are very few problems in language teaching that have not been written about or analyzed somewhere.

Designing the needs analysis

Designing a needs analysis involves choosing from among the various options discussed above and selecting those that are likely to give a comprehensive view of learners' needs and that represent the interests of the different stakeholders involved. Decisions have to be made on the practical procedures involved in collecting, organizing, analyzing, and reporting the information collected. It is important to make sure that the needs analysis does not produce an information overload. There needs to be a clear reason for collecting different kinds of information so as to ensure that only information that will actually be used is collected. In investigating the language needs of non-English-background students at a New Zealand university (Gravatt, Richards, and Lewis 1997), the following procedures were used:

1. literature survey
2. analysis of a wide range of survey questionnaires
3. contact with others who had conducted similar surveys
4. interviews with teachers to determine goals
5. identification of participating departments
6. presentation of project proposal to participating departments and identification of liaison person in each department
7. development of a pilot student and staff questionnaire
8. review of the questionnaires by colleagues
9. piloting of the questionnaires
10. selection of staff and student subjects
11. developing a schedule for collecting data
12. administration of questionnaires

13. follow-up interviews with selected participants
14. tabulation of responses
15. analysis of responses
16. writing up of report and recommendations

In smaller-scale needs analysis such as that of a teacher or group of teachers assessing the needs of new groups of students in a language program, needs analysis procedures may consist of:

• initial questionnaire
• follow-up individual and group interviews
• meetings with students
• meetings with other teachers
• ongoing classroom observation
• tests

Making use of the information obtained

The results of a needs analysis will generally consist of information taken from several different sources and summarized in the form of ranked lists of different kinds. For example, it might result in lists of the following kind:

• situations in which English is frequently used
• situations in which difficulties are encountered
• comments most often made by people on learners' performance
• frequencies with which different transactions are carried out
• perceived difficulties with different aspects of language use
• preferences for different kinds of activities in teaching
• frequencies of errors made in different types of situations or activities
• common communication problems in different situations
• suggestions and opinions about different aspects of learners' problems
• frequencies of linguistic items or units in different texts or situations

One of the findings of a needs analysis of problems of ESL students attending university lectures was a list of the frequency with which students experienced difficulties with speaking and listening skills (Gravett et al. 1997, 36). The most common difficulties reported were (by rank):

1. large-group discussions
2. class discussions
3. interactions with native speakers

4. out-of-class projects
5. small-group work
6. demonstrator interactions
7. class participation

However, such a listing provides little useful information about the precise type of problems the learners experience in relation to each event. Even if more detailed information had been provided, the results would still be impressionistic. For example, in relation to event 1 (large-group discussions), more detailed information could have been sought, from which a further listing might have resulted – the most difficult aspects of taking part in group discussions. Johns and Johns (1977) provide such a list based on a needs analysis of problems students have with discussions. The most frequent difficulties were:

1. comprehension of spoken English ('they speak too fast'; 'they mumble'; 'vocabulary is idiomatic')
2. the pressing need to formulate a contribution quickly ('I can't think what to say')
3. shyness about the value of a contribution ('I might say something wrong')
4. inability to formulate an idea in English ('I don't know how to say it in English')
5. awareness that a given function may be realized in different ways ('I don't know the best way to say it')
6. frustration about being unable to enter the discussion ('some students speak too much') (Johns and Johns 1977)

Yet even with this more detailed breakdown no direct application to program design is possible. In order to develop aims and objectives that addressed each problem, more analysis and research would be needed to further understand what is implied by "comprehension of spoken English" and before the information obtained could be used in course planning. The point here is that there is no direct application of the information obtained from needs analysis. Although the information gathered is useful, it still has to be subjected to a great deal of interpretation before it can be usefully applied in program planning.

In the course of carrying out a needs analysis, a large number of potential needs may be identified. However, these needs will have to be prioritized because not all of them may be practical to address in a language program, or perhaps the time frame available in the program is suitable for addressing only a portion of them. And the mere fact that needs have been identified does not automatically imply that changes will have to be made in the curriculum. First, the existing curriculum (when there is one) has to be examined to see to what extent the needs that have been identified are being met. Decisions will therefore have to be made concerning which of the needs are critical, which are important, and which are merely desirable. In addition, some needs will be immediate and others longer-term. For some, solutions will be feasible; for others, they may be impractical.

It is also important to remember that because needs are not objective facts but subjective interpretations of information from a large variety of sources, a great deal of consultation is needed with the various stakeholders to ensure that the conclusions drawn from a needs analysis are appropriate and relevant. It often happens that some of the information may be contradictory, Stufflebeam et al. (1985, 111) remind us:

> The process of analysis [of the results of a needs analysis] involves efforts that are thoughtful, investigatory, systematic, and carefully recorded so that they can be replicated and reviewed. The primary goal of analysis is to bring meaning to the obtained information and to do so in the context of some philosophy, relevant perspectives, and value positions that may be in conflict.

Thus, for example, in a needs analysis as part of curriculum renewal in a state education system, different views of problems in the curriculum emerged. A number of different points of view emerged as to what should be changed:

- *learners' view:* more support for learning needed and reduction of the amount of materials they had to study
- *academics' view:* better preparation for tertiary studies needed in terms of reading and writing skills
- *employers' view:* better preparation for employment required in terms of basic communication skills
- *teachers' view:* better grasp of grammar needed by learners

Brindley (1989) discusses differences between learners' and teachers' views of needs and suggests the need for a negotiation process in order to satisfy and clarify each other's assumptions. The same is true of other stakeholders in the curriculum.

Where there are several different audiences for the needs analysis (e.g., teachers, administrators, a funding body), the information obtained will have to be analyzed – and analyzed in a form that suits each group's interests. One group may require a brief overview of the findings while another may be interested in detailed findings. The format for reporting the findings may also vary. For example, it might include:

- a full written document
- a short summary document
- a meeting
- a group discussion
- a newsletter

Needs analysis thus produces information that can be used in different ways. For example:

- It may provide the basis for the evaluation of an existing program or a component of a program.
- It may provide the basis for planning goals and objectives for a future program.
- It may assist with developing tests and other assessment procedures.
- It can help with the selection of appropriate teaching methods in a program.
- It may provide the basis for developing a syllabus and teaching materials for a course.
- It may provide information that can be used as part of a course or program report to an external body or organization.

In none of these cases, however, is there a direct route from needs analysis to application. Some of these applications will be discussed in the chapters that follow. Although a major application of needs analysis is in the design of language programs, before a program can be designed additional information is needed on factors that can have an impact on the program. The identification of these factors and the assessment of their likely impact form the focus of Chapter 4.

Discussion questions and activities

1. Needs analysis is very applicable in situations where students have very specific language needs. However, it can also be used in situations where learners' needs are not so specific, as in the case of students learning English as a foreign language in a school setting. What might the focus of a needs analysis be in this situation?
2. If you were planning a needs analysis for the situation in which you teach, what information would you seek to obtain?
3. Discuss the concept of "stakeholders" in planning a needs analysis in relation to a context you are familiar with. How can the concerns of different stakeholders be addressed?

4. If you were designing a needs analysis for secretaries working in business offices, what target population would you include in the needs analysis? What kind of information would you need from each member of the target population?
5. Suggest four different needs analysis procedures that could be used to collect information about the language needs of hotel telephone operators. What are the advantages and limitations of each procedure?
6. Suggest situations in which a case study would provide useful information during a needs analysis.
7. Design a short questionnaire designed to investigate the language needs of tour guides. What issues will the questionnaire address? What type of items will you include in the questionnaire?
8. Critique the questionnaires in Appendixes 2 and 3 and suggest any improvements you think could be made to them.
9. Prepare a set of questions to be used in a structured interview for use in a needs analysis of the language needs of immigration officers at an airport.
10. Choose an occupation that you are familiar with or that you would be able to observe and prepare a task analysis of the tasks typically carried out by people in that occupation. Suggest the language requirements of each task.

Examples of needs analyses

Example 1: Needs analysis of non-English-background students and their English language needs at the University of Auckland

This is an example of needs analysis conducted in order to evaluate whether currently available language courses meet the needs of non-English-background learners at the university.

CONTEXT

The University of Auckland, Auckland, New Zealand. The largest of New Zealand's seven universities with a student population of some 26,000 in 1997.

BACKGROUND

The number of students for whom English is a second language has increased steadily since 1990, and continues to do so. In some faculties as many as 30 percent of the students are ESL students.

- The English competence of these students on entry varies considerably.
- A previous small-scale report within the university, addressing the issue of English-language skills of students and entrance requirements, strongly indicated that more data were needed regarding the problems experienced by ESL students.
- This prompted a needs analysis initiated to assess these problems, using two questionnaires to survey staff and ESL students' perceptions across the university.
- The study looked at the language demands placed on ESL students, problems, experiences, and suggestions for improving the situation.

METHOD

Staff questionnaire This included some questions from similar instruments developed in other institutions, as well as others specific to issues at the university. The questions were organized into the following sections.

- background information concerning the course or paper the lecturer was describing
- overview of problems experienced by ESL students in the course/paper
- linguistic demands of the course/paper in the areas of listening, speaking, reading, writing, as well as the difficulties experienced by the students in these areas
- suggestions as to which language skills should be focused on in courses for ESL students
- modifications made in teaching or in examinations as a result of the difficulties experienced by ESL students

The questionnaire was piloted and revised before it was distributed. Respondents were identified by the heads of all fifty-one departments at the university. The results were analyzed overall and by faculty.

Student questionnaire (see Appendix 3) The student questionnaire was a modified version of the staff questionnaire. The structure was similar but with less emphasis on language expectations and greater emphasis on problems being encountered. The questionnaire was piloted before distribution. The questionnaire was distributed to students enrolled in all courses that were identified in the staff questionnaire as having a high proportion of ESL students. In all, 302 student questionnaires were completed.

PRODUCT
A fifty-seven page report was produced that described the results of the two survey questionnaires together with a series of recommendations.

Example 2: A curriculum guide and teaching kit for tutors of English as a second language teaching Vietnamese refugees in London

This is an example of needs analysis "on the run," that is, conducted as part of the process of teaching and developing a course.

CONTEXT

As a result of the arrival of large number of Vietnamese refugees in London, the Kensington Institute in conjunction with the Inner London Education Authority Language and Literacy Unit planned an ESL program for the refugees. Six teachers and a tutor in charge were appointed to manage the program, with time budgeted to plan a syllabus, develop materials, and coordinate the program.

METHOD

Syllabus frameworks   On the basis of experience of students with similar needs, ten topic areas were chosen as the basis for the program.

Personal information	Work
Shopping	Services
Health and welfare	Education
House and home	Social
Travel	Food and drink

This was a starting point for the program to be revised in the light of ongoing information about the students' needs identified during the teaching of the program. Situations were then selected from the topic areas and the language needs of each situation predicted. This resulted in provisional syllabus frameworks organized by topic.

Student profiles   In order to develop the program, records were kept of information gathered during teaching, resulting in the building up of student and class profiles. The class profiles documented previous learning experience, strengths and weakness of each student, common areas of interest, individual and group needs, and reflected areas that would be useful to focus on in that class.

Cultural comparisons   Information was also collected through observation, discussions, and interviews on cultural differences between Vietnamese and British people with regard to such things as family relationships, old age, work, and leisure to help identify differences between the social norms in the two cultures. This information then fed into the course content.

PRODUCT

The project resulted in the preparation of a 156-page tutors' kit that contained the following elements:

a) description of the planning process
b) syllabus frameworks
c) discussion of teaching techniques and activities
d) literacy guidelines
e) worksheets
f) aids and materials
g) discussion of problem areas in English for speakers of Vietnamese

Appendix 1   Designing a questionnaire

The following questions need to be considered in designing a questionnaire.

1. Preliminary questions

a) Will it be useful to carry out some interviews before designing the questionnaire, in order to get a sense of appropriate topics and issues?
b) How large will the sample be? Is it representative of the whole population information is needed about?
c) How will the questionnaire be piloted?
d) How will it be administered (e.g., by mail, self-administered, or group-administered)?

2. The types of information asked for

a) Is the question really necessary? How will the information it provides be used?
b) Are other questions needed on this issue?
c) Can the respondents answer this question? Do they have sufficient information (e.g., to answer a question such as "How much English do your students use outside of class?")?
d) Should the question be made more specific and more closely related to the respondents' personal experience?
e) Is the question biased in one direction? (E.g., "Do you agree that a communicative approach is the best way to teach a language?")
f) Will the respondents be willing to give the information asked for? (E.g., "Does your teacher know how to teach English?")
g) Is it appropriate to ask this question? (E.g., "How old are you?")

3. How the questions are worded

a) Can the question be understood? Is the wording unambiguous?
b) Can the question be shortened? (Aim for not more than 20 words.)
c) Does it contain vocabulary likely to be known by the learner?
d) Does the question contain any unstated assumptions? (E.g., "In your college English course, did you. . . ?")
e) Are there any prestige questions, that is, which students are likely to try to answer to give a good impression of themselves? (E.g., "Have you used the things you have been taught out of class?")
f) Is the wording biased or emotionally loaded in any way?

g) Would a more personalized (or less personalized) version of the question be better?

h) Is the answer to the question likely to be influenced by the content of preceding questions?

4. The type of items in the questionnaire

a) Open question: one that can be answered freely and where no kind of choice is required in the answer

b) Closed question: one that is answered by choosing alternatives provided

c) Checklist: a set of terms that describe different attributes or values

d) Rating scale: a value is given on a scale (e.g., between "strongly agree" and "strongly disagree")

e) Ranking: items are ranked (e.g., from 1 to 9) according to some criteria

f) Inventory: a list that the respondents mark or check in some way

Appendix 2   Needs analysis questionnaire for Cantonese learners

Questionnaire used in needs analysis of learners of Cantonese in Hong Kong (from Li and Richards 1995).

Part A
In what situations is Cantonese (or would Cantonese be) useful for you?
Please check the appropriate column.

		Very useful	Useful	Not useful
A1.	Buying things in stores and supermarkets.	☐	☐	☐
A2.	Buying things in the market place.	☐	☐	☐
A3.	Getting information about services and goods I want to buy.	☐	☐	☐
A4.	Ordering food in a restaurant/canteen/cafeteria.	☐	☐	☐
A5.	Taking a taxi.	☐	☐	☐
A6.	Taking other public transport.	☐	☐	☐
A7.	Asking for directions.	☐	☐	☐
A8.	Talking to colleagues at work.	☐	☐	☐
A9.	Talking to office personnel at work.	☐	☐	☐
A10.	Talking to neighbours.	☐	☐	☐

		Very useful	Useful	Not useful
A11.	Talking to children.	☐	☐	☐
A12.	Talking to friends.	☐	☐	☐
A13.	Having casual conversations with people.	☐	☐	☐
A14.	Talking to students.	☐	☐	☐
A15.	Talking to a (Cantonese-speaking) domestic helper.	☐	☐	☐
A16.	Talking to workers in my place of residence.	☐	☐	☐
A17.	Talking to electricians, plumbers, etc.	☐	☐	☐
A18.	Receiving telephone calls.	☐	☐	☐
A19.	Making telephone calls.	☐	☐	☐
A20.	Joining hobby or interest group.	☐	☐	☐
A21.	Playing sports and participating in social clubs.	☐	☐	☐
A22.	Watching TV or movies.	☐	☐	☐
A23.	Listening to the radio.	☐	☐	☐
A24.	Listening to Cantonese music.	☐	☐	☐
A25.	Visiting friends' homes.	☐	☐	☐
A26.	Visiting different parts of the territory.	☐	☐	☐
A27.	Visiting Guangdong province.	☐	☐	☐
A28.	Making travel arrangements.	☐	☐	☐
A29.	Using Cantonese in situations related to my work.	☐	☐	☐

Please explain: _____

_____

_____

_____

Other: _____

_____

_____

_____

Part B
From the list above please choose five that are the most important for you. Write the numbers below.

_____

Part C

If you already speak some Cantonese, please indicate your present level of ability in Cantonese:

C1. Basic (lower): know a few words and fixed expressions; cannot manage conversational exchanges; respond to question and answer exchanges on a few topics; very limited vocabulary, grammar, and knowledge of idioms; pronunciation heavily influenced by mother tongue.

C2. Basic (upper): know a limited number of common words and expressions; able to manage limited, short conversations on a few predictable topics; survival level knowledge of vocabulary, grammar, and idioms; pronunciation heavily influenced by mother tongue.

C3. Intermediate (lower): reasonable fluency on a restricted range of topics but difficulty outside a limited range of topics; many problems with words, idioms, grammar, and pronunciation.

C4. Intermediate (upper): can manage comfortably in familiar situations and with familiar topics, though still some difficulty with vocabulary, idioms, grammar, and pronunciation.

C5. Advanced: able to converse fluently and naturally on most topics; little difficulty with vocabulary, idioms, grammar, and pronunciation.

C6. If you have studied Cantonese, please indicate under what circumstances.
  (a) I took a course.
  (b) I studied with a private tutor.
  (c) I picked up Cantonese informally.

  Other: _____
  _____
  _____
  _____

C7. If you attended a formal course, please indicate the length and frequency of the course (e.g., 6 weeks, 3 hours per week).

  _____
  _____

C8. How useful was the course? (Please circle your choice.)

  Very useful   Somewhat useful   Not useful

  Please explain: _____
  _____
  _____
  _____
  _____

C9. If you have used one or more textbooks, please indicate the name of each
     text and how useful or otherwise it was:

Name of text	Very useful	Useful	Not useful
(a) _____	☐	☐	☐
(b) _____	☐	☐	☐
(c) _____	☐	☐	☐
(d) _____	☐	☐	☐

C10. To what would you attribute your present level of ability in Cantonese?

	Very true	Somewhat true	Not true
(a) I attended a useful course.	☐	☐	☐
(b) I studied with a private tutor.	☐	☐	☐
(c) I make every effort to use Cantonese.	☐	☐	☐
(d) I enjoy studying Cantonese.	☐	☐	☐
(e) I need Cantonese for my job.	☐	☐	☐
(f) I am a good language learner.	☐	☐	☐
(g) I get a lot of help from Cantonese-speaking friends.	☐	☐	☐
(h) I spend a lot of time on Cantonese.	☐	☐	☐

Other: _____
_____
_____
_____
_____

C11. What activities or experiences were most helpful in your study of
     Cantonese? Please elaborate.

_____
_____
_____
_____
_____

Part D

If you have studied Cantonese before, but have since stopped studying Cantonese, please complete Part D below by checking the appropriate box.

I have studied Cantonese before, but I stopped because of the following reason(s):

		Very true	Somewhat true	Not true
D1.	I did not have time to continue.	☐	☐	☐
D2.	I felt that I was not making any progress.	☐	☐	☐
D3.	I was not given any opportunity to use Cantonese outside the classroom.	☐	☐	☐
D4.	The lessons were not useful because:			
	(a) We were not taught things that I could use.	☐	☐	☐
	(b) I found the language too difficult to master.	☐	☐	☐
	(c) I found the pronunciation too difficult to master.	☐	☐	☐
	(d) I found the grammar too difficult to master.	☐	☐	☐
	(e) I found the vocabulary too difficult to master.	☐	☐	☐
D5.	The teacher did not know how to teach Cantonese.	☐	☐	☐
D6.	I did not like the teaching methods used.	☐	☐	☐
D7.	The materials were:			
	(a) too difficult.	☐	☐	☐
	(b) not relevant to my needs.	☐	☐	☐
	(c) not interesting.	☐	☐	☐
	(d) not challenging.	☐	☐	☐

Other: _____

_____

_____

_____

_____

Part E

Have you ever used the following activities in studying Cantonese? If you indicate *yes,* how useful were they?

	Very useful	Useful	Not useful
E1. Practising dialogues from a book.	☐	☐	☐
E2. Practising drills on tones, sounds, and grammatical patterns.	☐	☐	☐
E3. Free conversation with native speakers.	☐	☐	☐
E4. Free conversation with other learners of Cantonese.	☐	☐	☐
E5. Memorizing bilingual vocabulary lists.	☐	☐	☐
E6. Studying Cantonese textbooks at home.	☐	☐	☐
E7. Studying the grammar of Cantonese.	☐	☐	☐
E8. Studying the tone system of Cantonese.	☐	☐	☐
E9. Studying the difference between English and Cantonese.	☐	☐	☐
E10. Doing pair-work exercises.	☐	☐	☐
E11. Doing group-work exercises.	☐	☐	☐
E12. Doing translation exercises.	☐	☐	☐
E13. Writing down Cantonese using a romanized system.	☐	☐	☐
E14. Watching TV in Cantonese at home.	☐	☐	☐
E15. Watching or listening to people speaking Cantonese around me.	☐	☐	☐
E16. Using cassettes at home.	☐	☐	☐
E17. Talking to friends in Cantonese.	☐	☐	☐
E18. Trying to use Cantonese whenever I have the opportunity.	☐	☐	☐
E19. Putting myself in situations in which I will be forced to speak in Cantonese.	☐	☐	☐
E20. Making myself understood even if I make a lot of mistakes.	☐	☐	☐
E21. Speaking a good Cantonese without making mistakes in grammar or pronunciation.	☐	☐	☐
E22. Studying with a private tutor.	☐	☐	☐

Other: _____

_____

_____

Part F

In class or with a tutor, I would like my teacher to:

F1.	explain new grammar points before practising them.	No	A little	Good	Best
F2.	practise before explaining new grammar points.	No	A little	Good	Best
F3.	correct any mistakes I made in front of others immediately.	No	A little	Good	Best
F4.	correct my mistakes of grammar.	No	A little	Good	Best
F5.	correct my mistakes of pronunciation.	No	A little	Good	Best
F6.	use Cantonese only.	No	A little	Good	Best
F7.	use both English and Cantonese.	No	A little	Good	Best

Part G

What are your feelings about Cantonese as a language?

G1.	Cantonese is a language with a rich vocabulary.	Very true	True	Not true
G2.	Cantonese is made up of many colloquial expressions.	Very true	True	Not true
G3.	Cantonese is made up of many idioms.	Very true	True	Not true
G4.	Cantonese is a very difficult language.	Very true	True	Not true
G5.	Cantonese is a language with a lot of grammar.	Very true	True	Not true
G6.	Cantonese is a language where pronunciation is very important.	Very true	True	Not true
G7.	Cantonese is a language where rhythm and intonation are important.	Very true	True	Not true
G8.	Cantonese is a very useful language in Hong Kong.	Very true	True	Not true
G9.	Cantonese is a fascinating language.	Very true	True	Not true
G10.	Cantonese is a beautiful sounding language.	Very true	True	Not true
G11.	Cantonese is a polite language.	Very true	True	Not true
G12.	The rhythm and intonation of Cantonese are pleasing to my ears.	Very true	True	Not true
G13.	Cantonese is a harsh sounding language.	Very true	True	Not true
G14.	Cantonese is a vulgar sounding language.	Very true	True	Not true

Other: _____

_____

_____

Appendix 3   Needs analysis questionnaire for non-English-background students

Student questionnaire used at the University of Auckland, New Zealand (from Gravatt, Richards, and Lewis 1997).

Institute of Language Teaching and Learning

NEEDS ANALYSIS OF ENGLISH AS A SECOND LANGUAGE
STUDENT – STUDENT VERSION

This questionnaire is part of a project being carried out by the Institute of Language Teaching and Learning to determine what the language needs of students whose first or dominant language is not English (ESL students) attending the University are, whether these are being adequately met and, if not, what can be done better. For this purpose the opinions of both staff and students in a variety of departments are being surveyed. It would be appreciated if you could complete this questionnaire, which should take approximately 20 minutes.

The term 'N/A' is used in this questionnaire. It means 'Not applicable' and is the appropriate response if a question does not apply to you.

With which of the following groups do you identify? (please tick the appropriate box):

☐ Pacific Island – which?
☐ Asian – which country?
☐ Other (please specify):

How many years have you been studying at Auckland University (including 1997)?

What is your current course of study?

Please complete this questionnaire with regard to the course you have specified here.

A. Overview of Skills Needed and Difficulties Encountered

In your course of study, how often are you expected to use the following skills? (please circle):

	Very often	Often	Sometimes	Rarely	Never
Reading	1	2	3	4	5
Writing	1	2	3	4	5
Speaking	1	2	3	4	5
Listening	1	2	3	4	5

How often do you have difficulty with each of these skills? (please circle):

	Very often	Often	Sometimes	Rarely	Never
Reading	1	2	3	4	5
Writing	1	2	3	4	5
Speaking	1	2	3	4	5
Listening	1	2	3	4	5

B. General Statements

Please circle the appropriate response:

How important to success in your course of study are the following abilities?

	High		Moderate		Low
1. Listening to English	1	2	3	4	5
2. Speaking English	1	2	3	4	5
3. Writing English	1	2	3	4	5
4. Reading English	1	2	3	4	5

How important to success in your field after graduation are the following abilities?

	High		Moderate		Low
1. Listening to English	1	2	3	4	5
2. Speaking English	1	2	3	4	5
3. Writing English	1	2	3	4	5
4. Reading English	1	2	3	4	5

C. Speaking and Listening Skills

How often do the following happen to you?

	Always	Often	Sometimes	Never	N/A
1. Receive low grades in tasks involving class participation.	1	2	3	4	5
2. Have difficulty working in small groups during class.	1	2	3	4	5
3. Have difficulty working with other students on out-of-class projects.	1	2	3	4	5
4. Have trouble leading class discussions.	1	2	3	4	5
5. Have difficulty participating in large group discussions or in debates.	1	2	3	4	5

	Always	Often	Sometimes	Never	N/A
6. Have difficulty interacting with student demonstrators in labs, tutorials, etc.	1	2	3	4	5
7. Struggle with out-of-class assignments which require interaction with native speakers of English.	1	2	3	4	5

D. Speaking Skills

How often do the following happen to you?

	Always	Often	Sometimes	Never	N/A
1. Have difficulty giving oral presentations.	1	2	3	4	5
2. Have trouble wording what you want to say quickly enough.	1	2	3	4	5
3. Worry about saying something in case you make a mistake in your English.	1	2	3	4	5
4. Not know how to say something in English.	1	2	3	4	5
5. Not know the best way to say something in English.	1	2	3	4	5
6. Have difficulty with your pronunciation of words.	1	2	3	4	5
7. Find it difficult to enter discussion.	1	2	3	4	5
8. Other (please specify):	1	2	3	4	5

_____

_____

_____

E. Listening Skills

How often do the following happen to you?

	Always	Often	Sometimes	Never	N/A
1. Have trouble understanding lectures.	1	2	3	4	5

	Always	Often	Sometimes	Never	N/A
2. Have trouble taking effective notes.	1	2	3	4	5
3. Have to ask staff questions to clarify material you have been taught.	1	2	3	4	5
4. Have trouble understanding lengthy descriptions in English.	1	2	3	4	5
5. Have trouble understanding spoken instructions.	1	2	3	4	5
6. Have trouble understanding informal language.	1	2	3	4	5
7. Have trouble understanding the subject matter of a talk, i.e., what is being talked about.	1	2	3	4	5
8. I also have difficulty with (please specify):	1	2	3	4	5

_____

_____

_____

I have problems understanding lecturers or other students because:

	Often	Sometimes	Never
9. They talk very fast.	1	2	3
10. They talk very quietly.	1	2	3
11. Their accents or pronunciation are different from what I am used to.	1	2	3
12. More than one person is speaking, e.g., in group discussions.	1	2	3
13. Other (please specify):	1	2	3

_____

_____

_____

F. Writing Skills

With regard to written assignments, please indicate for each of the following:

1. How important the skill is, and
2. How often you have problems with the skill:

Importance					**Frequency of problems**			
Very important	Important	Not important	Not sure		Often	Sometimes	Never	N/A
1	2	3	4	Using correct punctuation and spelling.	1	2	3	4
1	2	3	4	Structuring sentences.	1	2	3	4
1	2	3	4	Using appropriate vocabulary.	1	2	3	4
1	2	3	4	Organising paragraphs.	1	2	3	4
1	2	3	4	Organising the overall assignment.	1	2	3	4
1	2	3	4	Expressing ideas appropriately.	1	2	3	4
1	2	3	4	Developing ideas.	1	2	3	4
1	2	3	4	Expressing what you want to say clearly.	1	2	3	4
1	2	3	4	Addressing topic.	1	2	3	4
1	2	3	4	Adopting appropriate tone and style.	1	2	3	4
1	2	3	4	Following instructions and directions.	1	2	3	4
1	2	3	4	Evaluating and revising your writing.	1	2	3	4
1	2	3	4	Overall writing ability.	1	2	3	4
1	2	3	4	Completing written tasks (e.g., exams, tests) within the time available.	1	2	3	4
1	2	3	4	Other (please specify): _____	1	2	3	4

_____

_____

G. Reading Skills

The following questions concern the reading tasks required of you during the course. Please indicate:

a) which of the following types of material you are expected to read, and
b) how often you have difficulty doing so (please circle):

	Expected to read?	Frequency of difficulties		
		Often	Sometimes	Never
1. Journal articles	Yes / No	1	2	3
2. Newspaper articles	Yes / No	1	2	3

	Expected to read?	Frequency of difficulties		
		Often	Sometimes	Never
3. Works of fiction	Yes / No	1	2	3
4. Entire reference or text books	Yes / No	1	2	3
5. Selected chapters of books	Yes / No	1	2	3
6. Photocopied notes	Yes / No	1	2	3
7. Workbook or laboratory instructions	Yes / No	1	2	3
8. Computer-presented reading materials	Yes / No	1	2	3
9. Other (please specify):	Yes / No	1	2	3

_____

_____

_____

Indicate how often you have difficulty with each of the following:

	Very often		Sometimes		Never
10. Understanding the main points of text.	1	2	3	4	5
11. Reading a text quickly in order to establish a general idea of the content (skimming).	1	2	3	4	5
12. Reading a text slowly and carefully in order to understand the details of the text.	1	2	3	4	5
13. Looking through a text quickly in order to locate specific information (scanning).	1	2	3	4	5
14. Guessing unknown words in a text.	1	2	3	4	5
15. Understanding text organisation.	1	2	3	4	5
16. Understanding specialist vocabulary in a text.	1	2	3	4	5
17. Reading speed.	1	2	3	4	5
18. Reading in order to respond critically.	1	2	3	4	5
19. Understanding a writer's attitude and purpose.	1	2	3	4	5
20. General comprehension.	1	2	3	4	5
21. Other (please specify): _____	1	2	3	4	5

_____

_____

_____

H. Skills You Would Like to Improve

If you were to take a course to improve your English skills, which of the following would be useful to you? Rate the importance of each (please circle):

	High		Moderate		Low
1. Listening to pronunciation/intonation/ stress patterns of New Zealand English.	1	2	3	4	5
2. Lecture notetaking.	1	2	3	4	5
3. General listening comprehension.	1	2	3	4	5
4. Giving formal speeches/presentations.	1	2	3	4	5
5. Participating effectively in discussions.	1	2	3	4	5
6. Communicating effectively with peers in small group discussions, collaborative projects, or out-of-class study groups.	1	2	3	4	5
7. Communicating effectively with staff in or out of class.	1	2	3	4	5
8. Library skills.	1	2	3	4	5
9. Essay writing.	1	2	3	4	5
10. Lab report writing.	1	2	3	4	5
11. Creative writing.	1	2	3	4	5
12. Writing case studies.	1	2	3	4	5
13. Describing objects or procedures.	1	2	3	4	5
14. Writing introductions and conclusions.	1	2	3	4	5
15. Writing references and quotations.	1	2	3	4	5
16. Formulating coherent arguments.	1	2	3	4	5
17. Summarising factual information.	1	2	3	4	5
18. Synthesizing information from more than one source.	1	2	3	4	5
19. Analysing written materials.	1	2	3	4	5
20. Knowledge of vocabulary.	1	2	3	4	5
21. Reading quickly.	1	2	3	4	5
22. Reading critically.	1	2	3	4	5
23. Reading for author's viewpoint.	1	2	3	4	5
24. Summarizing material.	1	2	3	4	5
25. General reading comprehension.	1	2	3	4	5
26. Other (please specify and rate): _____	1	2	3	4	5

_____

_____

_____

I. Assistance Available

Are you aware of the course available at the Student Learning Centre for students for whom English is a second language? (please circle):   Yes / No

If you have taken any of these courses, please state which you have taken and how useful they were:

Course	Very useful				No use at all
_____	1	2	3	4	5
_____	1	2	3	4	5
_____	1	2	3	4	5

J. Catering for ESL Students

Do you believe any changes should be made to your course or the way it is taught as a result of difficulties students such as yourself have with English?
(please circle):   Yes / No

If you have answered Yes, please tick the modification which should be made:

☐ Using overheads more in lectures
☐ Simplifying the material covered
☐ Having less class involvement
   during lectures.
☐ Providing more photocopied notes
☐ Other (please specify): _____

☐ Having more multiple choice tests
☐ Providing summaries of important materials
☐ Reducing the amount of reading
☐ Giving additional tutorials

_____

K. Additional Comments

Do you have any other comments which might be helpful in assessing what English skills are expected of you by the University, what specific difficulties you encountered in this paper, how English courses could better prepare students such as yourself for this paper, or anything else relating to your English language skills and needs? If so, please write them here:

_____

_____

_____

_____

L. Additional Information

If we would like more information from you, would you be prepared to be interviewed?   Yes / No

If so, please give your:

Name: _____

Contact telephone number: _____

THANK YOU FOR YOUR ASSISTANCE

References

Auerbach, E. R. 1995. The politics of the ESL classroom: Issues of power in pedagogical choices. In Tollefson 1995. 9–33.

Berwick, R. 1989. Needs assessment in language programming: From theory to practice. In R. K. Johnson (ed.), *The second language curriculum*. New York: Cambridge University Press.

Brindley, G. 1984. *Needs analysis and objective setting in the adult migrant education program*. Sydney: N.S.W. Adult Migrant Education Service.

Brindley, G. 1989. The role of needs analysis in adult ESL programme design. In R. K. Johnson (ed.), *The second language curriculum*. New York: Cambridge University Press.

Burnett, L. 1998. *Issues in immigrant settlement in Australia*. Sydney: National Centre for English Language Teaching and Research.

Connelly, E. M., and D. J. Clandinin. 1988. *Teachers as curriculum planners*. New York: Teachers College, Columbia University.

Elley, W. 1984. Tailoring the evaluation to fit the context. In R. K. Johnson (ed.), *The second language curriculum*. New York: Cambridge University Press. 270–285.

Gravatt, B., J. Richards, and M. Lewis. 1997. *Language needs in tertiary studies*. Auckland: Occasional Paper Number 10, University of Auckland Institute of Language Teaching and Learning.

Hudelson, S. (ed.). 1993. *English as a second language curriculum resource handbook*. New York: Krause International.

Johns, A. M., and T. F. Johns. 1977. Seminar discussion strategies. In A. P. Cowie and J. B. Heaton (eds.), *English for academic purposes*. Reading: University of Reading, BAAL/SELMOUS.

Li, D., and J. Richards. 1995. *Cantonese as a second language: A study of learner needs and Cantonese course books*. Hong Kong: City University of Hong Kong.

Linse, C. T. 1993. Assessing student needs. In Hudelson 1993. 35–48.

Porcher, L. 1977. Une notion ambigue: les 'besoins langagiers'. *Les cahiers du CRELEF* 3.

Pratt, D. 1980. *Curriculum: Design and development*. New York: Harcourt Brace.

Richards, J. C., and B. Gravatt. 1998. *Students' beliefs about foreign languages*. Auckland: Occasional Paper Number 11, University of Auckland Institute of Language Teaching and Learning.

Shaw, J., and G. Dowsett. 1986. *The evaluation process in the adult migrant education program*. Adelaide: Adult Migrant Education Program.

Stufflebeam, D., C. McCormick, R. Brinkerhoff, and C. Nelson. 1985. *Conducting educational needs assessment*. Hingham, MA: Kluwer-Nijhoff Publishing.

Tollefson, J. W. (ed.). 1995. *Power and inequality in language education*. Cambridge: Cambridge University Press.

4 Situation analysis

The goal of needs analysis is to collect information that can be used to develop a profile of the language needs of a group of learners in order to be able to make decisions about the goals and content of a language course. However, other factors apart from learner needs are relevant to the design and implementation of successful language programs. Language programs are carried out in particular contexts or situations. Clark (1987, xii) comments:

A language curriculum is a function of the interrelationships that hold between subject-specific concerns and other broader factors embracing socio-political and philosophical matters, educational value systems, theory and practice in curriculum design, teacher experiential wisdom and learner motivation. In order to understand the foreign language curriculum in any particular context it is therefore necessary to attempt to understand how all the various influences interrelate to give a particular shape to the planning and execution of the teaching/learning process.

The contexts for language programs are diverse and the particular variables that come into play in a specific situation are often the key determinants of the success of a program. Some language curricula are planned for centrally organized state school systems where a great deal of direction and support for teaching is provided. Others take place in settings where there are limited human and physical resources. Some proposals for curriculum change are well received by teachers, but others may be resisted. In some situations, teachers are well trained and have time available to plan their own lesson materials. In other situations, teachers may have little time for lesson planning and materials production and simply teach from their textbooks. Each context for a curriculum change or innovation thus contains factors that can potentially facilitate the change or hinder its successful implementation (Markee 1997). It is important, therefore, to identify what these factors are and what their potential effects might be when planning a curriculum change (Bean 1993). Pratt (1980, 117) observes:

The designer should estimate both the direct and indirect effects a proposed curriculum will have on the students, on other programs, and on other people in and outside the institution. These effects must be taken into account in the design and made clear to decision-makers when the curriculum proposal is submitted.

This is the focus of situation analysis. *Situation analysis* is an analysis of factors in the context of a planned or present curriculum project that is made in order to assess their potential impact on the project. These factors may be political, social, economic, or institutional. Situation analysis complements the information gathered during needs analysis. It is sometimes considered as a dimension of needs analysis, and can also be regarded as an aspect of evaluation (see Chapter 9).

Some examples of language teaching changes that were attempted without an adequate analysis of the context of the innovation will clarify the importance of situation analysis in curriculum planning.

Example 1: A team of foreign experts under contract to an international funding body is given a contract to write a new series of English textbooks for the state school system in an EFL country. They base themselves in an attractive small town in a rural setting and set up their writing project. They do a series of interviews with educational officials and teachers to determine students' language needs and make use of the latest thinking on language teaching and textbook design to produce an oral-based language course that reflects the recommended language teaching methodology of the time – Audiolingualism. Textbooks are developed and provided to secondary schools at no cost and teachers are given the choice of using the new books or their old outdated government textbooks. After a period of initial enthusiasm, however, very few teachers end up using the new course and most revert to using the old government-provided textbooks.

Comment: The project team members spent insufficient time familiarizing themselves with the local school situation. Most English teachers had a limited command of English. Teachers found the new materials difficult to teach because they required a high level of oral fluency in English and an English-only methodology that was difficult to implement in large classes. A more successful reception might have occurred if the introduction of the new materials had been gradual, so that problems were addressed as they occurred. In addition, there could have been more provision for teacher training.

Example 2: The education department in an EFL country decides to introduce English from the third year of elementary school rather than in high school. New textbooks are required. A group of teachers is seconded from schools to join a curriculum unit in the ministry to produce the books for the next school year. There is an element of secrecy in the work of the unit and few people have an opportunity to review the materials before they are published. When the books are published, they receive many complaints from teachers. They are found to be difficult to teach, they contain too much material, and they are prepared to poor standards of design and production.

Comment: Several factors had not been addressed in planning the project. None of the members of the writing team had experience or training in writing elementary language teaching materials. More consultation with classroom teachers should have been provided, as well as pilot testing of the materials. In addition, there was an unrealistic budget for design and production. And the time framework the writers were working with did not allow for adequate development and review of the materials.

Example 3: A large private university of an EFL country decides that, rather than use commercial materials in its language institute, it will produce its own materials and publish them. It is hoped that they will compete on the market with materials produced by commercial publishers. A large amount of money is invested in setting up a materials writing team and the books are prepared. When they are finally published, however, it is found that few other institutes or schools want to use them.

Comment: Private universities in this country are highly competitive, and the fact that the materials were produced by one institution meant that other institutions did not want to use them. Some basic market research should have been carried out at the initial stages of the project to determine if there would be a commercial market for the materials.

These examples illustrate the kinds of factors that can have an impact on the success of a curriculum project and emphasize the importance of determining the potential influence of such factors on the implementation of a curriculum change. In this chapter, we will consider societal factors, project factors, institutional factors, teacher factors, learner factors, and adoption factors. (Some of these factors will be considered further in later chapters in relation to issues of teaching, methodology, and materials design.) Analysis and appraisal of the potential impact of these factors at the initial stages of a curriculum project can help determine the kinds of difficulties that might be encountered in implementing a curriculum change. Procedures used in situation analysis are similar to those involved in needs analysis, namely, *(a)* consultation with representatives of as many relevant groups as possible, such as parents, students, teachers, administrators, and government officials; *(b)* study and analysis of relevant documents, such as course appraisal documents, government reports, ministry of education guidelines, and policy papers, teaching materials, curriculum documents; *(c)* observation of teachers and students in relevant learning settings; *(d)* surveys of opinions of relevant parties; *(e)* review of available literature related to the issue.

Societal factors

Second or foreign language teaching is a fact of life in almost every country in the world. Yet countries differ greatly in terms of the role of foreign languages in the community, their status in the curriculum, educational traditions and experience in language teaching, and the expectations that members of the community have for language teaching and learning. Van Els, T. Bongaerts, G. Extra, C. Van Os, and A. Janssen-van Dieten (1984, 156), for example, comparing foreign language teaching experience in Holland and the United States, point out that the circumstances of foreign language teaching are completely different in both countries. In Holland, a command of one or more foreign languages has long been accepted as a necessity. Schools are expected to offer a range of foreign languages, and there is both a strong tradition and considerable expertise in foreign language teaching. New proposals are therefore met with informed skepticism. In the United States, by comparison, there is much less collective wisdom or experience in foreign language teaching. The position of foreign languages in the school curriculum is neither strong nor secure. More promotion of foreign language teaching is consequently needed, and there is a greater interest in novel teaching methods. In examining the impact of societal factors on language teaching, therefore, the aim is to determine the impact of groups in the community or society at large on the program. These groups include:

- policy makers in government
- educational and other government officials
- employers
- the business community
- politicians
- tertiary education specialists
- educational organizations
- parents
- citizens
- students

In the case of projects of community or national scope, questions such as the following may be relevant:

- What current language teaching policies exist and how are they viewed?
- What are the underlying reasons for the project and who supports it?
- What impact will it have on different sectors of society?
- What language teaching experience and traditions exist in the country?
- How do members of the public view second languages and second language teaching?
- What are the views of relevant professionals such as academics and teacher trainers?
- What do professional organizations such as teachers' unions think of the project?
- What are the views of parents and students?
- What are the views of employers and the business community?
- What community resources are available to support the innovations, such as radio, television, and the media?

The following examples illustrate the impact of societal factors on language curriculum projects.

Example 1: A new English curriculum has been prepared for English at secondary level in an EFL context. The new curriculum is described as a communicative curriculum and downplays the importance of grammar, which traditionally received a strong focus in the English curriculum. When textbooks to support the new curriculum are published, concerns are expressed by parents and parents' groups because they feel that their children "are not being taught the basics" and the textbooks will not provide sufficient preparation for school exams.

Comment: Mechanisms should have been established for communicating the intentions of the new curriculum to parents and other interested parties and to identify and address their concerns. Perhaps parents misunderstood the way grammar was addressed in the new curriculum and would be satisfied once they understood better how the program worked. In addition, the textbooks should be reviewed to ensure that they address the skills covered in the exams.

Example 2: In an EFL country, a new 6-year English course is developed for secondary schools. The course seeks to prepare students both for employment and for entry to English-medium universities. The course is based on an integrated-skills syllabus that was prepared by a group of consultants and materials writers and is carefully reviewed by teachers before it is published. After the course has been in use for two years, however, employers complain that school leavers have insufficient language skills for work purposes.

Comment: The course was largely planned around the needs of students going on to university studies. The needs of learners going to vocational schools or into the employment sector should also have been considered. Employers should have been consulted during the planning stage to find out what language skills they felt school leavers should have. The course could then have been examined to see if these skills were adequately covered.

Project factors

Curriculum projects are typically produced by a team of people. Members of the team may be specialists who are hired specifically for the purpose, they may be classroom teachers who are seconded to the project for a fixed period of time, or the project may be carried out by teachers and other staff of a teaching institution as part of their regular duties. Projects are completed under different constraints of time, resources, and personnel, and each of these variables can have a significant impact on a project. There should be sufficient members in the project team to do the job and they should represent a balance of skills and expertise. Some projects are generously resourced while others operate on a shoestring budget. The time frame for a project needs to be carefully planned. If a curriculum development team takes on too ambitious a task for the time available, the quality of their efforts may be compromised. The working dynamics of the team are also essential to the smooth progress of the project. If the team members are highly committed to the project and share a common vision, it is likely to encounter fewer difficulties than one where the project team experiences internal feuds and power struggles.

The following project factors need to be considered:

- Who constitutes the project group and how are they selected?
- What are the management and other responsibilities of the team?
- How are goals and procedures determined?
- Who reviews the progress of the project and the performance of its members?
- What experience do members of the team have?
- How do members of the team regard each other?
- What resources do they have available and what budget to acquire needed resources?
- What is the time frame of the project? Is it realistic, or is more or less time needed?

The following examples illustrate how these kinds of factors can affect curriculum planning;

Example 1: A private institute decides to develop a set of course materials for some of its major courses. A group of teachers is assigned to the task and given release time to work on the project as materials writers. One of the senior teachers is put in charge. However, the team members cannot agree on the goals of the project or the best approach to take in writing the materials. There is constant tension within the team and a rapid turnover of writers. Consequently, the project takes much longer to accomplish than planned.

Comment: A person who is a good teacher may not make a good materials developer or project leader. Better direction of the project was needed through recruitment of someone with appropriate qualifications and experience. In addition, better communication was needed so that different perceptions of the project could be aired and differences resolved before they became problems. Clearer specifications of roles might also have led to fewer problems.

Example 2: A full-time textbook writer needs help in developing a textbook series. She hires three graduate students who appear to have the necessary skills and experience. A contract is signed and the project commences. It soon emerges, however, that the graduate students do not have the skills needed to write independently and are able to undertake little more than secretarial roles within the project. The experienced writer finds it necessary to take on the major part of the writing, leading to tension and bad feeling because the contract is already signed.

Comment: The graduate students should have been given a trial period to prove their worth before they were offered a contract. Problems that emerged early on in the project should have been aired so that replacement writers could have been recruited if necessary.

Example 3: A project team within a ministry of education is assigned to develop a national textbook project in an EFL country. Team members are recruited by a professional recruitment agency. There is little difficulty recruiting writers, but there are few appropriate applicants for the role of project director. As a consequence, a succession of inexperienced or unsuitable appointees fill the post of project director, leading to serious problems within the team and to disruption of the project deadlines.

Comment: The role of project director might have to be reconsidered and the responsibilities assigned to members of the team. Alternatively, terms of employment for the project director might need to be reconsidered to enable a suitable candidate to be found. In addition, members of the project team should be consulted on how to resolve communication difficulties and other problems within the team.

Institutional factors

A language teaching program is typically delivered in an institution such as a university, school, or language institute. Different types of institutions create their own "culture," that is, settings where people interact and where patterns emerge for communication, decision making, role relations, and conduct. Morris (1994, 109) observes:

Schools are organizations and they develop a culture, ethos or environment which might be favorable or unfavorable to encouraging change and the implementation of innovations. A school with a relatively open climate, where the teachers collaborate with each other and where the principal and [senior teachers] are supportive of teachers, is more likely to try to implement a change. In contrast, a school where the principle focuses on administrative matters, the teachers work in isolation or in narrow subject-based groups and where there is no mechanism to discuss and try to solve problems is less likely to change.

A teaching institution is a collection of teachers, groups, and departments, sometimes functioning in unison, sometimes with different components functioning independently, or sometimes with components in a confrontational relationship. Within an institution there may be a strong and positive climate to support innovation, one where there is effective and positive leadership and where change is received positively. On the other hand, there may be a climate where teachers distrust one another and the administration and have no firm commitment to the school.

Institutions also have their own ways of doing things. In some institutions, textbooks are the core of the curriculum and all teachers must use the prescribed texts. In other institutions, teachers work from course guidelines and supplement them as they see fit. Institutions also differ greatly in their levels of professionalism. In some institutions, there is a strong sense of professional commitment and a culture of quality that influences every aspect of the institution's operations. In others, the driving force of the school may be monetary. As a cost-saving measure, heavy reliance is made on part-time teachers or teachers with little training and experience. They are not paid for lesson preparation time and consequently teach their classes and then depart for their next teaching assignment, perhaps in another school.

In addition to the human side of the institution, the physical aspects need to be considered. What kinds of resources are available for teachers? Is there a good teachers' reference room? What access do teachers have to the photocopier? Who chooses textbooks and materials? Institutional factors thus relate to the following kinds of questions:

- What leadership is available within the school to support change and to help teachers cope with change?
- What are the school's physical resources, including classroom facilities, media and other technological resources, and library resources?
- What is the role of textbooks and other instructional materials?
- What is staff morale like among English teachers?
- What problems do teachers face and what is being done about them?
- What administrative support is available within the school and what is communication like between teachers and the administration?
- What kind of reputation does the institution have for delivering successful language programs?
- How committed is the institution to attaining excellence?

Example 1: A new director is appointed to a private language institute. The owners of the institute are concerned at falling student enrollments and feel that the institute's programs need to be reviewed to make them more competitive and attractive to potential clients. The director prepares an excellent rationale for revamping existing courses, for replacing the textbooks currently in use with more up-to-date texts, and develops a plan for marketing new courses. However, she meets a wall of resistance from teachers who feel that they are undervalued, underpaid, and that proposed changes will not bring any benefits to them.

Comment: Perhaps the teachers could have been involved in rethinking the institute's programs from the start and ways found to build in some incentives for the teachers themselves. This might involve negotiating with the school's owners for better service conditions for teachers as part of the overall curriculum renewal plan. In addition, some of the teachers may have to be replaced with teachers who are more open to the kinds of changes the director is proposing.

Example 2: There is an unacceptably high amount of staff turnover in a language institute and several excellent teachers have moved on, claiming that the school does not provide them with the continued source of professional satisfaction they need. As a consequence, the institute is short of key teachers. New teachers complain that they do not have the support they need from senior teachers in order to enable them to successfully carry out their teaching and materials development responsibilities.

Comment: The institute should review its staff structure and consider creating special roles for key senior teachers with appropriate remuneration. These could be mentor teachers, teacher trainers, or teacher researchers.

Teacher factors

Teachers are a key factor in the successful implementation of curriculum changes. Exceptional teachers can often compensate for the poor-quality resources and materials they have to work from. But inadequately trained teachers may not be able to make effective use of teaching materials no matter how well they are designed. In any institution, teachers may vary according to the following dimensions:

- language proficiency
- teaching experience
- skill and expertise
- training and qualifications
- morale and motivation
- teaching style
- beliefs and principles

In planning a language program it is therefore important to know the kinds of teachers the program will depend on and the kinds of teachers needed to ensure that the program achieves its goals.

Within schools, teachers also have many different kinds of responsibilities. Some teachers have mentoring or leadership roles within their schools and assist in orienting new teachers to the school or leading groups of teachers in materials development and other activities. Other teachers have time for little more than teaching. They may have very heavy teaching loads or teach in several different institutions in order to make ends meet. Some teachers may welcome the chance to try out a new syllabus or materials. Others may resent it because they see it as disrupting their routine and not offering them any financial or other kind of advantage.

Among the teacher factors that need to be considered in situation analysis are the following:

- What kinds of teachers currently teach in the target schools or institutions? What is their typical background, training, experience, and motivation?

- How proficient are they in English?
- What kinds of beliefs do the teachers typically hold concerning key issues in teaching?
- What teaching loads do teachers have and what resources do they make use of?
- What are the typical teaching methods teachers use and believe in?
- To what extent are teachers open to change?
- What opportunities do they have for retraining through in-service or other kinds of opportunities?
- What benefits are the proposed new syllabus, curriculum, or materials likely to offer teachers?

The following examples illustrate the potential impact of some of these issues.

Example 1: As part of an overall reform of the school curriculum, the curriculum department in an EFL country decides to implement a new task-based approach to teaching across the whole curriculum in all subject areas. The new curriculum involves a greater use of teacher-made criterion-referenced tests that are linked to graded tasks in different subject areas. However, when the plan is introduced to teachers, it meets with great resistance. Teachers are happy with the current curriculum; they have great difficulty understanding the philosophy of the new approach and see it as creating a much heavier workload. The teachers' union organizes a number of teachers' meetings to discuss and criticize the new curriculum. In the face of public opposition, the curriculum department decides to delay the introduction of the new curriculum and to modify it, despite having spent a large sum of money in developing the curriculum and supporting materials.

   Comment. Much wider consultation should have taken place before deciding to change the existing curriculum. Teachers should have been consulted to see if they saw the need for change. Teachers should have been involved in preparing the new curriculum rather than imposing it on them as a fait accompli. Adequate provision should have been made to train teachers to use the new curriculum and the curriculum piloted first to identify the demands it created for teachers and students.

Example 2: A program director in a private institute believes that teachers in his school should not use commercial textbooks but should prepare their own teaching materials. Most teachers are untrained and on short-term contracts so they feel that they cannot contest his ruling and pay lip service to the policy. However, most teachers ignore the policy. They teach from photocopied sections taken from commercial materials or type out sections from textbooks and pass these off as teacher-made materials.

Comment: The program director's policy serves no obvious purpose. If the director wants teachers to prepare their own materials, he will need to consider hiring better-qualified teachers or provide materials writing workshops for teachers. In addition, a set of goals related to materials writing needs to be agreed on to give some purpose to the requirement.

Learner factors

Learners are the key participants in curriculum development projects and it is essential to collect as much information as possible about them before the project begins. In Chapter 3 the focus was learners' language needs. Here the focus is on other potentially relevant factors such as the learners' backgrounds, expectations, beliefs, and preferred learning styles. The project designers may be operating from a set of assumptions about education, schools, teachers, and students that is culturally bound and at odds with the beliefs and assumptions of the learners. Nunan (1989, 176) comments:

the effectiveness of a language program will be dictated as much by the attitudes and expectations of the learners as by the specifications of the official curriculum. . . . Learners have their own agendas in the language lessons they attend. These agendas, as much as the teacher's objectives, determine what learners take from any given teaching/learning encounter.

Learners may affect the outcomes of a project in unexpected ways. For example, a textbook or set of materials may be engaging, at a suitable level, and provide a lot of useful practice but not be appreciated by students because they fail to see any links between the book and an examination they are working toward. A language program that is dependent on students' bringing to school a student book, a workbook, and a dictionary may encounter difficulties because students' schoolbags are not big enough to provide space for three English books in addition to books required for other subjects. Or a program in business English for company employees sensibly predicated on the assumption that the students really want to be able to discuss business topics in English may turn out to be off target because what the employees really want is an hour's escape from the pressures of their jobs and the chance to practice social and conversational English.

Among relevant learner factors therefore are the following:

- What are the learners' past language learning experiences?
- How motivated are the learners to learn English?

- What are their expectations for the program?
- Do the learners' views on language teaching reflect any culturally specific factors?
- Are they a homogeneous or a heterogeneous group?
- What type of learning approach do they favor (e.g., teacher-led, student-focused, or small-group work)?
- What type of content do they prefer?
- What expectations do they have for the roles of teachers, learners, and instructional materials?
- How much time can they be expected to put into the program?
- What learning resources will they typically have access to?

Example 1: A private institute in an EFL country offers an intermediate-level conversation course. Teachers in the course make extensive use of fluency activities, including pair and group activities, role plays, songs and games, and discussion activities. These activities are thought to reflect current views on second language acquisition. However, the first cohort of learners through the program are very critical of it because they cannot see the point of many of the classroom activities they were asked to take part in. They request more teacher-directed activities and more error correction. "We don't want to come to class to clap and sing" is a typical student comment.

Comment: Learners have their own views on how conversation skills can be developed and their own preferences for classroom activities. If the goals of fluency activities are not clearly explained and if students are not convinced of their value, they may not understand what their intent is and judge them to be ineffective. A questionnaire could have been administered prior to the course to determine students' views of different kinds of classroom activities. In addition, a better orientation to the goals and methodology of the program should have been provided.

Example 2: A group of foreign experts in an EFL context devise a program in oral communication skills for adults. The program reflects current Western views of teaching and learning and is built around such concepts as *autonomous learning, the learner-centered curriculum,* and *the negotiated curriculum.* The teachers decide that rather than develop the detailed content of the program in advance, they will involve the students in the development of the program's goals and content. Once the program commences, however, the students judge that the teachers do not know what they are doing and complain that the program is unstructured and unfocused.

Comment: The teachers and the students have different expectations about the requirements of a sound program as a result of cultural differences in their approach to teaching and learning. The students expect a program with clear goals and with an organization laid out in advance. This clashes with the beliefs of the teachers. Some sort of compromise should have been decided on early on in the project to prevent the students from misunderstanding the nature of the program. More time should have been spent explaining the purpose of different activities within the program and the philosophy it was based on.

Example 3: A young Western English teacher takes his first overseas teaching assignment at an Asian university. He wants to be viewed by his students as a peer rather than as a teacher and seeks to create an informal and friendly classroom atmosphere. Students are asked to address him by his first name. He likes to seat himself on the teacher's desk rather than conduct his classes standing. The program coordinator soon receives feedback that the teacher is unprofessional and that students do not take him seriously.

Comment: The teacher should have received a better orientation to his teaching context and become informed of students' (and the institution's) expectations for appropriate and acceptable teacher behavior.

Adoption factors

Any attempt to introduce a new curriculum, syllabus, or set of materials must take into account the relative ease or difficulty of introducing change into the system. Curriculum changes are of many different kinds. They may affect teachers' pedagogical values and beliefs, their understanding of the nature of language or second language learning, or their classroom practices and use of teaching materials. Some changes may be readily accepted while others might be resisted. The following questions therefore need to be asked of any proposed curriculum innovation:

- What advantages does the curriculum change offer? Is the innovation perceived to be more advantageous than current practices?
- How compatible is it? Is the use of the innovation consistent with the existing beliefs, attitudes, organization, and practices within a classroom or school?
- Is the innovation very complicated and difficult to understand?
- Has it been used and tested out in some schools before all schools are expected to use it?
- Have the features and benefits of the innovation been clearly communicated to teachers and institutions?

- How clear and practical is it? Are the expectations of the innovation stated in ways which clearly show how it can be used in the classroom?

(Morris 1994, 109)

Although curriculum planners might provide many compelling reasons for adopting a communicative teaching methodology, teachers might feel that it makes testing more difficult compared with a more traditional grammar-based approach. Hence it is perceived as offering few relative advantages for teachers. A language teaching approach that requires teachers to adopt new roles in the classroom, such as needs analyst, resource person, and language tutor, might not be compatible with learners' expectations for the role of teachers. The complexity and clarity of a curriculum change might also be crucial in its successful adoption. Compare the following pairs of items, for example, and consider which would be easier to explain to a group of teachers:

- computer-based learning versus cooperative learning
- communicative pair work versus consciousness-raising activities
- a functional syllabus versus a task-based syllabus
- a product syllabus versus a process syllabus
- a content-based curriculum versus a negotiated curriculum
- audiolingualism versus the Natural Approach
- the Structural Approach versus Communicative Language Teaching

Practicality is also a significant issue. A methodology that can readily be turned into teaching materials and textbooks will generally be easier to adopt than one that exists only as a set of guidelines. For this reason *Communicative Language Teaching* is much more widely adopted as a teaching approach than the *Natural Approach*. The support networks available in promoting or explaining an innovation may also be crucial. Are the ministry of education, key educational administrators, professional bodies, and recognized educational authorities committed to the project, and what level of support will they provide? Rodgers (1984, 41), discussing implementation of a communicative syllabus in Malaysia in the 1980s, describes some of the societal agencies that were involved:

Implementation of a new syllabus needs to involve the cooperation of many agencies. In Malaysia these include the Ministry of Education Directorship, the Curriculum Development Center, the Inspectorate, the Examinations Syndicate, teacher Training, The Textbook Bureau, textbook publishers, State Education officers, School Headmasters, the National Union of Teachers, and the formal and informal groups of teachers, themselves. As well, external agencies need to be informed about and, perhaps, directly involved in discussion of syllabus changes. These include the National Parliament, the press, the universities and language advisory agencies (e.g. the British Council). Feelings of being left out or uninformed create the adversary stance that representatives of such agencies often take with regard to new programs.

Example 1: A new state textbook series is prepared by the ministry of education in an EFL country. The series assumes a very different type of methodology from that currently used in schools because it is less transmission-oriented and more experientially based. When the program is introduced, however, a number of problems quickly emerge: teachers find the materials difficult to use and unsuitable for large classes; some of the content in the materials is thought to be unsuitable for the target population.

Comment: The materials could have been introduced in selected schools first (perhaps in a pilot version) in order to identify what problems teachers encountered using the materials. These problems could then have been addressed before full-scale implementation was carried out.

Example 2: English is being introduced at the elementary level for the first time in an EFL country. A teacher-training program is set in place to prepare teachers for teaching at this level. To provide the training, local teacher trainers are hired and given a "training-of-trainers course" by a foreign expert. However, a number of the local trainers are found to have very traditional views about teacher education and are opposed to the training model being used in the training course. Once they return to their own training centers, they try to use their own training principles that are not consistent with the philosophy of the new course.

Comment: More time should have been spent on selecting trainers to take part in the training-of-trainers program. In the process, those who did not support the philosophy of the training program could have been rejected. Ongoing feedback on the trainers' performance through workshops and visits might also help to make sure the trainers were using an appropriate training model.

Profiling the factors identified in the situation analysis

The goal of situation analysis is to identify key factors that might positively or negatively affect the implementation of a curriculum plan. This is sometimes known as a SWOT analysis because it involves an examination of "a language program's internal *strengths* and *weaknesses* in addition to external *opportunities* and *threats* to the existence or successful operation of the language program" (Klinghammer 1997, 65). These can be summarized in the form of a list and the profile developed for discussion within the project team, ministry, funding body, or institute (see Appendix 1). Rodgers (1984) describes a more elaborate matrix that can also be used for estimating the difficulty of implementing new programs (see Appendix 2) (see also Leidecker and Bruno 1987). Ways of addressing the negative factors that were identified can then be considered. Alternatively, the goals of a project might need to be modified to reflect the realities of the situation in which the curriculum will be implemented.

Situation analysis thus serves to help identify potential obstacles to implementing a curriculum project and factors that need to be considered when planning the parameters of a project. The next step in curriculum planning involves using the information collected during needs analysis and situation analysis as the basis for developing program goals and objectives. Procedures for this stage in planning are the focus of Chapter 5.

Discussion questions and activities

1. Discuss a language teaching context you are familiar with and list some of the most important factors that are likely to influence the success of the program. Then rank the factors in order of importance. Compare your information with others.
2. How do societal factors influence or have an impact on a language program that you are familiar with? Which factors are negative and which are positive? How can negative factors be addressed?
3. Are you familiar with a situation in which a curriculum change was attempted (e.g., the introduction of a new teaching approach, a new textbook, or a new program design) and met with difficulties? What factors in the situation contributed to these difficulties? Could the problems have been avoided?
4. List the factors that you think are most crucial in a school or institution in creating a favorable context for curriculum change, such as when a new course or language program is being offered for the first time.
5. What groups in the community or society at large would be most relevant to consult in your country (or the country in which you work) in relation to planned changes in the English- or foreign language curriculum in public schools?
6. Have you worked as a member of a curriculum project team (as a materials writer, course planner, etc.)? Discuss your experience on the

project and whether project factors had an impact on the dynamics and outcome of the project.

7. What can be done in circumstances where teachers and learners have different expectations and beliefs about the nature of a language course?

8. What support is provided for teachers in your teaching situation? How effective is the support provided? What other forms of support would you recommend?

9. Imagine that a new technology-based learning program is to be introduced into schools in your country or the country in which you work. The program employs print materials but also makes extensive use of CALL software, CD-ROMS, videos, and other electronic media. What factors might affect the reception of the program and how could any negative factors be addressed?

10. Examine the situation analysis profile in Appendix 1 and adapt it to make it applicable to a context for curriculum change (e.g., introduction of a new curriculum, new teaching methods, new textbooks, a new language program) that you are familiar with. Identify positive and negative factors in the situation that will affect the curriculum change.

Appendix 1   Situation analysis profile

Societal factors   Positives: _____

                        Negatives: _____

Project factors   Positives: _____

                        Negatives: _____

Institutional factors   Positives: _____

                        Negatives: _____

Teacher factors   Positives: _____

                        Negatives: _____

Learner factors   Positives: _____

                        Negatives: _____

Adoption factors   Positives: _____

                        Negatives: _____

Appendix 2   Matrix for identifying factors in curriculum renewal process

This matrix includes an estimate of the difficulty in fulfilling the requirements of the factor (from Rodgers 1984).

	Low difficulty		High difficulty
A. *The educational requirement sought:*			
1. The subject matter is familiar or unfamiliar.	— —	—	—

	Low difficulty			High difficulty
2. The knowledge domain (skill, or other) is simple or complex.	—	—	—	—
3. The learning group is relatively easy to teach or difficult to teach.	—	—	—	—
4. The instructional design is simple or complex.	—	—	—	—
5. The instructional design is familiar or unfamiliar.	—	—	—	—
6. The curricular and instructional designs are well or inadequately researched.	—	—	—	—
7. Instructional materials are "off the shelf" or nonexistent.	—	—	—	—
8. The instructional materials are to be technically simple or sophisticated.	—	—	—	—
9. The renewal is to be made in an individual or local arena or in a nation-wide (worldwide?) arena.	—	—	—	—
10. The proportion of concern with the "full renewal process" (from theory, through design and development, publications, training, and support) is partial or complete.	—	—	—	—

B. Renewal activities and resources required:

	Low difficulty			High difficulty
1. Time available is extensive or limited.	—	—	—	—
2. Funds available are extensive or limited.	—	—	—	—
3. Professional resources are extensive or limited.	—	—	—	—
4. Professional resources are experienced and accomplished or inexperienced.	—	—	—	—
5. The "standing" of the renewal agency/ persons (status, reputation, track record) is excellent or poor.	—	—	—	—
6. The role or position in the "system" of the renewal agency(ies) – (individual, school, system, university, publisher, etc.).	—	—	—	—
7. The theory and practice of curriculum renewal is adequate to nonexistent.	—	—	—	—

C. The content of the renewal program:

	Low difficulty			High difficulty
1. The target school system(s) is (are) well organized or unorganized.	—	—	—	—
2. The competing renewal programs are few or many.	—	—	—	—
3. The target school system(s) has (have) simple or profound educational problems.	—	—	—	—
4. The idea of curriculum renewal is well or poorly accepted.	—	—	—	—
5. The idea of the renewal effort is consistent with or inconsistent with the current view.	—	—	—	—

References

Bean, W. C. (ed.). 1993. *Strategic planning that makes things happen: Getting from where you are to where you want to be.* Amherst, MA: Human Resources Development Press.

Clark, J. 1989. *Curriculum renewal in school foreign language learning.* Oxford: Oxford University Press.

Klinghammer, S. 1997. The strategic planner. In M. A. Christisòn and F. Stoller (eds.), *A handbook for language program administrators.* Burlingame, CA: ALTA Books. 61–76.

Leidecker, J. K., and A. V. Bruno. 1987. Critical success factor analysis and the strategy development process. In W. R. King and D. I. Cleland (eds.), *Strategic planning and management handbook.* New York: Van Nostrand Reinhold. 333–351.

Markee, N. 1997. *Managing curricular innovation.* New York: Cambridge University Press.

Morris. P. 1994. *The Hong Kong school curriculum.* Hong Kong: Hong Kong University Press.

Nunan, D. 1989. Hidden agendas: The role of the learner in programme implementation. In R. K. Johnson (ed.), *The second language curriculum.* New York: Cambridge University Press. 176–187.

Pratt, D. 1980. *Curriculum: Design and development.* New York: Harcourt Brace.

Rodgers, T. 1984. Communicative syllabus design and implementation: Reflection on a decade of experience. In J. Read (ed.), *Trends in language syllabus design.* Singapore: Regional Language Center (RELC). 28–53.

Van Els, T., T. Bongaerts, G. Extra, C. Van Os, and A. Janssen-van Dieten. 1984. *Applied linguistics and the learning and teaching of foreign languages.* London: Arnold.

5 *Planning goals and learning outcomes*

It was suggested in Chapter 1 that early planners of English-language courses saw the purpose of language teaching as self-evident. It was sufficient to state that the goal of a course was to teach English. The ESP movement argued that this approach was inadequate and that in order to teach English it was necessary to find answers to much more specific questions: What kind of English? At what level of proficiency? And for what purposes? Needs analysis seeks to provide answers to these questions and situation analysis seeks to identify the role of contextual factors in implementing curriculum change. In this chapter we will consider another crucial dimension of decision making in curriculum planning: determining the goals and outcomes of a program.

Several key assumptions about goals characterize the curriculum approach to educational planning. These can be summarized as follows:

- People are generally motivated to pursue specific goals.
- The use of goals in teaching improves the effectiveness of teaching and learning.
- A program will be effective to the extent that its goals are sound and clearly described.

These principles appear to be self-evident and uncontroversial, and most language programs describe their goals in terms of aims and objectives. The nature of aims and objectives, however, is not necessarily straightforward because they refer to knowledge, skills, and values that educational planners *believe* learners need to develop. In deciding on goals, planners choose from among alternatives based on assumptions about the role of teaching and of a curriculum. Formulating goals is not, therefore, an objective scientific enterprise but a judgment call. For this reason, the nature of goals in the design of educational programs has aroused considerable controversy and debate in the curriculum literature, and continues to do so. This debate is reflected in such issues as the following, which are all related to questions of curriculum goals:

- Is there any value in teaching students a foreign language at school if they have no practical need for it?
- Should a language program for immigrants just teach practical life skills or should it seek to prepare immigrants to confront racial and other forms of prejudice?
- Should learners participate in the shaping of the curriculum or is it something best left to teachers?
- Should students study the literature and culture of speakers of the language they are learning, or just learn to speak and use the language as a tool?
- Is it the language teacher's job to raise students' awareness of social injustices?
- Should teachers just prepare students to pass a flawed language exam (such as the English tests used as part of the entry examination at many universities) or should teachers and students together seek ways of finding fairer methods of assessment?
- What role should the learner's native language play in the curriculum and in the classroom?

Eisner (1992, 302) observes: "Because educational practice is concerned with the achievement of certain desired end states, it relies on a larger value matrix to secure and justify the directions in which it moves." In order to appreciate how value systems shape decisions about what schools should teach and the outcomes they seek to achieve, we will begin our discussion of goals by considering five curriculum ideologies (borrowing Eisner's term) that shape the nature of the language curriculum and the practices of language teaching in different ways: academic rationalism, social and economic efficiency, learner-centeredness, social reconstructionism, and cultural pluralism.

The ideology of the curriculum

In developing goals for educational programs, curriculum planners draw on their understanding both of the present and long-term needs of learners and of society as well as the planners' beliefs and ideologies about schools, learners, and teachers. These beliefs and values provide the philosophical underpinnings for educational programs and the justification for the kinds of aims they contain. At any given time, however, a number of competing or complementary perspectives are available concerning the focus of the curriculum. Kliebard comments:

We do not find a monolithic supremacy exercised by one interest group; rather we find different interest groups competing for dominance over the curriculum and, at different times, achieving some measure of control depending on local as well as general social conditions. Each of these interest groups, then, represents a force for a different selection of knowledge and values from the culture and hence a kind of lobby for a different curriculum. (Kliebard, 1986, 8)

Each of the five curriculum perspectives examined here emphasizes a different approach to the role of language in the curriculum.

Academic rationalism

This justification for the aims of curriculum stresses the intrinsic value of the subject matter and its role in developing the learner's intellect, humanistic values, and rationality. The content matter of different subjects is viewed as the basis for a curriculum and mastery of content is an end in itself rather than a means to solving social problems or providing efficient means to achieve the goals of policy makers. The role of schools is to provide access to the major achievements of a particular cultural tradition and to know the insights gained from studying enduring fields of knowledge. Greek and Latin have traditionally appeared in many high school curricula in the West because they were believed to develop "mental discipline" in students. Also known as "classical humanism," this view "is characterized above all by the desire to promote broad intellectual capacities such as memorization and the ability to analyze, classify, and reconstruct elements of knowledge so that these capacities can be brought to bear on the various challenges likely to be encountered in life" (Clark 1987, 5). Academic rationalism is sometimes used to justify the inclusion of certain foreign languages in school curricula, where they are taught not as tools for communication but as an aspect of social studies. Ozolins (1993) documents the debate over foreign language teaching in Australian schools and the reasons why French has gradually replaced Latin and other foreign languages. In discussing the role of foreign languages, the education minister for the state of Victoria in 1964, Bloomfield, argued that the issue was not one of languages alone. Ozolins comments:

The intellectual justification for teaching French was, in Bloomfield's view, 'the understanding of other nations, so that foreign language teaching is an intensive and specialized form of social studies'. The purely linguistic and communicative aspects of languages were not the primary objective, at least not for Victorian schools. (Ozolins 1993: 87)

This ideology is also sometimes used as a justification for including courses on literature, or American or British culture, in a language program. In some parts of the world (e.g., Hong Kong, Singapore, Malaysia), under colonial rule the English curriculum was traditionally a literature-based one. "The basic educational aim was the assimilation of British culture through the medium of English literature. There was no provision for language work specially designed to help the non-native learner" (Ho 1994, 223). The curriculum aimed at maintaining the elitist status of English-medium education. Such curricula were gradually replaced with more functional and practically oriented ones as English-medium education became more widely available (Ho 1994).

Clark (1987, 6) points out that in the United Kingdom academic rationalism is concerned with:

- The maintenance and transmission through education of the wisdom and culture of previous generations. This has led to the creation of a two-tier system of education – one to accord with the "higher" cultural traditions of an elite, and the other to cater for the more concrete and practical lifestyles of the masses.
- The development for the elite of generalizable intellectual capacities and critical faculties.
- The maintenance of stands through an inspectorate and external examination boards controlled by the universities.

In the United States, the debate over "cultural literacy" that emerged with the publication of Hirsch's book *Cultural Literacy* in 1987 indicated that this educational ideology still has both influential proponents and critics.

Social and economic efficiency

This educational philosophy emphasizes the practical needs of learners and society and the role of an educational program in producing learners who are economically productive. People can improve themselves and their environment through a process of rational planning. Social, economic, and other needs of society can be identified and planned for "by task analysis, by forming objectives for each task, and by teaching skills as discrete units" (Uhrmacher 1993, 4). It is an ends–means approach. One of the founders of curriculum theory, Bobbitt, advocated this view of the curriculum. Curriculum development was seen as based on scientific principles, and its practitioners were "educational engineers" whose job it was to "discover the total range of habits, skills, abilities, forms of thought, etc. that its members need for the effective performance of their vocational labors" (1918, 43). Bobbitt concluded that an appropriate metaphor for curriculum development was that of the factory and production. In language teaching, this philosophy leads to an emphasis on practical and functional skills in a foreign or second language.

Socioeconomic ideology stresses the economic needs of society as a justification for the teaching of English. Successful economies in the twenty-first century are increasingly knowledge-based, and the bulk of the world's knowledge is in the English language. In a recent debate over standards of English in Japan, poor standards of English were cited as one reason for Japan's economic malaise in the late 1990s. "The learning of English, now a global language, is essential for Japan to have a bright future. . . . the linguistic handicap of the Japanese could hold them back in an increasingly Internet-oriented world, where the bulk of information is written in English" (Kin 1999).

In foreign language teaching, the debate over skills-based versus academically based instruction in language teaching has a long history, as is seen in discussions over the relative merits of classical languages versus modern languages, literature versus language, and even grammar versus conversation in a language program. In many countries where English is a foreign language, over the past two decades there has been a move away from academic rationalism as the underpinnings of the English curriculum toward one based more on a socioeconomic efficiency model. The Threshold Level, the notional-functional syllabus, and outcomes-based approaches such as the use of graded objectives and competency-based outcomes in foreign language learning reflect this move toward an efficiency model in curriculum planning, one that Clark (1987) suggests often also reflects a *Research, Development, and Diffusion* model.

It generally involves the setting up of a central committee of selected 'experts' to develop a new curriculum product. The committee conducts initial research into what is required, produces draft materials, obtains feedback from classroom teachers who use the draft material in a number of designated pilot areas chosen to be representative of a range of contexts, and finally revises the materials for publication. (Clark 1987, 33)

Auerbach cites an example of this approach – the Texas Adult Performance Level Study – in which "university-based researchers surveyed literacy usage in a wide variety of contexts and identified sixty-five competencies that they claimed were characteristic of successful functioning in society" (Auerbach 1995, 13).

Critics of this view of the curriculum have argued that such a view is reductionist and presupposes that learners' needs can be identified with a predetermined set of skills and objectives. Knowledge is seen as something external to the learner that is transmitted in pieces. Freire describes this as a "banking model": "Education thus becomes an act of depositing, in which the students are depositories and the teacher is the depositor" (1975, 138). Advocates of the social-efficiency approach argue that the curriculum should above all focus on knowledge and skills that are relevant to the learner's everyday life needs and that the curriculum should be planned to meet the practical needs of society.

Learner-centeredness

This term groups together educational philosophies that stress the individual needs of learners, the role of individual experience, and the need to develop awareness, self-reflection, critical thinking, learner strategies, and other qualities and skills that are believed to be important for learners to develop. Within this tradition, *reconceptualists* emphasize the role of experience in learning. "What is missing from American schools . . . is a deep respect for personal purpose, lived experience, the life of the imagination, and those forms of understanding that resist dissection and measurement" (Pinar 1975, 316).

Constructivists emphasize that learning involves active construction and testing of one's own representation of the world and accommodation of it to one's personal conceptual framework. All learning is seen to involve relearning and reorganization of one's previous understanding and representation of knowledge (Roberts 1998, 23). Dewey, one of the founders of this philosophy, observed that "there is no intellectual growth without some reconstruction, some reworking" (Dewey 1934, 64). Roberts (1998) comments that constructivism has had a strong influence on language curriculum design, influencing the way, for example, reading and listening comprehension are taught with an emphasis on the prior knowledge, beliefs, and expectations that learners bring to listening and reading. Clark (1987, 49) (who uses the term *progressivism* to refer to this philosophy) suggests that it involves seeing education "as a means of providing children with learning experiences from which they can learn by their own efforts. Learning is envisaged as a continuum which can be broken up into several broad developmental stages. . . . Growth through experience is the key concept."

Marsh (1986, 201) points out that the issue of child-centered or learner-centered curricula reappears every decade or so and can refer to any of the following:

- individualized teaching
- learning through practical operation or doing
- laissez faire – no organized curricula at all but based on the momentary interests of children

- creative self-expression by students
- practically oriented activities directed toward the needs of society
- a collective term that refers to the rejection of teaching-directed learning

In language teaching, Clark sees this educational philosophy as leading to an emphasis on process rather than product, a focus on learner differences, learner strategies, and learner self-direction and autonomy.

Social reconstructionism

This curriculum perspective emphasizes the roles schools and learners can and should play in addressing social injustices and inequality. Curriculum development is not seen as a neutral process. Schools likewise do not present equal opportunities for all (Freire 1972; Apple 1986) but reflect the general inequalities in society. Schools must engage teachers and students in an examination of important social and personal problems and seek ways to address them. This process is known as "empowerment." Teachers must empower their students so that they can recognize unjust systems of class, race, or gender, and challenge them. Morris (1995, 10) observes:

The curriculum derived from this perspective focuses on developing knowledge, skills and attitudes which would create a world where people care about each other, the environment, and the distribution of wealth. Tolerance, the acceptance of diversity and peace would be encouraged. Social injustices and inequality would be central issues in the curriculum.

The most persuasive and currently popular representatives of this viewpoint are associated with the movement known as *critical theory* and *critical pedagogy*. The assumptions of "criticalists" are summarized by Kincheloe and McLaren (1994, 139):

that all thought is fundamentally mediated by power relations that are socially and historically constituted; that facts can never be isolated from the domain of value or removed from some form of ideological inscription; that the relationship between concept and object and between signifier and signified is never stable or fixed and is often mediated by the social relations of capitalist production and consumption; that language is central to the formation of subjectivity (conscious and unconscious awareness); that certain groups in any society are privileged over others . . . the oppression that characterizes contemporary societies is most forcefully reproduced when subordinates accept their social status as natural, necessary, or inevitable; that oppression has many faces and that focusing on only one at the expense of the others . . . often elides the interconnections between them; and, finally, that mainstream research practices are generally . . . implicated in the reproduction of systems of class, race, and gender oppression.

One of the best-known critical pedagogues is Freire (1972), who argued that teachers and learners are involved in a joint process of exploring and constructing knowledge. Students are not the "objects" of knowledge: they must find ways of recognizing and resisting various forms of control. In language teaching, Auerbach's (1992) work is an important application of critical pedagogy, stressing that teaching must seek to empower students and help them bring about change in their lives. Critics of this position argue that teachers and students may not be able to change the structure of the systems in which they work and that other channels are often available to address such changes.

Cultural pluralism

This philosophy argues that schools should prepare students to participate in several different cultures and not merely the culture of the dominant social and economic group. Banks (1988) argues that students in multicultural societies such as the United States need to develop cross-cultural competency or what is sometimes termed intercultural communication. This means that one cultural group is not seen as superior to others and that multiple perspectives representing the viewpoints of different cultural groups should be developed within the curriculum. Cultural pluralism seeks to redress racism, to raise the self-esteem of minority groups, and to help children appreciate the viewpoints of other cultures and religions (Uhrmacher 1993). In the United States, the American Council on the Teaching of Foreign Languages (ACTFL) has recently identified three dimensions to intercultural competence in foreign language programs: the need to learn about cultures, to compare them, and to engage in intercultural exploration (Phillips and Terry 1999). Crozet and Liddicoat (1999) explore the implications of these dimensions for the design of language programs in Australia. In multicultural societies such as Canada, the United States, and Australia, cultural pluralism has motivated demands for a bilingual approach to English-language teaching (Burnett 1998). Auerbach has questioned the rationale for the exclusive use of English in ESL classrooms and argues that literacy in the first language is a significant factor in the learning of a second language (Auerbach 1995, 25). Collingham (1988) emphasizes the importance of valuing learners' language knowledge: "to treat adult learners as if they know nothing of language is to accept the imbalance of power and so ultimately to collude with institutional racism; to adopt a bilingual approach and to value the knowledge that learners already have is to begin to challenge that unequal power relationship" (Collingham 1988, 85).

In reviewing the immigrant experience in Australia, Martin (1978) commented on the "lack of migrant participation – which could have been forth-coming if the medium of instruction had not been English alone, if bilingual teachers had been employed and if ethnic communities had been involved" (1978, 68).

The extent to which one or other of the curriculum ideologies discussed in this section serves as the ideological underpinning of the curriculum and the relative emphasis they receive in the curriculum will reflect the particular context in which the curriculum occurs. The philosophy of the curriculum is the result of political judgment in that it reflects a particular set of choices about curriculum options. It reflects what the participants in the planning process believe to be worthwhile goals to attain and the changes they feel the curriculum should bring about. Because these judgments and values are often not stated explicitly, identifying them, making them explicit, and reflecting on the unstated values and assumptions driving the curriculum are an essential part of the process of curriculum planning.

Stating curriculum outcomes

Aims

In curriculum discussions, the terms *goal* and *aim* are used interchangeably to refer to a description of the general purposes of a curriculum and *objective* to refer to a more specific and concrete description of purposes. We will use the terms *aim* and *objective* here. An aim refers to a statement of a general change that a program seeks to bring about in learners. The purposes of aim statements are:

- to provide a clear definition of the purposes of a program
- to provide guidelines for teachers, learners, and materials writers
- to help provide a focus for instruction
- to describe important and realizable changes in learning

Aims statements reflect the ideology of the curriculum and show how the curriculum will seek to realize it. The following statements describe the aims of teaching English at the primary level in Singapore:

Our pupils learn English in order to:

- communicate effectively, in both speech and writing, in everyday situations to meet the demands of society
- acquire good reading habits to understand, enjoy, and appreciate a wide range of texts, including the literature of other cultures
- develop the ability to express themselves imaginatively and creatively

- acquire thinking skills to make critical and rational judgments
- negotiate their own learning goals and evaluate their own progress
- acquire information and study skills to learn the other subjects taught in English
- cope effectively and efficiently with change, extended learning tasks, and examinations
- acquire knowledge for self-development and for fulfilling personal needs and aspirations
- develop positive attitudes toward constructive ideas and values that are transmitted in oral and/or written forms using the English language
- develop a sensitivity to, and an appreciation of, other varieties of English and the culture they reflect

These statements reflect several of the philosophies discussed in the preceding section. The following are examples of aim statements from different kinds of language programs.

A business English course

- to develop basic communication skills for use in business contexts
- to learn how to participate in casual conversation with other employees in a workplace
- to learn how to write effective business letters

A course for hotel employees

- to develop the communication skills needed to answer telephone calls in a hotel
- to deal with guest inquiries and complaints
- to explain and clarify charges on a guest's bill

Aim statements are generally derived from information gathered during a needs analysis. For example, the following areas of difficulty were some of those identified for non-English-background students studying in English-medium universities:

- understanding lectures
- participating in seminars
- taking notes during lectures
- reading at adequate speed to be able to complete reading assignments
- presenting ideas and information in an organized way in a written assignment

In developing course aims and objectives from this information, each area of difficulty will have to be examined and researched in order to understand what is involved in understanding lectures, participating in seminars, and so on. What knowledge and skills does each activity imply? Normally the overall aims of a short course can be described in two or three aim statements; however, in a course spanning a longer time period, such as the primary school course referred to earlier, a greater number of aim statements will be needed.

In developing aim statements, it is important to describe more than simply the activities that students will take part in. The following, for example, are not aims:

Students will learn about business-letter writing in English.
Students will study listening skills.
Students will practice composition skills in English.
Students will learn English for tourism.

For these to become aims, they need to focus on the changes in the learners that will result. For example:

Students will learn how to write effective business letters for use in the hotel and tourism industries.
Students will learn how to listen effectively in conversational interactions and how to develop better listening strategies.
Students will learn how to communicate information and ideas creatively and effectively through writing.
Students will be able to communicate in English at a basic level for purposes of tourism.

Objectives

Aims are very general statements of the goals of a program. They can be interpreted in many different ways. For example, consider the following aim statement:

Students will learn how to write effective business letters for use in the hotel and tourism industries.

Although this provides a clear description of the focus of a program, it does not describe the kinds of business letters students will learn or clarify what is meant by effective business letters. In order to give a more precise focus to program goals, aims are often accompanied by statements of more specific purposes. These are known as *objectives.* (They are also sometimes referred to as *instructional objectives* or *teaching objectives.*) An objective refers to a statement of specific changes a program seeks to bring about and results from an analysis of the aim into its different components. Objectives generally have the following characteristics:

- They describe what the aim seeks to achieve in terms of smaller units of learning.
- They provide a basis for the organization of teaching activities.
- They describe learning in terms of observable behavior or performance.

The advantages of describing the aims of a course in terms of objectives are:

- They facilitate planning: once objectives have been agreed on, course planning, materials preparation, textbook selection, and related processes can begin.
- They provide measurable outcomes and thus provide accountability: given a set of objectives, the success or failure of a program to teach the objectives can be measured.
- They are prescriptive: they describe how planning should proceed and do away with subjective interpretations and personal opinions.

In relation to the activity of "understanding lectures" referred to above, for example, aims and objectives such as the following can be described (Brown 1995):

Aim
- *Students will learn how to understand lectures given in English.*

Objectives
- *Students will be able to follow an argument, theme, or thesis of a lecture.*
- *Students will learn how to recognize the following aspects of a lecture:*
  cause-and-effect relationships
  comparisons and contrasts
  premises used in persuasive arguments
  supporting details used in persuasive arguments

Statements of objectives have the following characteristics:

Objectives describe a learning outcome. In writing objectives, expressions like *will study, will learn about, will prepare students for* are avoided because they do not describe the result of learning but rather what students will do during a course. Objectives can be described with phrases like *will have, will learn how to, will be able to.* (For exceptions, see the next section, "Nonlanguage outcomes and process objectives" on page 133.)

Objectives should be consistent with the curriculum aim. Only objectives that clearly serve to realize an aim should be included. For example, the objective below is unrelated to the curriculum aim *Students will learn how to write effective business letters for use in the hotel and tourism industries.*

Objective
The student can understand and respond to simple questions over the telephone.

Because the aim relates to writing business letters, an objective in the domain of telephone skills is not consistent with this aim. Either the aim statement should be revised to allow for this objective or the objective should not be included.

Objectives should be precise. Objectives that are vague and ambiguous are not useful. This is seen in the following objective for a conversation course:

Students will know how to use useful conversation expressions.

A more precise objective would be:

Students will use conversation expressions for greeting people, opening and closing conversations.

Objectives should be feasible. Objectives should describe outcomes that are attainable in the time available during a course. The following objective is probably not attainable in a 60-hour English course:

Students will be able to follow conversations spoken by native speakers.

The following is a more feasible objective:

Students will be able to get the gist of short conversations in simple English on topics related to daily life and leisure.

The following objectives (adapted from Pratt 1980) from a short course on English for travel and tourism designed to prepare students for travel in English-speaking countries illustrate the relationship between aims and objectives:

Course aim
To prepare students to communicate in English at a basic level for purposes of travel and tourism.

Course objectives
1. The student will have a reading vocabulary of 300 common words and abbreviations.

2. The student will have a listening vocabulary of 300 common words plus numbers up to 100.
3. The student can understand simple written notices, signs, and menus.
4. The student can understand simple questions, statements, greetings, and directions.
5. The student can get the gist of simple conversations in spoken English.
6. The student can pick out unfamiliar phrases from conversations and repeat them for clarification.
7. The student can use in speech 200 common words plus numbers up to 100 for time, quantity, and price.
8. The student can use about 50 useful survival phrases, questions, requests, greetings, statements, and responses.
9. The student can hold a bilingual conversation, speaking English slowly and clearly in simple words.
10. The student can use and understand appropriate gestures.
11. The student will have the confidence to initiate conversations in English, be unafraid of making mistakes, and attempt utterances outside his or her competence.
12. The student will be willing to learn from a native speaker's correction of his or her errors.
13. The student will have a "success experience" of making himself or herself understood in, and understand, a foreign language.

Frankel (1983, 124) gives the example of aims and objectives for a course in foundation reading skills for first-year university students in a Thai university:

Aim
To read authentic, nonspecialist, nonfiction texts in English with comprehension and at a reasonable speed.

Objectives
1. To use linguistic information in the text as clues to meaning, including:

   • deducing the meaning and use of unfamiliar lexical items through an understanding of word formation and context clues
   • decoding complex phrases and sentences including premodification, postmodification, complex embedding, and clause relations in compound and complex sentences
   • recognizing and interpreting formal cohesive devices for linking different parts of a text
   • recognizing and interpreting discourse markers

2. To understand the communicative value of a text, including:

- its overall rhetorical purpose (e.g., giving instructions, reporting an event)
- its rhetorical structure, including ways of initiating, developing, and terminating a discourse

3. To read for information, including:

- identifying the topic (theme)
- identifying the main ideas, stated and implied
- distinguishing between the topic and the main idea
- reading for detail
- distinguishing important from unimportant details
- skimming to obtain the gist or a general impression of the semantic content
- scanning to locate specifically required information

4. To read interpretatively including:

- extracting information not explicitly stated by making inferences
- distinguishing fact from opinion
- interpreting the writer's intention, attitude, and bias
- making critical judgments

Examples of objectives for the teaching of listening comprehension from the Singapore Primary Syllabus referred to earlier are:

At the end of the course, pupils should be able to demonstrate listening competence in the following ways:

- recognize and distinguish the basic sounds and phonological features of the English language
- understand and carry out instructions (simple to complex) given orally
- answer questions of differing levels based on what is heard
- recognize a range of spoken and written text types/speech situations and respond appropriately when required
- recognize discourse features in extended spoken texts in order to follow effectively what is spoken (e.g., words/expressions signaling, introduction, conclusion, exemplification, digression)
- observe conversation etiquette as a listener in group discussion
- listen critically for a specific purpose and respond appropriately

The difficulty of drawing up statements of objectives should not be underestimated. In developing language objectives one is doing more than creating a wish list off the top of one's head (though in the real world this is what often happens). Sound objectives in language teaching are based on an understanding of the nature of the subject matter being taught (e.g., listening, speaking, reading, writing), an awareness of attainable levels of learning for basic, intermediate, or advanced-level learners, and the ability to be able to describe course aims in terms of logical and well-structured units of organization. Objectives are therefore normally produced by a group of teachers or planners who write sample objectives based on their knowledge and experience and revise and refine them over time. In developing objectives, it is necessary to make use of a variety of sources, such as diagnostic information concerning students' learning difficulties, descriptions of skilled performance in different language domains, information about different language levels as is found in the *ACTFL Proficiency Guidelines* (see Chapter 6), as well as characterizations of the skills involved in different domains of language use (see Appendix 2). Objectives cannot therefore be regarded as fixed. As instruction proceeds, some may have to be revised, some dropped because they are unrealistic, and others added to address gaps.

Criticisms of the use of objectives

Although in many institutions the use of objectives in course planning is seen as a way of bringing rigor and structure to the process of course planning, the use of objectives either in general form or in the form of behavioral objectives has also attracted some criticism. The major criticisms of their use are:

Objectives turn teaching into a technology. It is argued that objectives are linked to an efficiency view of education, that is, one based on the assumption that the most efficient means to an end is justified. There is a danger that curriculum planning becomes a technical exercise of converting statements of needs into objectives. In the process, the broader goals of teaching and learning (e.g., to provide meaningful and worthwhile learning experiences) may be lost.

    Comment: This criticism is more applicable to the form of objectives known as "behavioral objectives" (see Appendix 1). To ensure that the curriculum addresses educationally important goals, objectives should be included that address "meaningful and worthwhile learning experiences." One way to do this is to include objectives that cover both language outcomes and nonlanguage outcomes: the latter will be discussed later in this chapter.

Objectives trivialize teaching and are product-oriented. By assuming that every purpose in teaching can be expressed as an objective, the suggestion is that the only worthwhile goal in teaching is to bring about changes in student behavior.

Comment: Objectives need not be limited to observable outcomes. They can also describe processes and experiences that are seen as an important focus of the curriculum.

Objectives are unsuited to many aspects of language use. Objectives may be suitable for describing the mastery of skills, but less suited to such things as critical thinking, literary appreciation, or negotiation of meaning.

Comment: Objectives can be written in domains such as critical thinking and literary thinking but will focus on the experiences the curriculum will provide rather than specific learning outcomes.

Competency-based program outcomes

An alternative to the use of objectives in program planning is to describe learning outcomes in terms of competencies, an approach associated with Competency-Based Language Teaching (CBLT). CBLT seeks to make a focus on the outcomes of learning a central planning stage in the development of language programs (Schneck 1978; Grognet and Crandall 1982). Traditionally, in language teaching planners have focused to a large extent on the content of teaching (as reflected in a concern for different types of syllabuses) or on the process of teaching (as reflected in a concern for different types of teaching methods). Critics of this approach argue that this concern with content or process focuses on the means of learning rather than its ends. CBLT shifts the focus to the ends of learning rather than the means. As a general educational and training approach, CBLT seeks to improve accountability in teaching through linking instruction to measurable outcomes and performance standards.

CBLT first emerged in the United States in the 1970s and was widely adopted in vocationally oriented education and in adult ESL programs. By the end of the 1980s, CBLT had come to be accepted as "the state-of-the-art approach to adult ESL by national policymakers and leaders in curriculum development as well" (Auerbach 1986, 411). In 1986, any refugee in the United States who wished to receive federal assistance had to be enrolled in a competency-based program (Auerbach 1986, 412). CBLT has recently reemerged in some parts of the world (e.g., Australia) as the major approach to the planning of language programs. The characteristics of CBLT are described by Schneck (1978, vi):

Competency-based education has much in common with such approaches to learning as performance-based instruction, mastery learning and individualized instruction. It is outcome-based and is adaptive to the changing needs of students, teachers and the community. . . . Competencies differ from other student goals and objectives in that they describe the student's ability to apply basic and other skills in situations that are commonly encountered in everyday life. Thus CBE is based on a set of outcomes that are derived from an analysis of tasks typically required of students in life role situations.

THE NATURE OF COMPETENCIES

Competencies refer to observable behaviors that are necessary for the successful completion of real-world activities. These activities may be related to any domain of life, though they have typically been linked to the field of work and to social survival in a new environment. Docking (1994, 11) points out the relationship between competencies and job performance:

A qualification or a job can be described as a collection of units of competency, each of which is composed of a number of elements of competency. A unit of competency might be a task, a role, a function, or a learning module. These will change over time, and will vary from context to context. An element of competency can be defined as any attribute of an individual that contributes to the successful performance of a task, job, function, or activity in an academic setting and/or a work setting. This includes specific knowledge, thinking processes, attitudes, and perceptual and physical skills. Nothing is excluded that can be shown to contribute to performance. An element of competency has meaning independent of context and time. It is the building block for competency specifications for education, training, assessment, qualifications, tasks, and jobs.

Tollefson (1986) observes that the analysis of jobs into their constituent functional competencies in order to develop teaching objectives goes back to the mid-nineteenth century. In the 1860s, Spencer "outlined the major areas of human activity he believed should be the basis for curricular objectives." Similarly, in 1926 Bobbitt developed curricular objectives according to his analysis of the functional competencies required for adults living in America. This approach has been picked up and refined as the basis for the development of competency-based programs since the 1960s. Northrup (1977) reports on a study commissioned by the U.S. Office of Education in which a wide variety of tasks performed by adults in American society were analyzed and the behaviors needed to carry out the tasks classified into five knowledge areas and four basic skill areas. From this analysis sixty-five competencies were identified. Docking (1994) describes how he was part of a project in Australia in 1968 that involved specifying the competencies of more than one hundred trades.

Mrowicki (1986) describes the process of developing a competency-based curriculum for a refugee program designed to develop language skills for employment. The process included:

- reviewing existing curricula, resource materials, and textbooks
- needs analysis (interviews, observations, survey of employers)
- identifying topics for a survival curriculum
- identifying competencies for each of the topics
- grouping competencies into instructional units

Examples of competencies are (Mrowicki 1986):

Topic: housing
1. Identify common household furniture/rooms.
2. Answer simple questions about basic housing needs.
3. Ask for simple information about housing, including rent, utilities, and date available.
4. Report household problems and emergencies.
5. Request repairs.
6. Arrange time for repairs.

Topic: shopping
1. Read a limited number of basic signs.
2. Ask the price of items.
3. State basic food (or other) needs.
4. State intention to purchase items.
5. Request correct change when incorrect change is received.
6. Read abbreviations for common weights and measure.
7. Ask for food using common weights and measures.
8. State clothing needs, including color and size.
9. Differentiate sizes by reading tags and tape measure.

In the Australian Migrant Education Program, one of the world's largest providers of language training to immigrants, a competency-based approach is used. Learning outcomes are specified in terms of work-related competencies such as the following:

Job-seeking skills: sample competencies
- Can inquire about an employment opportunity
- Can read and interpret advertisements for employment
- Can prepare a job-application letter

Workplace language: sample competencies
- Can follow and give oral instructions relevant to the workplace
- Can read diagrammatic and graphic workplace texts

- Can write formal letters relevant to a workplace context

In the Australian program competencies are described in terms of:

- elements that break down the competency into smaller components and refer to the essential linguistic features involved
- performance criteria that specify the minimal performance required to achieve a competency
- range of variables that sets limits for the performance of the competency
- sample texts and assessment tasks that provide examples of texts and assessment tasks that relate to the competency

As the examples above illustrate, competency descriptions are very similar to statements of objectives. They can be regarded as objectives that are linked to specific domains or activities.

CRITICISMS OF THE USE OF COMPETENCIES

The use of competencies in program planning is not without its critics. These criticisms focus on the following issues:

Definition of competencies   Tollefson (1986) argues that no valid procedures are available to develop competency specifications. Although lists of competencies can be generated intuitively for many areas and activities, there is no way of knowing which ones are essential. Typically, competencies are described based on intuition and experience, a process similar to the one used to develop statements of objectives. In addition, focusing on observable behaviors can lead to a trivialization of the nature of an activity. Therefore, competencies related to effective performance on a job will tend to include such things as "reading directions or following orders on a job," but not "to change or question the nature of the job."

Hidden values underlying competency specifications   CBLT is based on a social and economic efficiency model of curriculum design that seeks to enable learners to participate effectively in society. Consequently, as Tollefson and others have pointed out, the competencies selected as a basis for instruction typically represent value judgments about what such participation involves. Tollefson gives examples of value-based competency descriptions developed as part of a refugee resettlement training program in the Philippines:

- To develop the belief "that self-sufficiency is highly regarded in American society, that upward mobility is possible by hard work and persever-

ance . . . and that men and women have equal access to employment opportunities"
- To discourage attending school while receiving welfare
- To develop the attitude that the purchasing and use of secondhand items is appropriate
- To identify common entry-level jobs that can be held by those with limited English ability
- To respond appropriately to supervisors' comments about quality of work on the job, including mistakes, working too slowly, and incomplete work

(Tollefson 1986, 655–656)

Tollefson (1986, 656–657) points out that such competencies encourage refugees "to consider themselves fortunate to find minimum-wage employment, regardless of their previous education. Moreover, the competencies attempt to inculcate attitudes and values that will make refugees passive citizens who comply rather than complain, accept rather than resist, and apologise rather than disagree."

Criticisms such as these essentially argue for a different curriculum ideology than CBLT, such as a learner-centered or social-reconstructionist model. CBLT is not necessarily linked to the ideology Tollefson exposes. As with the use of objectives, appropriately described and chosen competency descriptions can provide a useful framework for course planning and delivery, though they may be more appropriate for certain types of courses than others. They seem particularly suited to programs that seek to teach learners the skills needed to perform specific tasks and operations, as found in many kinds of ESP programs.

The standards movement

The most recent realization of a competency perspective in the United States is seen in the "standards" movement, which has dominated educational discussions since the 1990s. As Glaser and Linn note:

In the recounting of our nation's drive towards educational reform, the last decade of this century will undoubtedly be recognized as the time when a concerted press for national educational standards emerged. The press for standards was evidenced by the efforts of federal and state legislators, presidential and gubernatorial candidates, teacher and subject-matter specialists, councils, governmental agencies, and private foundations. (Glaser and Linn 1993, xiii)

Standards are descriptions of the targets students should be able to reach in different domains of curriculum content, and throughout the 1990s there was a drive to specify standards for subject matter across the curriculum. These standards or benchmarks are stated in the form of competencies. In Australia, McKay (1999, 52) reports:

Literacy benchmarks at Years 3, 5 and 7 are currently under development centrally in consultation with States/Territories, literacy experts and professional associations. The benchmarks are to be short statements and to be "expressed in plain, accessible English, clearly understandable by a community audience". . . . They are to be accompanied by professional elaborations "to assist teachers and other educational professionals to assess and report student progress against the benchmarks."

Second and foreign language teaching in the United States has also embraced the standards movement. "It quickly became apparent to ESL educators in the United States at that time (1991) that the students we serve were not being included in the standards-setting movement that was sweeping the country" (Short 1997, 1).

The TESOL organization undertook to develop school standards for ESL for grades K–12. These are described in terms of competencies: "The standards . . . specify the language competencies ESOL students in elementary and secondary schools need to become fully proficient in English, to have unrestricted access to grade-appropriate instruction in challenging academic subjects, and ultimately to lead rich and productive lives" (TESOL 1997, 3). The standards are framed around three goals and nine standards. Each standard is further explicated by descriptors, sample progress indicators, and classroom vignettes with discussions (see Appendix 3).

Nonlanguage outcomes and process objectives

A language curriculum typically includes other kinds of outcomes apart from language-related objectives of the kind described above. If the curriculum seeks to reflect values related to learner centeredness, social reconstructionism, or cultural pluralism, outcomes related to these values will also need to be included. Because such outcomes go beyond the content of a linguistically oriented syllabus, they are sometimes referred to as *nonlanguage outcomes*. Those that describe learning experiences rather than learning outcomes are also known as *process objectives*. Jackson reports that a group of teachers of adult immigrants in Australia identified eight broad categories of nonlanguage outcomes in their teaching (Jackson 1993, 2):

- social, psychological, and emotional support in the new living environment

- confidence
- motivation
- cultural understanding
- knowledge of the Australian community context
- learning about learning
- clarification of goals
- access and entry into employment, further study, and community life

Objectives in these domains relate to the personal, social, cultural, and political needs and rights of learners. If these are not identified, they tend to
get forgotten or overlooked in the curriculum planning process. Jackson
(1993, 8) comments:

Non-language outcomes represent more than desirable or optional by-products
of the language learning process. They are essential prerequisites for on-going
and meaningful involvement with the process of language learning and learning
in general. Non-language outcomes are thus teaching and learning issues strongly
related to issues of access and equity for non-English-speaking background
learners and workers. It is important that the development of knowledge and
learning skills represent a significant component of the adult ESL curriculum.

Jackson gives the following examples of objectives in on-arrival programs
for immigrants that relate to understanding the context of local service institutions (1993, 45):

- to assist students to identify major local providers of services for:

  1. the unemployed
  2. employment
  3. education and training

- to assist students to identify the main functions of the above
- to situate main functions of above services in context of educational provision as a first step in the process of ongoing adult education
- to assist students to identify major services, including private/public for:

  1. migrants
  2. children
  3. women
  4. sport and recreation

- to provide task-oriented activities, including community visits, to famil-
  iarize students with above services
- to assist students to ascertain relevance of above services for themselves
  in terms of

1. eligibility
2. accessibility

Another category of outcomes is sometimes referred to as *process objectives.* In general education these are associated with the ideas of Bruner (1966) and Stenhouse (1975). Bruner argued that the curriculum should focus less on the outcomes of learning and more on the knowledge and skills learners need to develop. These include the concepts and procedures that children should acquire through the processes of inquiry and deliberation. Stenhouse argued that the curriculum should focus on activities that engage learners in such processes as investigation, decision making, reflection, discussion, interpretation, making choices, cooperation with others, and so on. Thus Hanley, Whitla, Moss, and Walter identified the aims of a course titled "Man: A Course of Study" as:

- To initiate and develop in youngsters a process of question posing
- To teach a research methodology where children can look for information
- To help youngsters develop the ability to use a variety of firsthand sources as evidence from which to develop hypotheses and draw conclusions
- To conduct classroom discussions in which youngsters learn to listen to others as well as to express their own view
- To legitimize the search, that is, to give sanction and support to open-ended discussions where definitive answers to many questions are not found
- To encourage children to reflect on their own experiences
- To create a new role for the teacher, who becomes a resource rather than an authority

(Hanley, et al. 1970, 5)

With this approach it is suggested that detailed specification of objectives is not needed. The curriculum specifies instead the content students will study and the activities and processes they are expected to engage in while studying the content. Stenhouse (1975) explains:

[The curriculum] is not designed on a pre-specification of behavioral objectives. Of course there are changes in students as a result of the course, but many of the most valued are not to be anticipated in detail. The power and the possibilities of the curriculum cannot be contained within objectives because it is founded on the idea that knowledge must be speculative and thus indeterminate as to student outcomes if it is to be worthwhile.

Objectives in the category of learning how to learn refer to learning strategies. Learning strategy theory suggests that effective learning involves:

- developing an integrated set of procedures and operations that can be applied to different learning – that is, strategies
- selecting strategies appropriate to different tasks
- monitoring strategies for their effectiveness and replacing or revising them if necessary

Many different kinds of learning strategies may be relevant to particular groups of learners. For example, a description of objectives for a national secondary school curriculum in an EFL country includes the following:

The course should develop students' awareness of the learning process and their role as learners by developing the following knowledge and skills:

1. ways of organizing learning and dividing learning tasks into smaller subtasks
2. familiarity with how to use reference words designed to assist them in independent learning (e.g., dictionaries, reference grammars, study guides)
3. awareness of their own learning styles and strengths and weaknesses
4. familiarity with various techniques of vocabulary learning and identification of techniques that are particularly useful to themselves
5. awareness of the nature of learning strategies and the difference between effective and ineffective strategies
6. ability to monitor their own learning progress and ways of setting personal goals for language improvement

Jackson (1993, 41) gives examples of objectives designed to help develop different types of learning strategies. The following relate to developing strategies for effective organization and management of time:

- to explicitly introduce students to the concept of time allocation in relation to study
- to assist students to identify realistic times and time spans for home study and individual study in the learning center
- to assist students to prioritize study time allocation in relation to other everyday activities and family commitments
- to assist students to create a daily/weekly timetable of study

The English Language Syllabus for the Teaching of English at Primary Level (1991) in Singapore includes a number of categories of process objectives. These are described as follows:

Thinking skills

At the end of the course, pupils should be able to:

- explore an idea, situation, or suggested solution for a specific purpose
- think creatively to generate new ideas, to find new meanings, and to deal with relationships
- analyse and/or evaluate an idea, a situation, or a suggested solution for a specific purpose

Learning how to learn

At the end of the course, pupils should be able to:

- apply a repertoire of library, information, and study skills
- take some responsibility for their own learning
- use some of the basic skills relating to information technology

Language and culture

At the end of the course, pupils should be able to:

- appreciate that there are varieties of English reflecting different cultures and use this knowledge appropriately and sensitively in communication
- adopt a critical, but not negative, attitude toward ideas, thoughts, and values reflected in spoken and written texts of local and foreign origin

The American Council on the Teaching of Foreign Languages in its National Standards for Foreign Language Learning (1996) (part of the standards movement referred to earlier) identifies a number of objectives for language programs that relate to the philosophy of cultural pluralism. For example:

- Students demonstrate understanding of the concept of culture through comparisons of the cultures studied and their own.
- Students acquire information and recognize the distinctive viewpoints that are only available through the foreign language and its cultures.

The planning of learning outcomes for a language course is closely related to the course planning process. Issues involved in developing and organizing course content are the focus of Chapter 6.

Discussion questions and activities

1. Choose a language teaching context you are familiar with and characterize the ideology underlying the curriculum. Are there any limitations of the ideology you have identified?

2. What limitations might there be in a focus on practical and functional skills in a language curriculum?

3. How has the philosophy of learner-centeredness influenced approaches to language teaching in recent years? What is such a philosophy a response to?

4. Do you think it is appropriate for language teachers to seek to empower students? If so, give examples of issues you think should be addressed and how these might be the focus of teaching.

5. To what extent is cultural pluralism an issue in the context in which you work or will work? If it is an issue, how would you address it in the curriculum?

6. What approach to planning learning outcomes is used in a program you are familiar with? How effective is it?

7. Give examples of aim statements that are appropriate for the following kinds of courses:

a course for English in primary school
a course in listening skills for intermediate-level learners

8. Rewrite the following aim statements so that they describe changes in learners:

Students will study English grammar
Students will improve their pronunciation

9. Prepare five sample objectives related to this aim:

Students will learn how to use effective office communication skills in English.

10. Look at the lists of listening skills and conversation skills in Appendix 2 and prepare three sample objectives related to any of the skills listed.

11. Prepare descriptions of competencies required to perform the following activities that are part of the target competencies of a program for English for hotel employees:

handling guest check-in at the hotel reception desk
taking guests' meal orders in a restaurant
dealing with guest inquiries at a tour desk

12. Discuss a teaching context you are familiar with and identify some non-language outcomes that are important in the context.

13. Discuss the advantages and limitations of using the following in planning learning outcomes: objectives, competencies, standards.

Appendix 1 Behavioral objectives

A particular form of expressing objectives known as behavioral objectives became popular at the time of the systems approach to educational planning. (The word *behavior* here refers to performance and is not related to behaviorist psychology.) Behavioral objectives take the idea of describing learning outcomes one step beyond the examples above by further operationalizing the definition of behavior. In a classic paper, Mager (1975) described three components for the description of behavioral objectives:

- performance: an objective says what a learner is expected to be able to do
- conditions: an objective describes the important conditions (if any) under which the performance is to occur
- criterion: wherever possible, an objective describes the criterion of acceptable performance, describing how well the learner must be able to perform in order to be considered acceptable

Findlay and Nathan (1980, 225–226) suggest that to meet the criterion of an operational definition of behavior, behavioral objectives need to include the following aspects:

1. the student as subject
2. an action verb that defines behavior or performance to be learned
3. conditions under which the student will demonstrate what is learned
4. minimum level of performance required after instruction, as specified by a criterion-referenced measurement strategy

The principal difference between behavioral objectives and instructional or teaching objectives as discussed above is the addition of statements of conditions and criterion. The statement of conditions is an attempt to specify the circumstances under which the learner demonstrates learning. For example, in showing that the learner has learned how to use certain conversational expressions will these be demonstrated by filling in the blanks in a cloze dialogue, by taking part in a question-and-answer exchange, or by performing a role play? The statement of criterion describes how well the learner must perform the action. For example, should the learner be able to complete a task within a time limit, with a minimum number of errors, or to a certain level of comprehensibility? The following are examples of behavioral objectives for a common-core ESL program (Findlay and Nathan 1980, 226):

- Given an oral request [condition] the learner [student as subject] will say [action that defines behavior] his/her/name, address and telephone number to a native speaker of English as spell his/her name, street and city so

that an interviewer may write down the data with 100% accuracy [level
of performance].
• Given oral directions for a 4-step physical action, the learner will follow
the directions with 100% accuracy.

Behavioral objectives of this kind are even more difficult to write than the
simpler objectives illustrated above and perhaps for this reason have not
been widely used in language teaching. In most circumstances, objectives
in the more general form illustrated earlier provide sufficient guidance for
program planning and instruction.

Appendix 2   Listening and conversation skills

1. An example of a skills taxonomy for the domain of listening skills (from
   Brindley 1997).

   1   Orienting oneself to a spoken text
   1.1 Identifying the purpose/genre of a spoken text
   1.2 Identifying the topic
   1.3 Identifying the broad roles and relationships of the participants (e.g.,
       superior/subordinate)

   2   Identifying the main idea/s in a spoken text
   2.1 Distinguishing main ideas from supporting detail
   2.2 Distinguishing fact from example
   2.3 Distinguishing fact from opinion when explicitly stated in text

   3   Extracting specific information from a spoken text
   3.1 Extracting key details explicitly stated in text
   3.2 Identifying key vocabulary items

   4   Understanding discourse structure and organisation
   4.1 Following discourse structure
   4.2 Identifying key discourse/cohesive markers
   4.3 Tracing the development of an argument

   5   Understanding meaning not explicitly stated
   5.1 Relating utterances to the social/situational context
   5.2 Identifying the speaker's attitudes/emotional state
   5.3 Recognising the communicative function of stress/intonation
       patterns
   5.4 Recognising the speaker's illocutionary intent
   5.5 Deducing meaning of unfamiliar words
   5.6 Evaluating the adequacy of the information provided
   5.7 Using information from the discourse to make a reasonable pre-
       diction

2. An example of a description of conversation skills.*

- turn taking
- giving feedback and backchanneling
- maintaining conversations
- initiating conversations
- closing interactions appropriately
- guessing the meanings of unfamiliar words
- seeking clarification
- asking for repetition
- structuring spoken information
- giving spoken instructions
- developing spoken texts as anecdotes
- using appropriate vocabulary
- using appropriate intonation and stress patterns

Appendix 3   ESOL standards for grades 4–8 (from TESOL 1997)

Descriptors
- sharing and requesting information
- expressing needs, feelings, and ideas
- using nonverbal communication in social interactions
- getting personal needs met
- engaging in conversations
- conducting transactions

Sample progress indicators
- ask peers for their opinions, preferences, and desires
- correspond with pen pals, English-speaking acquaintances, and friends
- write personal essays
- make plans for social engagements
- shop in a supermarket
- engage listener's attention verbally or nonverbally
- volunteer information and respond to questions about self and family
- elicit information and ask clarification questions
- clarify and restate information as needed
- describe feelings and emotions after watching a movie
- indicate interests, opinions, or preferences related to class projects
- give and ask for permission
- offer and respond to greetings, compliments, invitations, introductions, and farewells

* Extract reprinted from *Focus on Speaking* by A. Burns and H. Joyce (1997) with permission from the National Centre for English Language Teaching and Research (NCELTR), Australia. ©Macquarie University.

- negotiate solutions to problems, interpersonal misunderstandings, and disputes
- read and write invitations and thank-you letters
- use the telephone

References

ACTFL Proficiency guidelines. 1985. Hastings-on-Hudson: ACTFL Materials Center.

ACTFL. 1996. *Standards for foreign language learning: Preparing for the twenty-first century.* Lincolnwood, Ill.: National Textbook Co.

Apple, L. 1986. *Teachers and texts.* New York: Routlege and Kegan Paul.

Auerbach, E. R. 1986. Competency-based ESL: One step forward or two steps back? *TESOL Quarterly,* 20(3): 411–430.

Auerbach, E. R. 1992. *Making meaning, making change: Participatory curriculum development for adult ESL literacy.* Washington, DC: ERIC/Center for Applied Linguistics.

Auerbach, E. R. 1995. The politics of the ESL classroom: Issues of power in pedagogical choices. In Tollefson 1995. 9–33.

Banks, J. 1988. *Multi-ethnic education: Theory and practice.* Boston: Allyn and Unwin.

Bobbitt, F. 1918. *The curriculum.* Boston: Houghton Mifflin.

Bottomley, Y., J. Dalton, and C. Corbel. 1994. *From proficiency to competencies.* Sydney: National Centre for English Teaching and Resarch.

Brindley, G. 1997. Investigating second language listening ability: Listening skills and item difficulty. In G. Brindley and G. Wigglesworth (eds.), *Access: Issues in language test delivery and design.* Sydney: National Centre for English Teaching and Research. 65–86.

Brown, J. D. 1995. *The elements of language curriculum.* Boston: Heinle and Heinle.

Bruner, J. 1966. *The process of education.* Cambridge: Harvard Educational Press.

Burnett, L. 1998. *Issues in immigrant settlement in Australia.* Sydney: National Center for English Teaching and Research.

Burns, A., and H. Joyce. 1997. *Focus on speaking.* Sydney: National Center for English Teaching and Research.

Center for Applied Linguistics. 1983. *From the classroom to the workplace: Teaching ESL to adults.* Washington DC: Center for Applied Linguistics.

Clark, J. L. 1987. *Curriculum renewal in school foreign language learning.* Oxford: Oxford University Press.

Collingham, M. 1988. Making use of students' linguistic resources. In S. Nicholls and E. Hoadley-Maidment (eds.), *Current issues in teaching English as a second language to adults.* London: Arnold.

Crozet, C., and A. J. Liddicoat. 1999. Turning promises into practices. *Australian Language Matters* 7(1): 4–12.

Dewey, J. 1934. *Art as experience.* New York: Minton, Balch.

Docking, R. 1994. Competency-based curricula – the big picture. *Prospect* 9(2): 8–17.

Eisner, E. W. 1992. Curriculum ideologies. In Philip W. Jackson (ed.), *Handbook of research on curriculum.* New York: Macmillan. 302–306.

English language syllabus (primary). 1991. Singapore Curriculum Planning Division. Ministry of Education.

Findlay, C. A., and L. Nathan. 1980. Functional language objectives in a competency-based curriculum. *TESOL Quarterly* 14(2): 221–232.

Frankel, M. A. 1983. Designing a pre-EAP reading course: Practical problems. In R. R. Jordan (ed.), *Case studies in ELT.* London: Collins.

Freire, P. 1972. *Pedagogy of the oppressed.* New York: Herder and Herder.

Freire, P. 1975. *Pedagogy of the oppressed.* In M. Golby, J. Greenwald, and R. West (eds.), *Curriculum design.* London: Croom Helm. 138–149.

Glaser, R., and R. Linn 1993. Foreword. In L. Shepard, *Setting performance standards for student achievement.* Stanford, CA: National Academy of Education, Stanford University. xii–xiv.

Grognet, A. G., and Crandall, J. 1982. Competency based curricula in adult ESL. *ERIC/CLL New Bulletin* 6: 3–4.

Hagan, P. 1994. Competency-based curriculum: The NSW AMES experience. *Prospect* 9(2): 19–30.

Hanley, J., D. Whitla, E. Moss, and A. Walter. 1970. *Curiosity, competence, community – Man: A course of study.* Cambridge, MA: Education Development Center.

Hirsch, E. 1987. *Cultural literacy.* Boston: Houghton Mifflin.

Ho, W. K. 1994. The English language curriculum in perspective: Exogenous influences and indigenization. In S. Gopinathan, A. Pakir, W. K. Ho, and V. Saravana (eds.), *Language, society and education in Singapore.* Singapore: Times Academic Press. 221–244.

Hood, S., and A. Burns. 1994. The competency-based curriculum in action: Investigating course design practices. *Prospect* 9(2): 76–89.

Jackson, E. 1993. Nonlanguage outcomes in the language classroom. Sydney: NSW Adult Migrant English Service.

Kin, K. W. 1999. Mind your language. *Straights Time* (Singapore), September 2, 22.

Kincheloe, J., and P. McLaren. 1994. Rethinking critical theory and qualitative research. In N. Denzin and Y. Lincoln (eds.), *Handbook of qualitative research.* Thousand Oaks, CA: Sage. 138–157.

Kliebard, E. 1986. *The struggle for the American curriculum, 1893–1958.* Boston: Routledge and Kegan Paul.

Mager, R. F. 1975. *Preparing instructional objectives.* Belmont, CA: Fearon-Pitman.

Marsh, C. 1986. *Curriculum: An analytic introduction.* Sydney: Novak.

Martin, J. 1978. *The migrant presence: Australian reponses 1947–1977.* Sydney: George Allen and Unwin.

McDonald-Ross, M. 1975. Behavioural objectives: A critical review. In M. Golby, J. Greenwald, and R. West (eds.), *Curriculum design.* Kent: Croom Helm. 355–386.

McKay, P. 1999. Standards-based reform through literacy benchmarks: Comparisons between Australia and the United States. *Prospect* 14(2) (August): 52–65.

Ministry of Education, Singapore. 1991. *English language syllabus.* Singapore: Curriculum Planning Division.

Morris, P. 1995. *The Hong Kong curriculum.* Hong Kong: Hong Kong University Press.

Mrowicki, L. 1986. *Project Work English competency-based curriculum.* Portland: Northwest Educational Cooperative.

Northrup, N. 1977. *The adult performance level study.* Austin: University of Texas Press.

Nunan, D. 1989. *Designing tasks for the communicative classroom.* Cambridge: Cambridge University Press.

Ozolins, U. 1993. *The politics of language in Australia.* Sydney: Cambridge University Press.

Phillips, J., and R. Terry (eds.). 1999. *Foreign language standards: Linking research, theories, and practices.* Lincolnwood: National Textbook Company.

Pinar, W. (ed.). 1975. *Curriculum theorizing: The reconceptualists.* Berkeley: McCutchan.

Pratt, D. 1980. *Curriculum: Design and development.* New York: Harcourt Brace.

Roberts, J. 1998. *Language teacher education.* London: Arnold.

Schneck, E. A. 1978. *A guide to identifying high school graduation competencies.* Portland: Northwest Regional Educational Laboratory.

Short, D. 1997. Revising the ESL standards. *TESOL Matters* (February to March): 1, 6.

Stenhouse, L. 1975. *An introduction to curriculum research and development.* London: Heinemann.

Taba, H. 1962. *Curriculum development: Theory and practice.* New York: Harcourt Brace.

TESOL. 1997. *ESL standards for pre-K–12.* Alexandria, VA: TESOL.

Tollefson, J. 1986. Functional competencies in the US refugee program: theoretical and practical problems. *TESOL Quarterly* 20(40): 649–664.

Tollefson, J. (ed.). 1995. *Power and inequality in language education.* New York: Cambridge University Press.

Tyler, R. 1950. *Basic principles of curriculum and instruction.* Chicago: University of Chicago Press.

Uhrmacher, P. B. 1993. *English as a second language: Curriculum resource handbook.* Series introduction. New York: Krause International.

6 *Course planning and syllabus design*

A number of different levels of planning and development are involved in developing a course or set of instructional materials based on the aims and objectives that have been established for a language program. In this chapter we will examine the following dimensions of course development:

- developing a course rationale
- describing entry and exit levels
- choosing course content
- sequencing course content
- planning the course content (syllabus and instructional blocks)
- preparing the scope and sequence plan

These processes do not necessarily occur in a linear order. Some may take place simultaneously and many aspects of a course are subject to ongoing revision each time the course is taught. The types of decision making that we will examine in this chapter are also involved in developing instructional materials and many of the examples discussed apply to both course planning and materials design.

The course rationale

A starting point in course development is a description of the *course rationale.* This is a brief written description of the reasons for the course and the nature of it. The course rationale seeks to answer the following questions:

Who is this course for?
What is the course about?
What kind of teaching and learning will take place in the course?

The course rationale answers these questions by describing the beliefs, values and goals that underlie the course. It would normally be a two- or three-paragraph statement that has been developed by those involved in planning and teaching a course and that serves to provide the justification for the type of teaching and learning that will take place in the course. It provides a succinct statement of the course philosophy for anyone who may need such information, including students, teachers, and potential clients. Developing a rationale also helps provide focus and direction to some of the deliberations involved in course planning. The rationale thus serves the purposes of:

- guiding the planning of the various components of the course
- emphasizing the kinds of teaching and learning the course should exemplify
- providing a check on the consistency of the various course components in terms of the course values and goals

(Posner and Rudnitsky 1986)

The following is an example of a course rationale:

This course is designed for working adults who wish to improve their communication skills in English in order to improve their employment prospects. It teaches the basic communication skills needed to communicate in a variety of different work settings. The course seeks to enable participants to recognize their strengths and needs in language learning and to give them the confidence to use English more effectively to achieve their own goals. It also seeks to develop the participants' skills in independent learning outside of the classroom.

In order to develop a course rationale, the course planners need to give careful consideration to the goals of the course, the kind of teaching and learning they want the course to exemplify, the roles of teachers and learners in the course, and the beliefs and principles the course will reflect.

Describing the entry and exit level

In order to plan a language course, it is necessary to know the level at which the program will start and the level learners may be expected to reach at the end of the course. Language programs and commercial materials typically distinguish between *elementary, intermediate,* and *advanced* levels, but these categories are too broad for the kind of detailed planning that program and materials development involves. For these purposes, more detailed descriptions are needed of students' proficiency levels before they enter a program and targeted proficiency levels at the end of it. Information may be available on students' entry level from their results on international proficiency tests such as TOEFL or IELTS. Or specially designed tests may be needed to determine the level of students' language skills. Information from proficiency tests will enable the target level of the program to be assessed and may require adjustment of the program's objectives if they appear to be aimed at too high or too low a level.

An approach that has been widely used in language program planning is to identify different levels of performance or proficiency in the form of band levels or points on a proficiency scale. These describe what a student is able to do at different stages in a language program. An example of the use of proficiency descriptions in large-scale program planning was the approach used in the Australian Migrant Education On-Arrival Program.

> In order to ensure that a language program is coherent and systematically moves learners along the path towards that level of proficiency they require, some overall perspective of the development path is required. This resulted . . . in the development of the Australian Second Language Proficiency Ratings (ASLPR). The ASLPR defines levels of second language proficiency as nine (potentially 12) points along the path from zero to native-like proficiency. The definitions provide detailed descriptions of language behavior in all four macro-skills and allow the syllabus developer to perceive how a course at any level fits into the total pattern of proficiency development. (Ingram 1982, 66)

Similarly, in 1982 the American Council on the Teaching of Foreign Languages published proficiency guidelines in the form of "[a] series of descriptions of proficiency levels for speaking, listening, reading, writing, and culture in a foreign language. These guidelines represent a graduated sequence of steps that can be used to structure a foreign language program" (Liskin-Gasparro 1984, 11). The *ACTFL Proficiency Guidelines* (see Appendix 1) have been widely promoted as a framework for organizing curriculum and as a basis for assessment of foreign language ability, though they have also attracted controversy because they are not research-based (e.g., see Lowe 1986). Band descriptors such as those used in the IELTS examinations or the UCLES/RSA Certificate in Communicative Skills in English (Weir 1990, 149–179) can be similarly used as a basis for planning learner entry and exit levels in a program. (See Appendix 2 for an example of performance levels in *writing,* and Appendix 3 for band descriptors for "oral interaction.")

Choosing course content

The question of course content is probably the most basic issue in course design. Given that a course has to be developed to address a specific set of needs and to cover a given set of objectives, what will the content of the course look like? Decisions about course content reflect the planners' assumptions about the nature of language, language use, and language learning, what the most essential elements or units of language are, and how these can be organized as an efficient basis for second language learning. For example, a writing course could potentially be planned around any of the following types of content:

- grammar (e.g., using the present tense in descriptions)
- functions (e.g., describing likes and dislikes)
- topics (e.g., writing about world issues)
- skills (e.g., developing topic sentences)
- processes (e.g., using prewriting strategies)
- texts (e.g., writing a business letter)

Similarly a speaking course could be organized around:

- functions (expressing opinions)
- interaction skills (opening and closing conversations, turn taking)
- topics (current affairs, business topics)

The choice of a particular approach to content selection will depend on subject-matter knowledge, the learners' proficiency levels, current views on second language learning and teaching, conventional wisdom, and convenience. Information gathered during needs analysis contributes to the planning of course content, as do additional ideas from the following sources:

- available literature on the topic
- published materials on the topic
- review of similar courses offered elsewhere
- review of tests or exams in the area
- analysis of students' problems
- consultation with teachers familiar with the topic
- consultation with specialists in the area

Rough initial ideas are noted down as a basis for further planning and added to through group brainstorming. A list of possible topics, units, skills, and other units of course organization is then generated. One person suggests something that should go into the course, others add their ideas, and these are compared with other sources of information until clearer ideas about the content of the course are agreed on. Throughout this process the statements of aims and objectives are continually referred to and both course content suggestions and the aims and objectives themselves are revised and fine-tuned as the course content is planned. For example, a group of teachers listed the following initial ideas about what they would include in a course on listening and speaking skills for a group of intermediate-level learners:

- asking questions
- opening and closing conversations
- expressing opinions
- dealing with misunderstandings
- describing experiences
- social talk
- telephone skills
- situation-specific language, such as at a bank
- describing daily routines
- recognizing sound contrasts
- using communication strategies

These topics then have to be carefully reviewed and refined and the following questions asked about them:

Are all the suggested topics necessary?
Have any important topics been omitted?
Is there sufficient time to cover them?
Has sufficient priority been given to the most important areas?
Has enough emphasis been put on the different aspects of the areas identified?
Will the areas covered enable students to attain the learning outcomes?

Developing initial ideas for course content often takes place simultaneously with syllabus planning, because the content of a course will often depend on the type of syllabus framework that will be used as the basis for the course (discussed later in this chapter).

Determining the scope and sequence

Decisions about course content also need to address the distribution of content throughout the course. This is known as planning the scope and sequence of the course. *Scope* is concerned with the breadth and depth of coverage of items in the course, that is, with the following questions:

What range of content will be covered?
To what extent should each topic be studied?

For example, in relation to the course on listening and speaking skills referred to in the preceding section, one area of potential content identified was "describing experiences." But how much will be included in relation to this topic? And should two, four, or six class periods be devoted to it? The *sequencing* of content in the course also needs to be determined. This involves deciding which content is needed early in the course and which provides a basis for things that will be learned later. Sequencing may be based on the following criteria.

Simple to complex

One of the commonest ways of sequencing material is by difficulty level. Content presented earlier is thought to be simpler than later items. This is typically seen in relation to grammar content, but any type of course content can be graded in terms of difficulty. For example, in a reading course reading texts may be simplified at the beginning of the course and unsimplified at later levels. Or simple skills such as "literal comprehension" may be required early on, and more complex skills such as "inferencing" taught at a later stage.

Chronology

Content may be sequenced according to the order in which events occur in the real world. For example, in a writing course the organization might be based on the sequence writers are assumed to employ when composing: (1) brainstorming; (2) drafting; (3) revising; (4) editing. In a proficiency course, skills might be sequenced according to the sequence in which they are normally acquired: (1) listening; (2) speaking; (3) reading; (4) writing.

Need

Content may be sequenced according to when learners are most likely to need it outside of the classroom. For example, the rationale for the sequencing of content in a social survival curriculum is given as follows:

The topics and cross-topics in the curriculum are sequenced "in order of importance to students' lives, ease of contextualization and their relationship to other topics and cross-topics." The sequence is:

    i. basic literacy skills
   ii. personal identification
  iii. money
  iv. shopping
   v. time and dates
  vi. telephone

   vii. health
  viii. emergencies
    ix. directions
     x. transportation
    xi. housing
   xii. post office
  xiii. banking/bills
  xiv. social language
   xv. clarification

(Mrowicki 1986, xi)

Prerequisite learning

The sequence of content may reflect what is necessary at one point as a foundation for the next step in the learning process. For example, a certain set of grammar items may be taught as a prerequisite to paragraph writing. Or, in a reading course, word attack skills may be taught early on as a prerequisite to reading unsimplified texts at later stages of the course.

Whole to part or part to whole

In some cases, material at the beginning of a course may focus on the overall structure or organization of a topic before considering the individual components that make it up. Alternatively, the course might focus on practicing the parts before the whole. For example, students might read short stories and react to them as whole texts before going on to consider what the elements are that constitute an effective short story. Or, students might study how to write paragraphs before going on to practice putting paragraphs together to make an essay.

Spiral sequencing

This approach involves the recycling of items to ensure that learners have repeated opportunities to learn them.

Planning the course structure

The next stage in course development involves mapping the course structure into a form and sequence that provide a suitable basis for teaching. Some of the preliminary planning involved will have occurred while ideas for course content were being generated. Two aspects of this process, how-ever, require more detailed planning: *selecting a syllabus framework* and *developing instructional blocks.* These issues are closely related and some-times inseparable but also involve different kinds of decisions.

Selecting a syllabus framework

A syllabus describes the major elements that will be used in planning a lan-guage course and provides the basis for its instructional focus and content. For example, in planning a course on speaking skills based on the course content discussed earlier (in the section titled "Describing the entry and exit level"), a number of options are available. The syllabus could be:

- *situational:* organized around different situations and the oral skills needed in those situations
- *topical:* organized around different topics and how to talk about them in English
- *functional:* organized around the functions most commonly needed in speaking
- *task-based:* organized around different tasks and activities that the learn-ers would carry out in English

In choosing a particular syllabus framework for a course, planners are in-fluenced by the following factors:

- *knowledge and beliefs about the subject area:* a syllabus reflects ideas and beliefs about the nature of speaking, reading, writing, or listening
- *research and theory:* research on language use and learning as well as ap-plied linguistics theory sometimes leads to proposals in favor of particu-lar syllabus types
- *common practice:* the language teaching profession has built up consid-erable practical experience in developing language programs and this of-ten serves as the basis for different syllabus types
- *trends:* approaches to syllabus design come and go and reflect national or international trends

In the 1980s and 1990s, the communicative language teaching movement led to a reexamination of traditional approaches to syllabus design and a search for principles for the development of communicative syllabuses (see Chapter 2). A communicative syllabus is either an attempt to develop a framework for a general language course, such as a Threshold Level syl-labus, or one that focuses on communication within a restricted setting, such as English for Specific Purposes. Because many different syllabus approaches are available in developing "communicative" courses, many different syllabus frameworks can make a claim to be versions of a communicative syllabus: for example, competency-based, text-based, and task-based syllabuses. Other approaches to syllabus design are also possible and we will consider now the nature of these different syllabus options.

Grammatical (or structural) syllabus: one that is organized around grammatical items. Traditionally, grammatical syllabuses have been used as the basis for planning general courses, particularly for beginning-level learners. In developing a grammatical syllabus, the syllabus planner seeks to solve the following problems:

- to select sufficient patterns to support the amount of teaching time available
- to arrange items into a sequence that facilitates learning
- to identify a productive range of grammatical items that will allow for the development of basic communicative skills

Choice and sequencing of grammatical items in a grammar syllabus reflect not only the intrinsic ease or difficulty of items but their relationship to other aspects of a syllabus that may be being developed simultaneously. The syllabus planner is typically mapping out grammar together with potential lesson content in the form of topics, skills, and activities, and for this reason grammatical syllabuses often differ from one course to the next even when targeting the same proficiency level. Appendix 4 presents the grammatical syllabus underlying a typical first-year EFL course.

Grammatical syllabuses have been criticized on the following grounds:

- They represent only a partial dimension of language proficiency.
- They do not reflect the acquisition sequences seen in naturalistic second language acquisition.
- They focus on the sentence rather than on longer units of discourse.
- They focus on form rather than meaning.
- They do not address communicative skills.

These objections are true for traditional grammar-based courses and few language courses today are planned solely around grammatical criteria. Indeed, it is doubtful if they ever were. However, grammar remains a core component of many language courses. There are several reasons for this:

- Teaching a language through its grammar represents a familiar approach to teaching for many people. In many parts of the world, teachers and students expect to see a grammar strand in a course and react negatively to its absence.

- Grammar provides a convenient framework for a course: grammar can readily be linked to other strands of a syllabus, such as functions, topics, or situations.
- Grammar represents a core component of language proficiency: communicative competence includes the ability to use grammar and therefore deserves a place in the curriculum.

Grammatical syllabuses thus continue to be widely used in language teaching. Typically, however, they are seen as one stream of a multiskilled or integrated syllabus rather than as the sole basis for a syllabus.

Lexical syllabus: one that identifies a target vocabulary to be taught normally arranged according to levels such as the first 500, 1,000, 1,500, 2,000 words. We saw in Chapter 1 that vocabulary syllabuses were among the first types of syllabuses to be developed in language teaching. Today there is a large degree of consensus in English-language teaching concerning targets for vocabulary teaching at different levels and textbook and materials writers tend to keep materials within target vocabulary bands. Typical vocabulary targets for a general English course are:

Elementary level: 1,000 words
Intermediate level: an additional 2,000 words
Upper Intermediate level: an additional 2,000 words
Advanced level: an additional 2,000+ words

(Hindmarsh 1980; Nation 1990)

An example of a course planned systematically around lexical targets is the *Collins Cobuild English Course* (Willis and Willis 1988), of which Willis (1990, vi) comments:

The 700 most frequent words of English account for around 70% of all English text. That is to say around 70% of the English we speak and hear, read and write is made up of the 700 most common words in the language. The most frequent 1,500 words account for 76% of text and the most frequent 2,500 for 80%. Given this, we decided that word frequency would determine the contents of our course. Level 1 would aim to cover the most frequent 700 words together with their common patterns and uses. Level 2 would recycle these words and go on to cover the next 800 to bring us up to the 1,500 level, and Level 3 would recycle those 1,500 and add a further 1,000.

Because vocabulary is involved in the presentation of any type of language content, a lexical syllabus can only be considered as one strand of a more comprehensive syllabus.

Functional syllabus: one that is organized around communicative functions such as *requesting, complaining, suggesting, agreeing.* A functional syllabus seeks to analyze the concept of communicative competence into its different components on the assumption that mastery of individual functions will result in overall communicative ability. Functional syllabuses were first proposed in the 1970s as part of the communicative language teaching movement (see Chapter 2) and have formed the basis for many language courses and textbooks from that time. They were one of the first proposals for a communicative syllabus, that is, one that addresses communicative competence rather than linguistic competence. In *Threshold Level English,* basic functions were identified through analysis of the purposes for which learners use English, particularly younger learners up to the intermediate level using a language for social survival and travel purposes. This resulted in a widely used functional syllabus that consists of 126 functions grouped into the following categories (see Appendix 5):

- imparting and seeking factual information
- expressing and finding out attitudes
- deciding on courses of action
- socializing
- structuring discourse
- communication repair

Functional syllabuses such as *Threshold Level* provided the first serious alternative to a grammatical syllabus as a basis for general-purpose course design, and major courses published from the 1980s increasingly employed functional syllabuses, sometimes linked to a parallel grammatical syllabus. Because they often focus on communication skills, functional syllabuses are particularly suited to the organization of courses in spoken English. Functional syllabuses have proved very popular as a basis for organizing courses and materials for the following reasons:

- They reflect a more comprehensive view of language than grammar syllabuses and focus on the use of the language rather than linguistic form.
- They can readily be linked to other types of syllabus content (e.g., topics, grammar, vocabulary).
- They provide a convenient framework for the design of teaching materials, particularly in the domains of listening and speaking.

Functional syllabuses have also been criticized for the following reasons:

- There are no clear criteria for selecting or grading functions.
- They represent a simplistic view of communicative competence and fail to address the processes of communication.
- They represent an atomistic approach to language, that is, one that as-

sumes that language ability can be broken down into discrete components that can be taught separately.

- They often lead to a phrase-book approach to teaching that concentrates on teaching expressions and idioms used for different functions.
- Students learning from a functional course may have considerable gaps in their grammatical competence because some important grammatical structures may not be elicited by the functions that are taught in the syllabus.

These objections can be regarded as issues that need to be resolved in implementing a functional syllabus. Since their inception and enthusiastic reception in the 1980s, functional syllabuses are now generally regarded as only a partial component of a communicative syllabus. Alternative proposals for communicative syllabus design include task-based and text-based syllabuses (discussed later in this section).

Situational syllabus: one that is organized around the language needed for different situations such as *at the airport* or *at a hotel*. A situation is a setting in which particular communicative acts typically occur. A situational syllabus identifies the situations in which the learner will use the language and the typical communicative acts and language used in that setting. Situational syllabuses have been a familiar feature of language teaching textbooks for centuries (Kelly 1969) and are often used in travel books and books that focus on mastering expressions frequently encountered in particular situations. An example of a recent situationally organized textbook on English for travel is *Passport* (Buckingham and Whitney 1995), which contains the following situational syllabus:

1. On an airplane
2. At an immigration counter
3. At a bank
4. On the telephone
5. On the street
6. In the city
7. At home
8. At the doctors'
9. In an office
10. In a restaurant
11. In a café
12. In a bar
13. On a bus
14. In a store
15. At the post office
16. At the cinema
17. In a hotel
18. At the airport

Situational syllabuses have the advantage of presenting language in context and teaching language of immediate practical use. However, they are also subject to the following criticisms:

- Little is known about the language used in different situations, so selection of teaching items is typically based on intuition.

- Language used in specific situations may not transfer to other situations.
- Situational syllabuses often lead to a phrase-book approach.
- Grammar is dealt with incidentally, so a situational syllabus may result in gaps in a student's grammatical knowledge.

The role of situations in syllabus design has recently reentered language teaching, albeit in a different form from traditional situational syllabuses, with the emergence of communicative approaches to syllabus design and ESP. ESP approaches to curriculum development attribute a central role to the situation or setting in which communication takes place and to the following elements of the situation (Munby 1978; Feez 1998):

- the participants
- their role relations
- the transactions they engage in
- the skills or behaviors involved in each transaction
- the kinds of oral and written texts that are produced
- the linguistic features of the texts

Competency-based language teaching (see Chapter 5 and later in this section) is an approach to teaching that focuses on transactions that occur in particular situations and their related skills and behaviors. Text-based syllabus design (discussed later in this section) focuses on transactions, the texts that occur within transactions, and the linguistic features of the texts. The notion of situation has thus been incorporated as an element of more comprehensive approaches to syllabus design.

Topical or content-based syllabus: one that is organized around themes, topics, or other units of content. With a topical syllabus, content rather than grammar, functions, or situations is the starting point in syllabus design. Content may provide the sole criterion for organizing the syllabus or a framework for linking a variety of different syllabus strands together. "It is the teaching of content or information in the language being learned with little or no direct effort to teach the language separately from the content being taught" (Krahnke 1987, 65). All language courses, no matter what kind of syllabus they are based on, must include some form of content. But with other approaches to syllabus design, content is incidental and serves merely as the vehicle for practicing language structures, functions, or skills. In a typical lesson in a grammar-based course, for example, a structure is selected and then content is chosen to show how the item is used and to provide a context for practicing the structure. In a topic-based syllabus, in contrast, content provides the vehicle for the presentation of language rather than the other way around. Maximum use is made of content to provide links and continuity across the skill areas. Claims made for the advantages of courses based on content-based syllabuses are:

- They facilitate comprehension.
- Content makes linguistic form more meaningful.
- Content serves as the best basis for teaching the skill areas.
- They address students' needs.
- They motivate learners.
- They allow for integration of the four skills.
- They allow for use of authentic materials.

(Brinton, Snow, and Wesche 1989; Mohan 1986)

Topic-based syllabuses have often been a feature of ESL programs in elementary or secondary schools where the teaching of English is integrated with science, mathematics, and social sciences, as well as of ESL programs for students at the university level. Brinton et al. (1989, 27) give the following example of how a content-based course can be organized:

In a theme-based course, a high-interest topic such as "culture shock" could serve as the organizing principle for a 2-week integrated skills course, with the linguistic focus of the instruction determined by the students' needs, their proficiency level, and (last but not least) the degree to which the content "maps" onto the course objectives.

This approach was used in a German university program described in Brinton et al. (1989) that was built around the following themes:

television	modern architecture
religious persuasion	microchip technology
advertising	ecology
drugs	alternative energy
racism	nuclear energy
Native Americans	Dracula in myth, novel, and films

Issues that arise in developing a topic-based syllabus are:

- How are themes, topics, and content decided on?
- What is the balance between content and grammar or other strands in the syllabus?
- Are ESL teachers qualified to teach content-based courses?
- What should be the basis for assessment – learning of content or learning of language?

Although choosing appropriate content is an issue in the design of any language course, using topics as the overarching criterion in planning a course leaves other questions unresolved because decisions must still be made concerning the selection of grammar, functions, or skills. It may also be difficult to develop a logical or learnable sequence for other syllabus components if topics are the sole framework. Different topics may require language of differing levels of complexity and, as a consequence, it may not always be possible to reconcile the different strands of the syllabus. Appendix 3 in Chapter 8 describes how a topical syllabus was used in developing speaking materials.

Competency-based syllabus: one based on a specification of the competencies learners are expected to master in relation to specific situations and activities (see Chapter 5 for an extended discussion). Competencies are a description of the essential skills, knowledge, and attitudes required for effective performance of particular tasks and activities. For example, the work-skills curriculum in Mrowicki (1986) is organized according to topics and competencies.

The curriculum's language competencies are divided into topic and cross-topic areas. A topic refers to the context in which language is used. For example, the competency "Report basic household problems" is found in the topic "Housing." A cross-topic is a topic which can occur in other topic areas. For example, the competency "Read and write dates" from the cross-topic "Time and Dates" also occurs in the topics "Shopping" (reading expiration dates of food), "Health" (reading appointment times), "Banking and Bills" (reading the date due on bills), etc. (Mrowicki 1986, ix)

Examples of competencies related to the topic of "telephoning" are:

1. read and dial telephone numbers
2. identify oneself on the telephone when answering and calling
3. request to speak to someone
4. respond to request to hold
5. respond to offer to take message

Competency-based syllabuses are widely used in social survival and work-oriented language programs. Advantages and disadvantages of a competency-based approach are discussed in Chapter 5.

Skills syllabus: one that is organized around the different underlying abilities that are involved in using a language for purposes such as reading, writing, listening, or speaking. Approaching a language through skills is based on the belief that learning a complex activity such as "listening to a lecture" involves mastery of a number of individual skills or microskills that together make up the activity. Examples of skills that relate to different types of language use are:

writing:	creating a topic sentence
	distinguishing between main ideas and supporting sentences
	self-editing
listening:	recognizing key information
	using discourse markers to identify the flow of discourse
	following rapid speech
speaking:	recognizing turn-taking signals
	introducing a topic
	using communication strategies
reading:	reading for gist
	guessing words from context
	reading and making inferences

Skills have traditionally been a central focus in language teaching and there have been attempts to identify the *microskills* underlying the use of the four *macroskills* of reading, writing, listening, and speaking as a basis for syllabus design (e.g., Munby 1978). Yalden (1983) gives the following example of a skills syllabus for the teaching of study skills:

Basic reference skills: understanding and use of
• graphic presentation, namely, headings, subheadings, numbering, indentation, bold print, footnotes
• table of contents and index
• cross-referencing
• card catalog
• phonetic transcriptions/diacritics
• bibliography
• dictionaries

Skimming to obtain
• the gist of the text
• a general impression of the text

Scanning to locate specifically required information on
• a single point
• more than one point
• a whole topic

Transcoding information presented in diagrammatic display, involving
• completing a diagram/table/graph
• constructing one or more diagrams/tables/graphs

Note-taking skills
• completing note-frames

- deletions
- use of diagrams

Appendix 6 contains a skills syllabus for *listening* and *speaking* from a national curriculum document in an EFL country. Claims made in support of skills-based syllabuses are:

- They focus on behavior or performance.
- They teach skills that can transfer to many other situations.
- They identify teachable and learnable units.

Skills-based syllabuses have the advantage of focusing on performance in relation to specific tasks and therefore provide a practical framework for designing courses and teaching materials. They may be more relevant to situations in which students have very specific and identifiable needs (such as preparing for university-level studies in English). Skills syllabuses have been criticized, however, on the following grounds:

- There is no serious basis for determining skills.
- They focus on discrete aspects of performance rather than on developing more global and integrated communicative abilities.

Task-based syllabus: one that is organized around tasks that students will complete in the target language. A task is an activity or goal that is carried out using language such as *finding a solution to a puzzle, reading a map and giving directions,* or *reading a set of instructions and assembling a toy.* "Tasks are activities which have meaning as their primary focus. Success in tasks is evaluated in terms of achievement of an outcome, and tasks generally bear some resemblance to real-life language use" (Skehan 1996, 20).

All teaching makes use of tasks of different kinds. A task-based syllabus, however, is one based on tasks that have been specially designed to facilitate second language learning and one in which tasks or activities are the basic units of syllabus design. While carrying out these tasks, learners are said to receive comprehensible input and modified output, processes believed central to second language acquisition. A number of second language acquisition theorists have proposed tasks as a basis for syllabus planning. Long and Crookes (1991, 43) claim that tasks: "provide a vehicle for the presentation of appropriate target language samples to learners – input which they will inevitably reshape via application of general cognitive processing capacities – and for the delivery of comprehension and production opportunities of negotiable difficulty."

The basic claims made for a task-based syllabus are:

- Tasks are activities that drive the second language acquisition process.

- Grammar teaching is not central with this approach because learners will acquire grammar as a by-product of carrying out tasks.
- Tasks are motivating for learners and engage them in meaningful communication.

Two kinds of tasks have been proposed as a basis for syllabus design: *pedagogical tasks* and *real-world tasks*. Pedagogical tasks are based on SLA theory and are designed to trigger second language learning processes and strategies. The following are tasks of this kind:

- *jigsaw tasks:* These tasks involve learners in combining different pieces of information to form a whole (e.g., three individuals or groups may have three different parts of a story and have to piece the story together).
- *information-gap tasks:* Tasks in which one student or group of students has one set of information and another student or group has a complementary set of information. They must negotiate and find out what the other party's information is in order to complete an activity.
- *problem solving tasks:* Students are given a problem and a set of information. They must arrive at a solution to the problem. There is generally a single resolution of the outcome.
- *decision-making tasks:* Students are given a problem for which there a number of possible outcomes and they must choose one through negotiation and discussion.
- *opinion exchange tasks:* Learners engage in discussion and exchange of ideas. They do not need to reach agreement.

Although communicative activities of the type just described have long been a feature of communicative language teaching, advocates of task-based syllabuses propose them as the central feature of a syllabus rather than playing an incidental role. Real-world tasks are designed to practice or rehearse those activities that are found to be important in a needs analysis and that turn out to be important and useful in the real world. There is little difference between these kinds of tasks and those made use of in other situationally based approaches to syllabus design, such as Competency-Based Language Teaching.

At present, however, task-based syllabuses have not been widely implemented in language teaching. Among the concerns they raise are:

- *definition of task:* Definitions of tasks are sometimes so broad as to include almost anything that involves learners doing something.
- *design and selection of tasks:* Procedures for the design and selection of tasks remain unclear.

- *development of accuracy:* Excessive use of communicative tasks may encourage fluency at the expense of accuracy.

Although the notion of task appears useful as a component of methodology, it has yet to be widely adopted as a unit of syllabus design.

Text-based syllabus: one that is built around texts and samples of extended discourse. As already noted, this can be regarded as a type of situational approach because the starting point in planning a syllabus is analysis of the contexts in which the learners will use the language.

[This approach] starts with the texts which are identified for a specific context or which have been identified by students. This approach is often used when an overall context for language learning has been defined, such as in a specific workplace or a university or other further study context. Units of work are then developed in relation to the texts. For example, the spoken texts identified for a group of engineers in a workplace were: spoken instructions to field staff, presentations of report findings at meetings and telephone negotiations with contractors. (Burns and Joyce 1997, 17)

A text-based syllabus is a type of integrated syllabus because it combines elements of different types of syllabuses. Appendix 7 gives an example of the processes involved in developing a text-based syllabus. The following are examples of text types that can be used in planning a text-based syllabus (Feez 1998, 85–86):

exchanges	simple exchanges relating to information and goods and services
	complex or problematic exchanges
	casual conversation
forms	simple formatted texts
	complex formatted texts
procedures	instructions
	procedures
	protocols
information texts	descriptions
	explanations
	reports
	directives
	texts that combine more than one text types
story texts	recounts
	narratives
persuasive texts	opinion texts
	expositions
	discussions

In teaching from a text-based syllabus a five-part cycle is proposed that involves:

1. building the context for the text
2. modeling and deconstructing the text
3. joint construction of the text
4. independent construction of the text
5. linking related texts

The following advantages are suggested for a text-based syllabus:

- It teaches explicitly about the structures and grammatical features of spoken and written texts.
- It links spoken and written texts to the social and cultural contexts of their use.
- It allows for the design of units of work that focus on developing skills in relation to whole texts.
- It provides students with guided practice as they develop language skills for meaningful communication through texts.

(Feez 1998, v)

Criticisms of this approach are similar to those made of competency-based approaches, namely:

- It focuses on specific skills rather than a more general language proficiency.
- It may be impractical in many situations.

An integrated syllabus: Decisions about a suitable syllabus framework for a course reflect different priorities in teaching rather than absolute choices. The issue is, which foci will be central in planning the syllabus and which will be secondary? In most courses there will generally be a number of different syllabus strands, such as *grammar* linked to *skills* and *texts, tasks* linked to *topics* and *functions,* or *skills* linked to *topics* and *texts.* In arriving at a decision about which approach to syllabus planning to take, the course planners need to decide between macrolevel and microlevel planning units in the course. For example, a reading course might first be planned in terms of reading skills (the macrolevel planning category) and then further planned in terms of text types, vocabulary, and grammar (the microlevel planning category). A syllabus might be organized grammatically at the first level and then the grammar presented functionally. Or the first level of organization might be functional with grammar items selected according to the grammatical demands of different functions. In practical terms, therefore, all syllabuses reflect some degree of integration. Krahnke (1987, 75) concludes:

For almost all instructional programs, it is clear that some combination of types of instructional content will be needed to address the complex goals of the program. . . . for most general teaching applications, whose goal is functional ability in broadly defined settings and structural knowledge and communicative ability in specific situations, a combination of functional, structural, situational, and skill-based instruction is the probable choice. On the other hand, in some second language teaching settings, skills and tasks can be more narrowly specified, instructional resources are richer, or specific structural or formal knowledge is not required by the program for students to succeed, and a combination of task-based, skill-based, situational, functional, and content instruction may be chosen.

Developing instructional blocks

So far we have described the processes used to make decisions about the content of a course as well as its syllabus framework. A course also needs to be mapped out in terms of instructional blocks or sections. An instructional block is a self-contained learning sequence that has its own goals and objectives and that also reflects the overall objectives for the course. Instructional blocks represent the instructional focus of the course and may be very specific (e.g., a single lesson) or more general (e.g., a unit of work consisting of several lessons). Planning the organizational structure in a course involves selecting appropriate blocks and deciding on the sequence in which these will appear. In organizing a course into teaching blocks one seeks to achieve the following:

- to make the course more teachable and learnable
- to provide a progression in level of difficulty
- to create overall coherence and structure for the course

Two commonly used instructional blocks are planning by modules and by units.

Modules: This is a self-contained and independent learning sequence with its own objectives. For example, a 120-hour course might be divided into four modules of 30 hours each. Assessment is carried out at the end of each module. Modules allow for flexible organization of a course and can give learners a sense of achievement because objectives are more immediate and specific. Care needs to be taken, however, to ensure that the course does not appear fragmented and unstructured.

Units: This teaching block is normally longer than a single lesson but shorter than a module and is the commonest way of organizing courses and teaching materials. It is normally a group of lessons that is planned around a single instructional focus. (Sometimes units are referred to as a *scheme of work*.) A unit seeks to provide a structured sequence of activities that lead toward a learning outcome. The factors that account for a successful unit include:

- *Length:* Sufficient but not too much material is included.
- *Development:* One activity leads effectively into the next; the unit does not consist of a random sequence of activities.
- *Coherence:* The unit has an overall sense of coherence.
- *Pacing:* Each activity within the unit moves at a reasonable pace. For example, if there are five activities in the unit, one does not require four times as much time to complete as the others.
- *Outcome:* At the end of the unit, students should be able to know or do a series of things that are related.

The following comments by a learner indicate that the organization of the course units was not successful:

We did lots of different things in the course and many of them were quite useful. But it's hard to see where all the separate things fit together. Also, I never knew quite what to expect, where we were going from day to day.

The issue of unit structure is also crucial in developing instructional materials. In planning an upper-intermediate-level course with a topical organization of units and an integrated syllabus (Richards and Sandy 1998), the following solutions were reached with respect to unit structure (see Appendix 8).

- Each of the two books in the series would have 12 units.
- Each unit would consist of 8 pages that divide into two 4-page lessons.
- Each unit is organized around a general theme such as *creativity, communication, education* and *learning*.
- Each lesson focuses on a topic related to the unit theme. For example:

    Unit theme: *creativity*
    Lesson A: *creativity and jobs*
    Lesson B: *creative products*

Within each 4-page lesson, each page has a distinct focus in both terms of topic treatment and language focus. For example:

Lesson A
Page 1: Fluency activities introduce the topic of the first lesson through listening and oral work.

Page 2: Grammar exercises pick up an item that appears on page 1. Exercises provide controlled practice of grammar items leading to communicative practice.

Page 3: Fluency activities provide further listening and oral work on a topic related to the unit theme.

Page 4: Writing exercises on topics linked to the unit theme teach practical writing and composition skills.

Lesson B

Page 1: Fluency activities introduce the topic of the second lesson through listening and oral work.

Page 2: Grammar exercises provide controlled practice of grammar items leading to communicative practice.

Page 3: Fluency activities provide further listening and oral work.

Page 4: Reading activities develop reading skills and serve to initiate discussion.

With this unit structure two types of coherence are provided – horizontal and vertical. Horizontal coherence for a unit is created through the linked sequence of activities within each unit. Vertical coherence is created through the sequence that runs from the top of each page to the bottom with each page culminating in an appropriate activity to bring the page to closure.

Preparing the scope and sequence plan

Once a course has been planned and organized, it can be described. One form in which it can be described is as a scope and sequence plan. This might consist of a listing of the module or units and their contents and an indication of how much teaching time each block in the course will require. In the case of a textbook it usually consists of a unit-by-unit description of the course cross-referenced to the syllabus items included. Appendix 9 gives part of a scope and sequence plan for *New Interchange 1* (Richards, Proctor, and Hull 1997).

Having considered the different processes involved in planning and developing a language program, we can now turn to issues that arise in creating conditions for effective teaching of the course. These are the focus of Chapter 7.

Discussion questions and activities

1. How are different proficiency levels characterized and distinguished in a course or program you are familiar with? What are the advantages or limitations of using proficiency ratings or band descriptions as described in Appendixes 1–3?
2. Compare two or more textbooks for the same area (e.g., writing, speaking, listening) and for learners of the same level. How similar are the syllabuses in each book? Examine the teacher's books for each course. What justification do the authors of each book provide for the kind of syllabus they employ?
3. Choose three different approaches to syllabus design that are possible for the following types of courses and consider the advantages and limitations of each approach:

   a reading course
   a speaking course
   a writing course

4. Examine three different textbooks in a particular skill area (e.g., reading skills, writing). What approach to the selection and sequencing of content does each book adopt?
5. Do you think that grammar is a relevant component of a language course? If so, for what kind of courses? What would the role of grammar be in such a course? How would the choice of grammatical content be determined?
6. Select two or three related functions from the Threshold Level syllabus (see Appendix 5) and consider the language that would be needed to teach these functions to lower-intermediate learners in a speaking course. What decisions are involved in selecting the language realizations (or exponents) for functions in a functional syllabus?
7. Consider the design of a language course for airline employees working at the check-in counter at an airport. Suggest examples of the following:

   • the transactions they engage in
   • the skills or behaviors involved in each transaction
   • the kinds of oral and written texts that are produced
   • the linguistic features of the texts

8. How is a situational syllabus related to other syllabus options discussed in this chapter?
9. Plan a topic-based 4-hour unit of work in a course for a group of learn-

ers you are familiar with (or for intermediate-level ESL students in a general English class). Describe how the unit would do the following:

- integrate different language skills
- develop grammar from content

10. Compare two units from two course books that are designed for the same area and level. What unit structure does each book employ? How effective is the unit structure for each book?

11. Examine the skills listed in Appendix 6. How would you define "skills" based on the examples given in the syllabus?

12. Give an example of pedagogical tasks and real-world tasks that could be used in designing the following:

    a reading course
    a listening course

13. Examine the textbook unit in Appendix 8 and find examples of horizontal and vertical coherence as discussed on page 167.

Appendix 1   Proficiency descriptions for the domain of speaking

Proficiency descriptions for the domain of speaking from the *ACTFL Proficiency Guidelines* (American Council on the Teaching of Foreign Languages). The guidelines describe proficiency levels for speaking, listening, reading, and writing according to the levels of Novice, Intermediate, Advanced, and Superior. They are intended as guides for program planning and the development of objectives.

Generic descriptions – speaking

Novice   The Novice level is characterized by the ability to communicate minimally with learned material.

Novice-Low   Oral production consists of isolated words and perhaps a few high-frequency phrases. Essentially no functional communicative ability.

Novice-Mid   Oral production continues to consist of isolated words and learned phrases within very predictable areas of need, although quality is increased. Vocabulary is sufficient only for handling simple, elementary needs and expressing basic courtesies. Utterances rarely consist of more than two or three words and show frequent long pauses and repetition of interlocutor's words. Speaker may have some difficulty producing even the simplest utterances. Some Novice-Mid speakers will be understood only with great difficulty.

Novice-High   Able to satisfy partially the requirements of basic communicative exchanges by relying heavily on learned utterances but occasionally expanding these through simple recombinations of their elements. Can ask questions or make statements involving learned material. Shows signs of spontaneity although this falls short of real autonomy of expression. Speech continues to consist of learned utterances rather than of personalized, situationally adapted ones. Vocabulary centers on areas such as basic objects, places, and most common kinship terms. Pronunciation may still be strongly influenced by first language. Errors are frequent and, in spite of repetition, some Novice-High speakers will have difficulty being understood even by sympathetic interlocutors.

Intermediate   The Intermediate level is characterized by the speaker's ability to:
- create with the language by combining and recombining learned elements, though primarily in a reactive mode;
- initiate, minimally sustain, and close in a simple way basic communicative tasks; and
- ask and answer questions.

Intermediate-Low   Able to handle successfully a limited number of interactive, task-oriented, and social situations. Can ask and answer questions, initiate and respond to simple statements and maintain face-to-face conversation, although in a highly restricted manner and with much linguistic inaccuracy. Within these limitations, can perform such tasks as introducing self, ordering a meal, asking directions, and making purchases. Vocabulary is adequate to express only the most elementary needs. Strong interference from native language may occur. Misunderstandings frequently arise, but with repetition, the Intermediate-Low speaker can generally be understood by sympathetic interlocutors.

Intermediate-Mid   Able to handle successfully a variety of uncomplicated, basic and communicative tasks and social situations. Can talk simply about self and family members. Can ask and answer questions and participate in simple conversations on topics beyond the most immediate needs, e.g., personal history and leisure time activities. Utterance length increases slightly, but speech may continue to be characterized by frequent long pauses, since the smooth incorporation of even basic conversational strategies is often hindered as the speaker struggles to create appropriate language forms. Pronunciation may continue to be strongly influenced by first language and fluency may still be strained. Although misunderstandings still arise, the Intermediate-Mid speaker can generally be understood by sympathetic interlocutors.

Intermediate-High   Able to handle successfully most uncomplicated communicative tasks and social situations. Can initiate, sustain, and close a general conversation with a number of strategies appropriate to a range of circumstances and topics, but errors are evident. Limited vocabulary still necessitates hesitation and may bring about slightly unexpected circumlocution. There is emerging evidence of connected discourse, particularly for simple narration and/or description. The Intermediate-High speaker can generally be understood even by interlocutors not accustomed to dealing with speakers at this level, but repetition may still be required.

Advanced The Advanced level is characterized by the speaker's ability to:
– converse in a clearly participatory fashion;
– initiate, sustain, and bring to closure a wide variety of communicative tasks, including those that require an increased ability to convey meaning with diverse language strategies due to a complication or an unforeseen turn of events;
– satisfy the requirements of school and work situations; and
– narrate and describe with paragraph-length connected discourse.

Advanced Able to satisfy the requirements of everyday situations and routine school and work requirements. Can handle with confidence but not with facility complicated tasks and social situations, such as elaborating, complaining, and apologizing. Can narrate and describe with some details, linking sentences together smoothly. Can communicate facts and talk casually about topics of current public and personal interest, using general vocabulary. Shortcomings can often be smoothed over by communicative strategies, such as pause fillers, stalling devices, and different rates of speech. Circumlocution which arises from vocabulary or syntactic limitations very often is quite successful, though some groping for words may still be evident. The Advanced-level speaker can be understood without difficulty by native interlocutors.

Advanced-Plus Able to satisfy the requirements of a broad variety of everyday, school, and work situations. Can discuss concrete topics relating to particular interests and special fields of competence. There is emerging evidence of ability to support opinions, explain in detail, and hypothesize. The Advanced-Plus speaker often shows a well-developed ability to compensate for an imperfect grasp of some forms with confident use of communicative strategies, such as paraphrasing and circumlocution. Differentiated vocabulary and intonation are effectively used to communicate fine shades of meaning. The Advanced-Plus speaker often shows remarkable fluency and ease of speech but under the demands of Superior-level, complex tasks, language may break down or prove inadequate.

Superior   The Superior level is characterized by the speaker's ability to:
- participate effectively in most formal and informal conversations on practical, social, professional, and abstract topics; and
- support opinions and hypothesize using native-like discourse strategies.

Superior   Able to speak the language with sufficient accuracy to participate effectively in most formal and informal conversations on practical, social, professional, and abstract topics. Can discuss special fields of competence and interest with ease. Can support opinions and hypothesize, but may not be able to tailor language to audience or discuss in depth highly abstract or unfamiliar topics. Usually the Superior-level speaker is only partially familiar with regional or other dialectical variants. The Superior-level speaker commands a wide variety of interactive strategies and shows good awareness of discourse strategies. The latter involves the ability to distinguish main ideas from supporting information through syntactic, lexical, and suprasegmental features (pitch, stress, intonation). Sporadic errors may occur, particularly in low-frequency structures and some complex high-frequency structures more common to formal writing, but no patterns of error are evident. Errors do not disturb the native speaker or interfere with communication.

Appendix 2 Description of performance levels; writing (adapted by Paltridge from the IELTS test [Paltridge 1992])

Levels	Overall	Ideas & argument	Accuracy	Fluency	Appropriateness	Intelligibility
Beginner	Nonwriter. Cannot write in English at all.					
Elementary	Intermittent writer. Very difficult to follow.	Evidence of few ideas with no apparent development. Little apparent coherence to the text.	Very limited grasp of lexical, grammatical, and relational patterns. Little grasp of conventions of punctuation and spelling and use of cohesive devices.	Isolated words or short stock phrases only. Very short text.	Use of language (including layout) minimally appropriate to text type, function, and communicative goal.	Can convey only very simple meanings. Concentration and constant verification necessary on the part of the reader.
Intermediate	Limited writer. Rather difficult to follow.	Limited range of ideas expressed. Development may be restricted and often incomplete or unclear. Information is not arranged coherently.	Limited grasp of lexical, grammatical, and relational patterns and use of cohesive devices. Weaknesses in punctuation and/or spelling.	Texts may be simple, showing little development. Limited structures and vocabulary. Little subtlety and flexibility.	Use of language generally appropriate to function, text type, and communicative goal within a limited range of text types. Layout generally appropriate to text type.	Can convey basic meanings, although with some difficulty.
Upper-Intermediate	Moderate writer. Fairly easy to read and understand. Texts generally well organised.	Moderate range of ideas expressed. Topic development is present, but may still lack	Moderate grasp of lexical, grammatical, and relational patterns and use of cohesive devices	Texts show increased development. Writes with a fair range and variety of language.	Use of language generally appropriate to function, text type, and communicative	Broadly able to convey meanings, although errors can interfere with communication.

174

	some detail and supporting statements. Information is generally arranged coherently.	enabling the expression of a broader range of meanings and relationships between those meanings. Occasional faults in punctuation and spelling.	Moderate level of subtlety and flexibility.	goal within a moderate range of text types. Textual organisation and layout generally appropriate to text type.	Communicates meanings effectively. Only occasional interference due to errors.
Advanced	Competent writer. Easy to read from start to finish. Texts generally well organised.	Good range and progression of ideas expressed and coherently arranged, although there may still be isolated problems. Ideas and evidence are relevant, but more detail may still be desirable.	Competent grasp of lexical and grammatical patterns, although problems may still occur with punctuation and spelling. Relationships within and between propositions generally well managed.	Can generally write spontaneously on general topics. Competent use of a range of grammatical structures and vocabulary. Competent level of subtlety and flexibility.	Use of language generally appropriate to function, text type, and communicative goal within a range of text types. Textual organisation and layout appropriate to text type.	
Special Purpose	Good writer. Can write well within general and own special purpose areas. Able to produce organised, coherent, and cohesive discourse.	Good range of relevant ideas are coherently expressed. Evidence is presented and discussed. Where appropriate, a point of view is presented and developed.	Confident and generally accurate use of lexical and grammatical patterns, cohesive devices, punctuation, and spelling. Relationships within and between propositions well managed.	Writes well on general topics and on matters relevant to own special purpose interests. Good range of grammatical structures and vocabulary, subtlety, and flexibility.	Use of language mainly appropriate to function, text type, and communicative goal within a good range of text types. Textual organisation and layout appropriate to text type.	Communicates meanings competently and effectively; qualified intelligibility in certain special purpose areas. Can generally be understood without any difficulty.

Appendix 3   Band descriptors for oral interaction skills

These descriptors are from UCLES/RSA Certificates in Communicative Skills in English (Weir 1990). Certificates in all four areas – reading, writing, listening, and oral interaction – are offered at four different levels.

In order to achieve a pass at a given level, candidates must demonstrate the ability to complete the tasks set with the degree of skill specified by these criteria:

	Level 1	*Level 2*
Accuracy	It is acceptable for pronunciation to be heavily influenced by L1 if it is generally intelligible. With support, the candidate must be able to clarify any confusions caused by lexical or grammatical errors.	Pronunciation must be clearly intelligible even if still obviously influenced by L1. Grammatical/lexical accuracy is generally high, though some errors that do not destroy communication are acceptable.
Appropriacy	Use of the language must be broadly appropriate to function, though it may not correspond to native-speaker expectations. The intention of the speaker can be perceived by a sympathetic listener.	The use of language must be generally appropriate to function. The overall intention of the speaker must be generally clear.
Range	It is acceptable for the candidate to have a severely limited range of expression and to have to search often for a way to express the desired meaning.	A fair range of language must be available to the candidate. Only in complex utterances is there a need to search for words.
Flexibility	The candidate is not expected to take the initiative in conversation, or to respond immediately to a change in topic. The interlocutor may have to make considerable allowances and often adopt a supportive role.	There must be some evidence of the ability to initiate and concede a conversation and to adapt to new topics or changes of direction.

(continued)

	Level 1	Level 2
Size	Contributions limited to one or two simple utterances are acceptable.	Must be capable of responding with more than short-form answers where appropriate. Should be able to expand simple utterances with occasional prompting from the interlocutor.

	Level 3	Level 4
Accuracy	Pronunciation must be clearly intelligible, even if some influences from L1 remain. Grammatical/lexical accuracy is high, though occasional errors that do not impede communication are acceptable.	Pronunciation must be easily intelligible, though some residual accent is acceptable. Grammatical/lexical accuracy must be consistently high.
Appropriacy	The use of language must be generally appropriate to function and to context. The intention of the speaker must be clear and unambiguous.	The use of language must be entirely appropriate to context, function, and intention. There is nothing to cause confusion.
Range	A wide range of language must be available to the candidate. Any specific items that cause difficulties can be smoothly substituted or avoided.	There must be only occasional obvious limitations on the range of language. Few allowances have to be made for the fact that the candidate is not a native speaker.
Flexibility	There must be consistent evidence of the ability to "turn-take" in a conversation and to adapt to new topics or changes of direction.	The candidate must be able to "turn-take" and "direct" an interaction appropriately and keep it flowing.
Size	Must be capable of making lengthy contributions where appropriate. Should be able to expand and develop ideas with minimal help from the interlocutor.	Must be capable of making lengthy and complex contributions as appropriate. The interlocutor does not need to support the candidate.

Appendix 4   Grammar items and their sequence in a first-year English course (from Axbey 1997)

Present verb *be*
Subject pronouns
Possessive adjectives
Indefinite article: *a/an*
Plural nouns: *-s, -ies, -es*
Prepositions: *from, in, near, at, with, there is/are*
Countable nouns with *some* and *any*
Definite article: *the*
Plural nouns: irregular
Demonstrative pronouns: *this/that, these/those*
Adjectives
have/has got
Present simple
Object pronouns
Whose? How often?
enough
can/cannot (can't)
like + noun/*like* + gerund
Adverbs of frequency
Do you like?
Would you like?
Past verb *be*
Present continuous for present activities
Indefinite pronouns: *everyone, everybody, no one, nobody* + singular verb
most/some/a few + plural verb
ask/tell + infinitive
Past simple

Expressions with *go*
too + adjective/*not* + adjective *enough*
When clauses
want + infinitive
Imperatives
countable/uncountable nouns with *many/few, much/little*
Comparative adjectives
Superlative adjectives
Prepositions of place
Articles: definite/indefinite/zero
Present continuous for fixed plans
Verbs + prepositions
Expressions with *get*
going to for intentions
would you like + noun/infinitive
can for permission
cannot/can't for prohibition
should/shouldn't for advice about polite behavior
Possessive pronouns
Present perfect
Indefinite pronouns
should/shouldn't for giving opinions
will/won't for promises of help
promise/remember/forget + infinitive
have to for obligation
Adverbs of manner
Prepositions
will/won't for predictions
think so/hope so

Appendix 5   Threshold level syllabus

From *Threshold 1990* (Van Ek and Trim 1998).

Language functions for threshold level

  1 Imparting and seeking factual information
1.1 reporting (describing and narrating)
1.2 correcting
1.3 asking
1.4 answering questions

  2 Expressing and finding out attitudes
2.1 expressing agreement with a statement
2.2 expressing disagreement with a statement
2.3 enquiring about agreement and disagreement
2.4 denying statements
2.5 stating whether one knows or does not know a person, thing or fact
2.6 enquiring whether someone knows or does not know a person, thing or fact
2.7 stating whether one remembers or has forgotten a person, thing or fact or action
2.8 enquiring whether someone remembers or has forgotten a person, thing or fact or action
 2.9 expressing degrees of probability
2.10 enquiring as to degrees of probability
2.11 expressing or denying necessity (including logical deduction)
2.12 enquiring as to necessity (including logical deduction)
2.13 expressing degrees of certainty
2.14 enquiring about degrees of certainty
2.15 expressing obligation
2.16 enquiring about obligation
2.17 expressing ability/inability to do something
2.18 enquiring about ability or inability to do something
2.19 expressing that something is or is not permitted, or permissible
2.20 enquiring whether something is or is not permitted or permissible (including seeking permission)
2.21 granting permission
2.22 withholding permission
2.23 expressing wants/desires
2.24 enquiring about wants/desires
2.25 expressing intentions

2.26 enquiring about intentions
2.27 expressing preference
2.28 inquiring about preference
2.29 expressing pleasure, happiness
2.30 expressing displeasure, unhappiness
2.31 enquiring about pleasure/displeasure/happiness/unhappiness
2.32 expressing liking
2.33 expressing dislike
2.34 enquiring about likes and dislikes
2.35 expressing satisfaction
2.36 expressing dissatisfaction
2.37 enquiring about satisfaction/dissatisfaction
2.38 expressing interest
2.39 expressing lack of interest
2.40 enquiring about interest or lack of interest
2.41 expressing surprise
2.42 expressing lack of surprise
2.43 enquiring about surprise
2.44 expressing hope
2.45 expressing disappointment
2.46 expressing fear
2.47 giving reassurance
2.48 enquiring about fear/worries
2.49 expressing gratitude
2.50 reacting to an expression of gratitude
2.51 offering an apology
2.52 accepting an apology
2.53 expressing moral obligation
2.54 expressing approval
2.55 expressing disapproval
2.56 enquiring about approval/disapproval
2.57 expressing regret, sympathy

3 Deciding on courses of action (suasion)
3.1 suggesting a course of action
3.2 agreeing to a suggestion
3.3 requesting someone to do something
3.4 advising someone to do something
3.5 warning others to do something or to refrain from something
3.6 encouraging someone to do something
3.7 instructing or directing someone to do something
3.8 requesting assistance

3.9 offering assistance
3.10 inviting someone to do something
3.11 accepting an offer or invitation
3.12 declining an offer or invitation
3.13 enquiring whether an offer or invitation is accepted or declined
3.14 asking someone for something

4 Socialising

4.1 attracting attention
4.2 greeting people
4.3 when meeting a friend or acquaintance
4.4 replying to a greeting from a friend or acquaintance
4.5 addressing a friend or acquaintance
4.6 addressing a stranger
4.7 addressing a customer or a member of the general public
4.8 introducing someone to someone else
4.9 when being introduced to someone, or when someone is being introduced to you
4.10 congratulating someone
4.11 proposing a toast
4.12 taking leave

5 Structuring discourse

5.1 opening
5.2 hesitating
5.3 correcting oneself
5.4 introducing a theme
5.5 expressing an opinion
5.6 enumerating
5.7 exemplifying
5.8 emphasizing
5.9 summarizing
5.10 changing the theme
5.11 asking someone to change the theme
5.12 asking someone's opinion
5.13 showing that one is following a person's discourse
5.14 interrupting
5.15 asking someone to be silent
5.16 giving over the floor
5.17 indicating a wish to continue
5.18 encouraging someone to continue
5.19 indicating that one is coming to an end
5.20 closing

5.21 telephone opening
5.22 asking for [someone]
5.23 asking someone to wait
5.24 asking whether you are heard and understood
5.25 giving signals that you are hearing and understanding
5.26 announcing new call
5.27 opening [letter]
5.28 closing [letter]

  6 *Communication repair*
 6.1 signalling non-understanding
 6.2 asking for repetition of sentence
 6.3 asking for repetition of a word or phrase
 6.4 asking for confirmation of text
 6.5 asking for confirmation or understanding
 6.6 asking for clarification
 6.7 asking someone to spell something
 6.8 asking for something to be written down
 6.9 expressing ignorance of a word or expression
6.10 appealing for assistance
6.11 asking someone to speak more slowly
6.12 paraphrasing
6.13 repeating what one has said
6.14 asking if you have been understood
6.15 spelling out a word or expression
6.16 supplying a word or expression

Appendix 6   Skills syllabus for listening and speaking

From Malaysian Secondary School Syllabus form IV (1989).

1.0 Listening and Speaking

The component on listening and speaking deals with the skills of sound discrimination, extracting information, and prediction, in order to perform specific functions. The skills also include those of determining and using registers to suit different audiences, and for different purposes, so that students are able to express their thoughts clearly and succinctly and be able to fully participate in conversations and discussions.

The sub-skills that follow the main skills in this component are to be taught together with the main skills. These sub-skills are not arranged in a hierarchy and are thus not intended to be followed as a rigid sequence. They need to be repeated in different but meaningful combinations.

Objectives of the component on listening and speaking
Listening to and discriminating: consonant clusters, sentence stress and intonation, diphthongs and homonyms
Listening to and understanding: words, phrases and sentences; instructions, messages; stories; talks; reports; opinions; poems; dialogues; information in reports, guides, charts, graphs, manuals, forms, and letters; description of scenes, events, places, things, and processes and procedures
Speaking with correct pronunciation, intonation, word stress and sentence rhythm
Asking for and giving: meanings of words, phrases and sentences; instructions; messages; talks; reports; opinions; information in reports, guides, charts, graphs, manuals, forms and letters; descriptions of scenes, events, places, things, and processes and procedures; and
Telling stories

Skill specifications
At the end of the English Language Programme for Form IV, students should be able to

1.1   Listen to and discriminate between: consonant clusters, diphthongs and homonyms.
1.2   Listen to and understand, and ask for and give meanings of words, phrases and sentences.
1.3   Speak with correct intonation, word stress and sentence rhythm.
1.4   Listen to and understand, and ask for and give instructions on how to fix things, such as a leaking tap.
1.5   Listen to and understand, ask for and give and relay messages received through the mass media, such as the radio and the television.
1.6   Listen to and understand, and tell stories on moral values, such as self-reliance, diligence and public-spiritedness.
1.7   Listen to and understand, ask for and give information contained in talks on current issues, such as consumerism and health care.
1.8   Listen to and understand, ask for and give information contained in reports, such as newspaper reports and book reports.
1.9   Listen to and understand, ask for and give information contained in charts, graphs and manuals.
1.10 Listen to and understand, ask for and give information contained in informal letters, in newspapers and in formal letters of enquiry and complaint.

1.11 Listen to and understand, ask for and give descriptions of scenes, such as tourist spots in the ASEAN region.

1.12 Listen to and understand, ask for and give descriptions of events, such as the SEA games.

1.13 Listen to and understand, ask for and give opinions on current issues, such as unemployment.

1.14 Listen to and understand selected poems of writers from ASEAN region.

1.15 Listen to and understand, ask for and give descriptions of processes and procedures, such as the recycling of material.

1.16 Listen to and understand, and express displeasure and regret.

1.17 Practice social skills such as interrupting a conversation, and joining in and participating in a conversation.

The following sub-skills need to be combined and taught simultaneously with the above main skills where appropriate.

Sub-skills of listening
a. Discerning main ideas
b. Understanding sequence
c. Noticing specific details
d. Inferring
e. Comparing
f. Predicting
g. Determining relevance
h. Distinguishing fact and fiction
i. Differentiating between fact and opinion
j. Generalizing
k. Classifying

Sub-skills of speaking
l. Using correct pronunciation
m. Questioning
n. Paraphrasing
o. Supporting and clarifying
p. Summarizing
q. Using registers
r. Speaking coherently

Appendix 7   Designing a course from texts (from Burns and Joyce 1997)*

Step	Discussion and examples
1 Identify the overall context	University: course focus is preparing students for study at university
2 Develop an aim	To develop the spoken and written language skills required to undertake university study
3 Note the language event sequence within the context	These could include: • enrolling at university • discussing course selection • attending lectures • attending tutorials • using the library • reading reference books • writing essays • writing reports • undertaking examinations • participating in casual conversations

4 List the texts arising from the sequence	These could include:
	• enrollment forms
	• service encounter – selecting courses
	• lectures
	• tutorial discussions
	• service encounter – library enquiry
	• Range of possible written texts, for example:
	  – discipline-specific essays
	  – discipline-specific reports
	• Range of possible reading texts, for example:
	  – discipline-specific journal articles
	  – discipline-specific books
	  – library catalogues
	  – lecture notes
	• examination papers
	• genres within casual conversation (e.g., anecdote)

(continued)

* Extract adapted from *Focus on Speaking* by A. Burns and H. Joyce (1997) with permission from the National Centre for English Language Teaching and Research (NCELTR), Australia. ©Macquarie University.

Step	*Discussion and examples*
5 Outline the sociocultural knowledge students need	Students need knowledge about: • academic institutions • academic procedures and expectations • the role of the student

6 Record or gather samples of texts	• Written texts:
	   Gather examples of essays, catalogues, journals etc.
	• Spoken texts:
	   You may need to:
	   – find available recordings
	   – prepare some semi-scripted dialogues youself
	   – record authentic interactions

7 Develop units of work related to the texts and develop learning objectives to be achieved	Classroom tasks should be sequenced within units of work to provide students with: • explicit input • guided practice • an opportunity to perform independently

Appendix 8 A unit from *Passages 1* (Richards and Sandy 1998)

Unit 9 Putting the mind to work

Lesson A *Exploring creativity*

1 Qualities of creative people

starting point

A What qualities do you think creative people usually have? Rank them in terms of importance, and add others of your own. Then compare with a partner.

___ curiosity	___ independence	___ resourcefulness
___ decisiveness	___ intelligence	___ sensitivity
___ determination	___ originality	___ thriftiness
___ discipline	___ patience	___ _____

B Pair work Do you think these occupations demand a high level of creativity? Discuss some of the qualities you need in each job, and then compare around the class.

screenwriter

surgeon

cameraperson

sculptor

news announcer

animal trainer

> Originality is an important quality for a person who is working as a screenwriter. A screenwriter has to think up interesting, new stories.

2 Creativity at work

listening

A Listen to Angela, Simon, and Naomi talking about their jobs. What are their occupations? Why is creativity important in their work?

	Occupation	Why creativity is important
Angela		
Simon		
Naomi		

B Pair work Is creativity important in what you do every day? Why or why not?

grammar focus

Reduced relative clauses

You can shorten a relative clause by dropping *who* and the verb *be*.
Originality is an important quality for a person **(who is) working** as a screenwriter.

You can also drop *who* and change the verb to *-ing*.

Anyone $\left\{ \begin{array}{l} \text{who wants} \\ \text{wanting} \end{array} \right\}$ to be successful has to work hard.

A Rewrite these sentences by reducing each relative clause. Then compare with a partner.

1. Anyone who wants to become a journalist should be able to write under pressure.

Anyone wanting to become a journalist should be able to write under pressure.

2. Anyone who is hoping to succeed in business needs to have original ideas on how to market products.
3. A person who works as an inventor is always looking for new ways of solving common problems.
4. A person who is working as a detective has to try to get inside the mind of a criminal.
5. Anyone who is trying to become a successful actor will find that there is a lot more to it than he or she first thought.
6. Someone who works in advertising needs to be able to write catchy slogans.
7. A person who is responsible for a large staff has to be creative with scheduling.

B Now rewrite the sentences in Exercise A with your own ideas. Then compare with a partner.

Anyone wanting to become a journalist should keep up on current events.

---

discussion

Jobs that demand creativity

A Pair work How much creativity do these jobs require? Rank them from 1 (most creative) to 6 (least creative), and then compare with a partner. Ask and answer follow-up questions.

____ businessperson   ____ fashion designer
____ chef   ____ lawyer
____ radio DJ   ____ teacher

A: I think being a businessperson takes a lot of creativity, especially if you have your own company.
B: How so?
A: Well, someone running a business has a lot of problems to solve. . . .

B Group work Join another pair. Describe one more job that requires a high degree of creativity, one that requires a medium degree, and one that requires little creativity. Explain your choices and then share your answers with the class.

Creativity quiz

discussion **A** Creative people often answer "yes" to questions like these. Can you think of two more questions to add to the list?

1. Do you like to take risks?
2. Do you often question the way things work?
3. Do you like to come up with ways of improving things?
4. Are you sensitive to beauty?
5. Do you think it's OK if your ideas don't work at first?
6. Do you excel in many different fields?
7. Are you curious about the world in general?
8. Do you have a creative sense of humor?
9. _____
10. _____

Are you sensitive to beauty?   Do you like to take risks?

Source: From *Eccentrics* by David Weeks, M.D., and Jamie James

B Group work Answer the questions in Exercise A. Give examples to explain your answers.

> *I like to take risks. For example, last week I went bungee jumping.*

Creative solutions

discussion **A Pair work** Look at these situations, and think of at least three interesting suggestions for each one.

1. You manage a sports club and want to attract new members. What are the best ways?
2. You have to entertain some preschool children for an afternoon. What will you do?
3. It's your friend's birthday, and you want to plan a surprise he or she will never forget. What can you come up with?
4. You have an empty closet in your apartment and want to use it for something other than storage. What can you do with such a small space?

A: What would you do to attract new members to a sports club?
B: Well, there are many people who are embarrassed to exercise in public. I would try to attract them by . . .

B Group work Compare your ideas in groups. Which are the most creative?

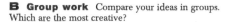

writing

7   Beginning new paragraphs

Begin a new paragraph each time you change focus.

A   Read this composition and decide where the writer changes focus. Write a (P) where you think each new paragraph should begin. Compare with a partner.

> Lucy Gomez is the most creative person I know. She started piano lessons when she was only 6 years old. At school, she was always creating interesting projects in her art class. When she was only 12 years old, she won a citywide poetry contest. Her parents were very proud of her. Now Lucy works as a sitcom writer for a popular TV show. She works with a group of writers, and together they have to think of fresh ideas. They also have to come up with funny dialog for the actors on their show because the actors have to play believable characters that will make the audience laugh. It is not an easy job, but Lucy does it well. She starts work late in the morning and often works until 7 or 8 at night. Lucy is very curious. She likes to travel and meet new people who have opinions that are different from hers. She often carries a notebook with her and writes down what she sees and hears. Lucy tells me that these new experiences are a good source of ideas for her work. I always enjoy talking to her and am happy to know someone as bright and creative as Lucy.

B   Write a three-paragraph composition about someone you know who is very creative or who is unique or different in some other interesting way. Use these questions or others of your own to get started.

1. In what ways is this person special or different?
2. How does this affect his or her life?
3. Would you like to be like this person? Why or why not?

C   Pair work   Read your partner's composition, and answer these questions.

1. Are the paragraphs divided where they should be?
2. Is the focus of each paragraph clear?
3. Is there any additional information that you would like to know that was not included in the composition?

Ideas that work

 1 **Everyday objects**

starting point

A Look at these "inventions." Why do people use them often? Why do you think they have been successful?

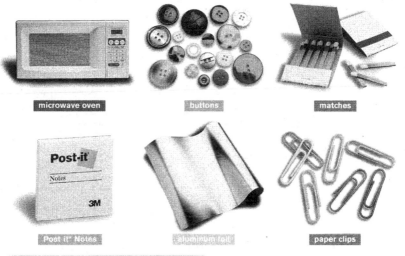

microwave oven   buttons   matches

Post-it® Notes   aluminum foil   paper clips

> *People need a quick and easy way to cook food, which is why the microwave oven has been so successful.*

B **Pair work** What everyday objects in your household are the most useful? Why do you think they have been so successful?

2 **Great ideas?**

listening

A Listen to John, Sandra, and Ted talking about what they would invent to make their lives easier. What are the inventions? What would they do?

	What are the inventions	What would they do
John		
Sandra		
Ted		

B **Pair work** Which invention would be most useful for you personally? Why?

78   Unit 9 Putting the mind to work

Non-defining relative clauses as sentence modifiers

grammar focus

Non-defining relative clauses with *which* can be used to make a comment about an entire sentence. Notice the use of the comma.

People need a quick and easy way to cook food, **which is why the microwave oven has been so successful.**

Seat belts are now required in all vehicles, **which means fewer people die in traffic accidents.**

A   Match these problems with the appropriate non-defining clauses. Then compare with a partner. Can you think of another clause to complete each sentence?

1. AIDS kills thousands of people each year, _i_
2. Cities are running out of safe places to dispose of trash, ____
3. It's very difficult to quit smoking, ____
4. Air travel became more dangerous in the 1980s because of terrorism, ____
5. Children used to get sick after opening medicine bottles and taking pills, ____
6. There are thousands of accidents in the workplace each year, ____
7. The postal service in many countries is not very efficient, ____
8. People already find today's computers inadequate, ____
9. It's easy to get lost when driving in a new city, ____
10. It used to be that people couldn't drive in the rain, ____

a. which means that more powerful models need to be developed.
b. which means that new methods of recycling will have to be invented.
c. which means engineers need to work harder to design safer workplaces.
d. which is why express delivery services have become very popular.
e. which is why scientists developed the nicotine patch.
f. which is why personal navigation systems were developed for rental cars.
g. which is why childproof bottle caps were invented.
h. which is why windshield wipers were invented.
i. which is why scientists are working so hard to find a vaccine.
j. which is why more sensitive types of metal detectors were invented.

B   Add non-defining clauses beginning with *which is why* . . . or *which means that* . . . to these statements. Then compare with a partner.

1. People today watch TV more than they buy books, . . .
2. The Internet is used by millions of people, . . .
3. Airplane design has improved tremendously, . . .
4. There have been many advances in medicine in recent years, . . .
5. It's becoming less expensive to use cellular phones, . . .

Inventions and discoveries

discussion   **Group work** What three inventions or discoveries have had the greatest impact on life in the twentieth century?

The jet engine has had a great impact on life in the twentieth century. People can now travel long distances in a short amount of time.

Collocations

vocabulary   **A**   Combine the verbs with the nouns to make common expressions. How many expressions can you find? Compare with a partner.

Verbs		Nouns	
analyze	make	a mistake	alternatives
explore	organize	a problem	possibilities
find	solve	a situation	information
		a solution	

analyze a situation   solve a problem

B   Pair work   How do people come up with ideas for new inventions? Answer using the expressions in Exercise A.

It's important not to be afraid to make a mistake.

 Making life better

discussion   **A   Pair work**   Why do inventors invent new products? Read this list of reasons, and add two more of your own.

- to make business more efficient
- to make daily life easier
- to help protect people's health
- to save lives
- to make life more enjoyable
- to protect the environment
- _____
- _____

B   Group work   Join another pair. Why do you think these things were invented? Use the reasons in Exercise A or others of your own.

air bags for cars	lie detectors	overnight delivery services
fax machines	life preservers	the Walkman
handheld computers	jet engines	virtual reality

Air bags for cars were invented in order to save lives. Without them, more people would be injured in car accidents.

194   *Chapter 6*

Innovative products and services

reading   **A Pair work** Why were these things developed or invented? Why have they
been so successful?

Sony Walkman

NIKE athletic shoes

FedEx overnight delivery

B Now read the article. What questions do you think inspired the inventors
of these products?

SILLY QUESTIONS, BRILLIANT ANSWERS

Several years ago, Masaru Ibuka, the chairman of Sony, was at a company planning meeting. Suddenly he had a brilliant idea. He stopped the meeting and asked everyone present what would happen if Sony removed the recording function and speaker and sold headphones with a tape player instead. Almost everyone thought he was crazy. Still, Ibuka kept thinking about his idea and worked at refining it. The result, of course, turned out to be the wildly successful Sony Walkman.

Good ideas often start with a really silly question. Bill Bowerman was making breakfast one day. As he stood there making waffles for his son, he wondered what would happen if he poured rubber into his waffle iron. Later, he tried it and the result looked something like the bottom of most sports shoes we see today. Still, when he took this idea to several existing shoe companies, he was literally laughed at. In fact, every single company turned him down. Though rather discouraged, Bowerman persevered and went on to form his own company, making NIKE athletic shoes.

Sometimes good ideas grow out of frustration. When Fred Smith was a student at Yale University, he had some paperwork that he needed to have delivered across the country the next day. Smith was amazed to find out that overnight delivery was impossible. He sat for a long while wondering why. Why couldn't there be a reliable overnight mail delivery service? He decided to design one. Smith did just that and turned his design into a class project. His business professor gave him only a C for his efforts. However, Smith was not through. He refined the ideas in that class project and eventually turned them into one of the first and most successful overnight mail services in the world – FedEx.

We know today, of course, that each of these ideas led to an incredibly successful product or service that has changed the way many of us live. The best questions are usually open-ended and are often silly. Children aren't afraid to ask such questions, but adults frequently are. Think how different the world might be if people never asked "silly" questions!

C Group work Discuss these questions. Then share your answers with the class.

1. Why do you think so many people turned down Bowerman's idea?
2. Why do you think Smith's professor gave him a C on the project?
3. Which idea has led to the most imitations?
4. Do you have any ideas for new products or services? What are they?

Lesson B Ideas that work   81

Appendix 9   Part of the scope and sequence chart from *New Interchange,* vol. 1 (Richards, Proctor, and Hull 1997)

Plan of Book 1

Title/Topics	Functions	Grammar
UNIT 1 — PAGES 2–7		
Please call me Chuck. Introductions and greetings; names and titles; countries and nationalities	Introducing yourself; introducing someone; checking information; asking about someone; exchanging personal information	Wh-questions and statements with *be*; yes/no questions and short answers with *be*; contractions; subject pronouns; possessive adjectives
UNIT 2 — PAGES 8–13		
How do you spend your day? Occupations, workplaces, and school; daily schedules; clock time	Describing work and school; asking for and giving opinions; talking about daily schedules	Simple present Wh-questions and statements; time expressions: *at, in, on, around, until, before, after, early,* and *late*
UNIT 3 — PAGES 14–19		
How much is it? Spending habits, shopping, and prices; clothing and personal items; colors and materials	Talking about prices; giving opinions; talking about preferences; making comparisons; buying and selling things	Demonstratives: *this, that, these, those; one* and *ones*; questions: *how much* and *which*; comparisons with adjectives
UNIT 4 — PAGES 20–25		
Do you like jazz? Music, movies, TV programs; entertainers; invitations and excuses; dates and times	Talking about likes and dislikes; giving opinions; making invitations and excuses	Simple present yes/no and Wh-questions with *do*; question: *what kind*; object pronouns; modal verb *would*; verb + *to* + verb
REVIEW OF UNITS 1–4 — PAGES 26–27		
UNIT 5 — PAGES 28–33		
Tell me about your family. Families and family life	Talking about families and family members; exchanging information about the present; describing family life	Present continuous yes/no and Wh-questions, statements, and short answers; determiners: *all, nearly all, most, many, a lot of, some, not many, a few,* and *few*
UNIT 6 — PAGES 34–39		
How often do you exercise? Sports and exercise; routines	Asking about and describing routines and exercise; talking about frequency; talking about abilities	Adverbs of frequency: *always, almost always, usually, often, sometimes, seldom, hardly ever, almost never, never*; questions with *how: how often, how much time, how long, how well, how good*; short answers
UNIT 7 — PAGES 40–45		
We had a great time! Free-time and weekend activities; vacations	Talking about past events; giving opinions about past experiences; talking about vacations	Past tense yes/no and Wh-questions, statements, and short answers with regular and irregular verbs; past tense of *be*
UNIT 8 — PAGES 46–51		
How do you like the neighborhood? Stores and places in a city; neighborhoods; houses and apartments	Asking about and describing locations of places; asking about and describing neighborhoods; asking about quantities	*There is/there are; one, any, some*; prepositions of place; questions: *how much* and *how many*; countable and uncountable nouns
REVIEW OF UNITS 5–8 — PAGES 52–53		

References

ACTFL Proficiency Guidelines. 1985. Hastings-on Hudson: ACTFL Materials Center.

Axbey, S. 1997. *Real times elementary.* London: Richmond.

Brinton, D., M. Snow, and M. Wesche. 1989. *Content-based second language instruction.* New York: Newbury House.

Buckingham, A., and N. Whitney. 1995. *Passport.* New York: Oxford University Press.

Burns, A., and H. Joyce. 1997. *Focus on speaking.* Sydney: National Centre for English Language Teaching and Research.

Feez, S. 1998. *Text-based syllabus design.* Sydney: National Centre for English Language Teaching and Research.

Hindmarsh, R. 1980. *The Cambridge English lexicon.* Cambridge: Cambridge University Press.

Ingram, D. 1982. Designing a language program. *RELC Journal* 13(2): 64–6.

Kelly, L. G. 1969. *Twenty-five centuries of language teaching.* Rowley, MA: Newbury House.

Krahnke, K. 1987. *Approaches to syllabus design for foreign language teaching.* Washington, DC: Center for Applied Linguistics.

Liskin-Gasparro, J. E. 1984. The ACTFL proficiency guidelines: A historical perspective. In T. V. Higgs (ed.), *Teaching for proficiency: The organizing principle.* Skokie, IL: National Textbook Company. 11–42.

Lowe, P. 1986. Proficiency: Panacea, framework, process? A reply to Kramsch, Schultz, and particularly to Bachman and Savigon. *Modern Language Journal* 70: 391–397.

Mohan, B. 1986. *Language and content.* Reading, MA: Addison-Wesley.

Mrowicki, L. 1986. *Project work English competency-based curriculum.* Portland: Northwest Educational Cooperative.

Munby, J. 1978. *Communicative syllabus design.* Cambridge: Cambridge University Press.

Nation, I. S. P. 1990. *Teaching and learning vocabulary.* New York: Newbury House.

Paltridge, B. 1992. EAP placement testing: An integrated approach. *ESP Journal* 11(3): 243–268.

Prabhu, N. S. 1987. *Second language pedagogy.* Oxford: Oxford University Press.

Pusat Perkembangan Kurikulum. 1989. *Bahasa Inggeris Tingkatan iv.* Kuala Lumpur.

Richards, J. C., and C. Sandy. 1998. *Passages 1.* New York: Cambridge University Press.

Richards, J. C., S. Proctor, and J. Hull. 1997. *New Interchange 1.* New York: Cambridge University Press.

Skehan, P. 1996. A framework for the implementation of task-based instruction. *Appled Linguistics* 17(1): 38–61.

Van Ek, J., and J. L. M. Trim. 1998. *Threshold 1990*. Cambridge: Cambridge University Press.

Weir, C. 1990. *Communicative language testing*. Oxford: Pergamon.

Willis, D. 1990. *The lexical syllabus*. London: Collins.

Willis, D., and J. Willis. 1998. *Collins Cobuild English course*. London: Collins ELT.

Yalden, J. 1983. *The communicative syllabus: Evolution, design and implementation*. Cambridge: Cambridge University Press.

7 *Providing for effective teaching*

Curriculum development processes as they have been described so far in this book are essential resources in helping schools achieve their goals. The other principal educational resource is teaching itself. The focus of this chapter is how quality teaching can be achieved and maintained in a language program. Whereas the preceding chapters have described some of the essential planning that is involved in developing a language course, the present chapter seeks to examine factors that are involved in creating conditions for good teaching to take place. Quality teaching is achieved not only as a consequence of how well teachers teach but through creating contexts and work environments that can facilitate good teaching. The following issues will be considered in this chapter:

- institutional factors
- teacher factors
- teaching factors
- learner factors

The institution

The organizational culture

The organizational culture of a school refers to the ethos and environment that exist within a school, the kinds of communications and decision making that take place, and the management and staffing structure they support. In Chapter 4, several aspects of a school's organizational culture were discussed, including the extent to which the school's organizational culture facilitates or hinders the reception of new ideas and practices. A school's organizational culture is revealed in the way the following questions are answered:

- What are the school's goals and mission?
- What is the school's management style?

- What shared values do staff have?
- What are the decision-making characteristics of the school?
- What roles do teachers perform?
- How are teaching and other work planned and monitored?
- What provision is made for staff development?
- How are courses and curriculum planned?
- How receptive is the school to change and innovation?
- How open are communication channels?

These and related questions will be examined throughout this chapter. Basic to the organizational culture of an institution is its management structure, because, as Davidson and Tesh point out (1997), its organizational design "is built by managerial decisions that delineate the number and type of jobs in the organization and the processes that subordinate, control, and link them, such as authority relationships, communication networks, and specific planning and organizational techniques" (Davidson and Tesh 1997, 177). Davidson and Tesh describe two types of organizational structure that are commonly found in schools and other kinds of organizations, the mechanistic model and the organic model. The mechanistic model is a bureaucratic approach to organizing collective activities that stresses "the need for authority, hierarchies of control, and an explicit chain of command" (Davidson and Tesh 1997, 178). Davidson and Tesh suggest that many language programs reflect this organizational model and cite the following examples.

1. Many programs value specialization; that is, they prefer that teachers specialize in one or two particular levels and skills. For example, a teacher may be assigned level-three reading and level-three writing, teaching those classes, and only those classes each term, and becoming an expert in those areas.
2. Many programs provide teachers not only with a course curriculum, but also with a class syllabus outlining which pages and exercises are to be covered each day. The more detailed the syllabus, the more uniformity there will be across each level in the program. Administrators in large programs, in programs that make use of graduate teaching assistants, or in multiple-site programs may find this advantageous because it eliminates uncertainty in teaching performance resulting from individual differences, professional inexperience, or the absence of propinquity.
3. Some programs have explicit chains of command. All communication in such programs is vertical. If moving upward, the communication must pass through each superior in the chain of command until it reaches the appropriate level. If moving downward, it must pass through each subordinate in like manner.

4. Many programs have hiring, promotion, and dismissal policies that match those of the mechanistic model. They hire based on professional qualifications such as degree, field, length and type of professional experience, and letters of recommendation; they promote based on seniority, program contributions, and professional achievements; and they terminate only after due process has occurred.

(Davidson and Tesh 1997, 179)

The organic model of organizational design, by comparison,

is one that maximizes flexibility and adaptability, encourages complete confidence and trust between superior and subordinates, and taps a wide range of human motivations to achieve organizational goals. Communication flows in all directions, both vertically and laterally. Teamwork is substantial, and decision-making and control functions are shared widely throughout the organization.

(Davidson and Tesh 1997, 179)

Aspects of the organic model are also found in many language programs. Davidson and Tesh cite the following examples:

1. Numerous program administrators value flexibility and adaptability; they expect their teachers to teach most, if not all, skills in most, if not all, levels. Thus they encourage a range of professional development activities for each faculty member. Level, skill, or content area specialization is viewed as an obstacle not only to the professional growth of the specialist, but also to other teachers who may wish to teach such classes, but cannot because they are not the "experts."
2. Many language programs provide opportunities for professional training that build up the value and worth of each faculty and staff member. They hold timely, well-organized, and appropriately focused in-service or residency meetings with internal or outside experts. They provide travel funding to relevant local, regional, and national professional meetings. They provide release time for materials development. They encourage research, publications, and grant proposal writing.
3. Numerous programs allow for communication not only vertically, but also laterally through cooperative teaching, peer coaching and observation, and joint piloting of new materials.
4. A large number of programs value teamwork and have established a committee system so that decision-making and control functions are shared widely throughout the program. Committee recommendations may be advisory or binding. Areas of concern include long-range plan-

ning, circular and personnel matters, professional development, and program marketing, to name a few.

(Davidson and Tesh 1997, 180)

Davidson and Tesh suggest that most language programs have features of both the organic and the mechanistic models, depending on the size of the program and the type of staff working in it. With a large program staffed by experienced and mature professionals, a more organic approach is likely. With smaller programs or programs dependent on less experienced staff, a more mechanistic approach may be needed.

Quality indicators in an institution

Language teaching institutions vary greatly in terms of how they view their educational mission. Some schools – hopefully the majority – are committed to providing quality educational services. They have a clearly articulated mission. They take seriously the development of a sound curriculum and set of programs, hire the best available teachers, and provide quality instruction and the kinds of support teachers need to achieve their best. The following characteristics are indicators of the quality of a school or educational institution (Morris 1994):

1. There are clearly stated educational goals.
2. There is a well-planned, balanced, and organized program that meets the needs of its students.
3. Systematic and identifiable processes exist for determining educational needs in the school and placing them in order of priority.
4. There is a commitment to learning, and an expectation that students will do well.
5. There is a high degree of staff involvement in developing goals and making decisions.
6. There is a motivated and cohesive teaching force with good team spirit.
7. Administrators are concerned with the teachers' professional development and are able to make the best use of their skills and experience.
8. The school's programs are regularly reviewed and progress toward their goals is evaluated.

Not all schools embrace a philosophy of quality, however. Some may be viewed by their owners as little more than business opportunities. Money spent on hiring qualified teachers and providing for teacher training and ongoing professional development is limited if nonexistent. An educational mission has not been developed, nor has a plan to achieve it. Teachers may be poorly motivated, poorly qualified, and on poor employment terms. Staff turnover is high, and the reputation of the institute low. Maintaining educational quality within a business environment is a challenge for many private language schools. It is increasingly the case that education is a business and the challenge is to meet educational objectives and standards while at the same time meeting financial imperatives, whether it be cost recovery or profit making. Being sound educationally and sound financially are not necessarily mutually exclusive. The following kinds of questions need to be addressed if an institution seeks to build quality and effectiveness into its programs (Henry 1997, 79):

1. How can we determine the quality of the language program?
2. How can we improve the quality of the language program?
3. What do we value most in the language program?
4. What type of curriculum best meets student needs?
5. What do we need to support the curriculum?
6. What kind of language proficiency testing is needed for accurate student placement?
7. What qualities are we looking for in faculty?

In the following sections, we will examine some of the key dimensions of quality and how quality can become a focus in a school or language program.

A SENSE OF MISSION

What goals does the institution have? Does it exist to serve an important educational purpose that provides the rationale for the range of courses and services it offers? A useful format for articulating a school's sense of mission is in the form of a mission statement. Such a statement should be developed collectively by those who have a commitment to the success of the institution. Appendix 1 gives an example of a mission statement for a university English department that was developed collectively by its staff. Once it is developed, a mission statement can serve as a reference point to assess proposals for new initiatives or programs within an institution and to provide a basis for evaluation of its performance over time.

A STRATEGIC PLAN

A strategic plan is a description of the long-term vision and goals of an institution and the means it undertakes for fulfilling them. Based on approaches used in successful businesses and industries, the notion of strategic planning is now increasingly seen as essential to the success of any organization, including schools. Klinghammer (1997, 64) provides a useful overview of the function of strategic planning in effective language programs, and identifies six elements of a good strategic plan:

- *vision:* a statement of where a language program is going in the long term and what its members hope to accomplish
- *values:* the principles that guide the conduct of a program, in terms of responsibility to students, teachers, and other stakeholders
- *purpose:* the basic reasons for the institution's existence
- *mission:* a description of the institution's vision in terms of specific goals that it seeks to achieve, usually within a particular time period. This is expressed in the form of the *mission statement*
- *goals:* specific steps that relate to each aspect of the mission, such as increasing student enrollments, developing teaching materials, or providing an environment in which teachers can carry out classroom research
- *strategies:* the methods and activities that will be used to attain the goals

QUALITY ASSURANCE MECHANISMS

Quality assurance refers to systems a school has in place to ensure the quality of its practices. For example, how does one ensure that the best-quality staff are employed? Is there a transparent recruitment process or is staff recruitment made through personal networks? What process is in place to select and review textbooks? Are textbooks chosen by teachers on the basis of quality and relevance or because of other factors? What systems are in place to ensure that tests and other forms of assessment are sound and fair? Are grades sometimes adjusted up or down by the administration based on unknown criteria? Factors relevant to creating a culture of quality assurance in an institution are:

- A formulated policy on quality assurance has been articulated and is familiar to all staff.
- Reasonable and acceptable standards have been determined for all aspects of quality, such as employment, publicity, materials, facilities, and teachers' dress codes.
- Systems are in place to ensure that quality is regularly assessed and corrections are made where necessary.
- A reward system is in place to ensure that those who attain high quality in their work are recognized.

• Support is available to enable staff to improve quality (e.g., of their teaching or materials) if necessary.

A SOUND CURRICULUM

A sound curriculum is reflected in the following features of a school's programs:

• The range of courses offered corresponds to the needs of learners.
• The curriculum is coherent: The courses represent a rationale approach to achieving the school's mission.
• Courses have been developed based on sound educational principles with due attention to recognized curriculum development processes.
• Course descriptions, including aims, goals, syllabuses, and course organization, have been developed.
• Teaching materials and tests are of high quality, have been carefully selected or developed, and are regularly reviewed and revised.
• Mechanisms are in place to monitor the quality of teaching and learning.
• The curriculum is subject to ongoing review and renewal. There is ongoing interest in identifying strengths and weaknesses and bringing about improvements in all aspects of the curriculum.

FLEXIBLE ORGANIZATIONAL FRAMEWORK

We noted earlier that effective schools and language programs are characterized by administrators who are open to change, flexible, and who encourage teachers to innovate. There is an atmosphere of trust and support and staff are supported by reasonable teaching loads, rewards, and opportunities for professional development. The management style is participatory rather than top-down (Stoller 1997).

GOOD INTERNAL COMMUNICATIONS

Good internal communications depend on setting up systems that facilitate communications among teachers and between teachers and administrators. Such systems include:

• regular meetings and briefings that bring people up to date on important issues and provide opportunities for input
• access to administrative leaders and visibility of administrators in the institutional setting; in addition the administration is receptive to teachers' suggestions

- shared decision making resulting from opportunities for multiple sources of input on key decisions
- availability of relevant course documentation and information for those who need it
- written guidance for staff on their different roles and job duties so that boundaries and expectations are clear
- a system for collecting feedback on all aspects of the program and procedures for making constructive use of feedback
- a system for staff support and for getting constructive comments on other people's course outlines and teaching materials
- regular evaluation or feedback sessions in which staff can describe and compare experiences, problems, and solutions
- regular newsletters, bulletins, or E-mail communication in which colleagues can pass on experiences, give and ask for suggestions, and report on successful teaching experiences
- informal gatherings that allow staff to get to know one another and develop collegial relations and friendships

PROFESSIONAL TREATMENT OF TEACHERS

Language teachers often suffer from poor employment conditions. They are not always recognized as trained professionals with specialized skills and knowledge. Leung and Teasdale (1998, 5) point out that the status of ESL teachers in mainstream education in many parts of the world is problematic and one of the major obstacles teachers face.

In the primary and secondary sectors ESL teachers work in mainstream classrooms, often in highly varied and unpredictable situations. ESL is not a curriculum subject and it has to be delivered through the content of other subjects. ESL teachers do not generally have sole control of classroom management; they often work as support or collaborative teachers and are with particular classes usually only for a limited number of hours per week. The pupils can, and do, arrive at different times of the year, their English language learning needs varying according to their previous schooling and circumstances. There are no clearly established and widely accepted disciplinary based teaching procedures (in the way that, for instance, science or music may have) and no clearly defined outcomes which are tailored to the specific needs of ESL pupils.

The broader issue here is whether teachers are treated as professionals or simply regarded as members of a workforce. Eskey (1997, 24) comments on the low academic status of Intensive English Programs in American universities, and the fact that they often have to deal with oppressive budgetary arrangements:

Most are required to be self-supporting and many are frankly regarded as cash cows that are expected to generate large surpluses for the support of more prestigious programs. . . . This means maximizing income and minimizing costs, which in practice means radical understaffing, low salaries for both staff and faculty, large numbers of part-time faculty with few or no benefits, and major corner-cutting with respect to equipment, facilities, and faculty perks such as support for curriculum development, in-service training, and attending professional conferences.

The extent to which teachers are regarded as professionals is indicated by the following:

- *Employment terms and conditions:* Do teachers have a written contract that clearly lays out their roles and responsibilities? Are they given full-time contracts or employed simply on a casual basis with few or no benefits? A program that is staffed entirely by teachers on casual terms cannot hope to attract the same level of commitment as one staffed by teachers on long-term contracts.
- *Support and reward systems:* What support is available to help teachers carry out their varying roles and what rewards are given for quality service?

Both factors are likely to influence teacher morale. Do teachers speak positively of their school or institute and are they proud to work there, or do they feel undervalued and exploited?

OPPORTUNITIES FOR TEACHER DEVELOPMENT

Teachers need to develop long-term career goals and expand their roles and responsibilities over time if they are to continue to find teaching rewarding. A quality institution provides opportunities for teachers to develop their careers. ESL/EFL is a rapidly changing field, and teachers need regular opportunities to update their professional knowledge and skills. Such opportunities may be provided for in a number of ways.

- *Conference participation:* Teachers can participate in professional conferences and seminars networking with other teachers and learning about trends, issues, and practices.
- *Workshops and in-service seminars:* Specialists from outside the school or staff from the school can offer workshops and seminars on topics of interest to the staff.
- *Reading groups:* Teachers can put together reading groups and read and discuss articles or books of interest.
- *Peer observation:* Teachers can take turns observing each other's classes as a basis for critical reflection and discussion about teaching approaches.

- *Writing about teaching:* Teachers can keep a reflective diary or journal and share it with colleagues.
- *Project work:* Teachers can be given the opportunity to develop projects such as classroom materials, videos, and other teaching resources.
- *Action research:* Teachers can conduct small-scale classroom research on their teaching.

(Richards and Lockhart 1994)

The extent to which an institution provides such opportunities for its teachers or encourages them to participate in such activities is a good indicator of how it views its teachers.

Appendix 2 represents the efforts of a group of language schools to articulate a philosophy of "Best Practice" that addresses many of these issues.

The teaching context

The last set of factors that affect the quality of teaching in a program relate to the institution context in which teachers work.

SIZE AND STAFF STRUCTURE

The size of a school and its administrative structure influences many aspects of a teacher's work. Working in an institute with a staff of five teachers is very different from working in one with a staff of one hundred. In the former case, the teachers are likely to be a closely knit team whose members know each other well. In the latter case, teachers may work more independently and may not feel that their individual contribution is crucial to the success of the program. In this case, the school will need to ask what can be done to enable teachers to get to know one another and to develop a sense of collegiality. Options available include informal professional activities such as "brown-bag lunches" as well as social activities. The administration will also need to develop mechanisms for communicating with such a large group of teachers.

EQUIPMENT

Schools vary greatly in the amount they have invested in equipment and technology. Some schools make extensive investments in such things as computers, cassette and CD players, video recorders, overhead transparency (OHT) machines, and photocopiers, recognizing that these are essential tools for teachers and can have a positive effect on teaching, staff workload, and morale. Where such investment is lacking, there may be a negative impact on teachers' workload.

SUPPORT STAFF

Adequate support staff can also facilitate teachers' work. Is there secretarial or administrative staff to help with typing, time-tabling, duplicating, and administration? If not, what percentage of teachers' time is spent on noninstructional chores and at what cost?

TEACHER WORK SPACE

One way of determining how seriously a school regards its teachers and the work they do is the work space it provides for its teachers. Is there a staff room for teachers where they can interact with colleagues, carry out lesson preparation, mark assignments, and prepare teaching materials and handouts?

TEACHER RESOURCE ROOM

Teachers need access to a good range of current ESL textbooks, resource books, materials, and magazines located in a resource room or similar facility in order to update their professional knowledge and get new ideas to feed into their teaching.

TEACHING FACILITIES

Where does teaching take place and how adequate are teaching facilities? In addition to classrooms, is there a multimedia lab or computer lab, language lab, self-access center, and student reading room? What impact do these facilities have on the quality of the program?

CLASS SIZE

What is the size of classes? Current wisdom suggests that class size should not exceed fifteen for most language classes, though in many contexts teachers have to work with much larger groups. Sometimes class size is outside the control of language providers. However, it should be made known to the client that class size affects the quality of instruction. The optimal class-size needs for each type of course should be established based on teacher, learner, and school factors, and when needed, the reasons for standards set need to be explained to clients.

The teachers

Many things can be done to create a context for good teaching, but it is teachers themselves who ultimately determine the success of a program. Good teachers can often compensate for deficiencies in the curriculum, the materials, or the resources they make use of in their teaching. In this section, we will consider the teachers themselves and how their role can be supported in a program.

Skills and qualifications

Language teaching institutions vary greatly in the type of teachers they employ. In some situations, there may be a choice between native speakers of English and nonnative speakers of English with varying levels of English-language proficiency. Within both groups there may be further choices possible based on teaching experience and professional qualifications in TESL/TEFL. Views concerning the appropriate qualifications of language teachers have changed in recent years as the field of TESOL has become more professionally demanding of itself and has sought to develop standards for language teachers (Leung and Teasdale 1998; TESOL 1986b). There is a much greater awareness today that an expert language teacher is a highly skilled professional. According to Lortie (1975), a profession is characterized by:

- a homogeneous consensual knowledge base
- restricted entry
- high social status
- self-regulation
- the legal right to govern daily work affairs

Although Lortie argues that many branches of teaching cannot be classed as a profession by these criteria, the field of language teaching has done much in recent years to conceptualize and define its knowledge base, to regulate entry to the profession, and to monitor the practices of teaching institutions. Increasingly, language schools are recruiting better trained and better qualified language teachers and operating within defined standards of quality (see Appendix 3). But what do skill and expertise in teaching English as a second or foreign language consist of? A number of attempts have been made to conceptualize the nature of teacher knowledge and skill (e.g., Roberts 1998). Core components of teacher knowledge include the following:

- *practical knowledge:* the teacher's repertoire of classroom techniques and strategies

- *content knowledge:* the teacher's understanding of the subject of TESOL, e.g., pedagogical grammar, phonology, teaching theories, second language acquisition, as well as the specialized discourse and terminology of language teaching
- *contextual knowledge:* familiarity with the school or institutional context, school norms, and knowledge of the learners, including cultural and other relevant information
- *pedagogical knowledge:* ability to restructure content knowledge for teaching purposes, and to plan, adapt, and improvise
- *personal knowledge:* the teacher's personal beliefs and principles and his or her individual approach to teaching
- *reflective knowledge:* the teacher's capacity to reflect on and assess his or her own practice

In describing teachers' skills, it is possible to compare teachers according to whether they are *untrained* or *trained* and whether they are *novice* or *experienced.* The training dimension refers to possession of a professional qualification in language teaching; the experience dimension refers to classroom experience. Initial teacher training typically sets out to give teachers what can be called "basic technical competence." This consists of an introductory understanding of the subject matter of TESOL, mastery of basic classroom teaching processes, as well as approaches to teaching the four skills. For example, the UCLES Certificate in Language Teaching to Adults (CELTA) (UCLES 1996), a widely taught initial qualification for language teachers, focuses on six areas of basic teaching skills:

- language awareness
- the learner, the teacher, and the teaching/learning context
- planning for effective teaching of adult learners of English
- classroom management and teaching skills
- resources and materials for teaching
- professional development

If an institution recruits teachers with a good command of English (or who are native speakers of English) but without a good command of basic teaching skills, then opportunities for basic training will need to be provided. Roberts (1998, 67–68) suggests that compared to experienced teachers, novice teachers tend to have the following characteristics:

- Novice teachers' perceptions of classroom events are relatively undiscriminating and simpler than those of experienced teachers.
- They are less able to select which information is salient when planning a lesson.

- They lack knowledge of what to expect of pupils, what challenges to set, and what difficulties to anticipate.
- They tend to work from the textbook rather than in terms of pupil attainment levels.
- They lack practical classroom management routines to keep pupils on task.
- Their concern with control makes it difficult for them to focus on pupil learning.
- They lack an established "pedagogic content knowledge."
- They lack the practical experience from which to construct personal meanings for theoretical or specialized terms.
- They lack a coherent system of concepts with which to think about teaching.
- They lack a specialized vocabulary with which to analyze and discuss teaching.

Opportunities to develop these skills can be provided in the following ways:

- observation of experienced teachers
- observation of training videos
- short theory courses
- practice teaching under the supervision of experienced teachers
- working with a mentor teacher

When the teacher is a nonnative speaker of English (NNS) additional issues may arise. Roberts (1998, 97) suggests that the following characteristics may be relevant to their needs:

- NNS teachers may lack confidence in their English language ability and give their own language improvement a high priority;
- NNS teachers may undergo an erosion in their English language performance through its restriction to classroom discourse;
- They may not have native-speaker (NS) intuitions about the language and may need linguistic rules as a source of security; they may avoid classroom activities which demand unpredictable language use and where rapid and intuitive assessment of accuracy and appropriacy are needed; they may need the support of a textbook more than NS teachers;
- They have the personal experience to understand their learners' difficulties;
- Where teachers and learners share a common culture, group norms may exert a powerful influence on their behavior, whereas NS teachers may be exempt from such norms;

- Language teaching behavior cannot be separated from pedagogic models inherited from the mother tongue culture (Koranic, Confucian, African, etc.) in such attributes as institutional culture, attitudes to authority and knowledge, adult-child relationships, etc.;
- The place of English in society at large has a profound influence on the purposes of English language education, the English language curriculum, and therefore the nature of the teacher's work.

As teachers develop experience in teaching, the institution needs to create an environment in which teachers can further develop their teaching skills and subject-matter knowledge, deepen their understanding of teaching and themselves as teachers, and have the opportunity for further professional development. Teachers now need to be given opportunities to do the following:

- engage in self-reflection and evaluation
- identify their areas of strength and weakness
- develop specialized knowledge and skills about many aspects of teaching
- develop curiosity and interest in many different aspects of teaching
- expand their knowledge base about research, theory, and issues in teaching
- take on new roles and responsibilities, such as supervisor, mentor teacher, teacher-researcher, or materials writer
- develop involvement in professional organizations

Activities of the kind mentioned earlier in the discussion of teacher development will be appropriate here.

Support for teachers

If teachers are expected to teach well and to develop their teaching skills and knowledge over time, they need ongoing support. This may take a number of forms:

ORIENTATION

New teachers need a careful orientation to teaching assignments in order to clarify the goals of the program, teaching approaches, resources, problems to anticipate, and solutions. Many programs use a "buddy system" for this purpose which links new teachers with experienced teachers for mentoring and support as needed during their first months in the program. New teachers need to feel that they are valued and their concerns appreciated and responded to.

ADEQUATE MATERIALS

Teachers need good materials to teach from either in the form of commercial textbooks or institutionally prepared materials. Nothing is more demotivating to teachers than having to use a textbook that no one likes or materials that are poorly prepared or presented. Teachers need to be involved in the choice of materials and guidelines may be needed on the role of materials in the program.

COURSE GUIDES

Course guides should be provided for each course offered in the program with information on the course, aims and objectives, recommended materials and methods, suggested learning activities, and procedures for assessment.

DIVISION OF RESPONSIBILITIES

Teachers have many different responsibilities apart from teaching. They may be involved in course planning, course coordination, testing, preparation of materials, and mentoring. Deciding which members of a team are best suited to different tasks and providing the support and training needed for specific roles is important. If a senior teacher's responsibilities include writing progress reports on other teachers' performance, training may be needed in how to prepare useful reports. Creating job descriptions for different responsibilities can also establish clear lines of demarcation and responsibility, which are important in strengthening staff morale.

FURTHER TRAINING

Teachers in an institution may not always have the particular knowledge and skills a program needs, so it may be important to select staff for specialized training to meet these needs. For example, a staff member may be sent to a workshop on using multimedia resources in the classroom or on alternative assessment.

TEACHING RELEASE

If teachers are expected to play a key role in some aspect of the program such as materials development or mentoring, they may need to be given release time from teaching to enable them to devote time to this. This acknowledges the value with which the institution regards such activities.

MENTORS

A system of mentoring is often helpful in a school where there are teachers of different levels of experience and training. The role of a mentor is to give teachers, particularly less experienced teachers, someone with whom they can sound off ideas, share problems, and get advice. Typically, this person is not a manager but another teacher in whom the teacher has confidence and trust.

FEEDBACK

Teachers need to be told when they are doing well and when there are problems with their performance. Good teaching sometimes goes unnoticed. In the case of negative feedback, ways need to be found for providing constructive and non-threatening feedback. Feedback can be face-to-face, in writing, or on the telephone, depending on the kind of feedback it is.

REWARDS

Teachers who perform well should receive acknowledgment for good service. This could include being sent to a conference or in-service course or having their name listed in a staff newsletter.

HELP LINES

Teachers often work for long periods in relative isolation. Whom should they turn to when they have problems with student discipline, difficulties working with another teacher, or difficulties in using course materials? Teachers should know exactly whom to turn to for help in solving different kinds of problems.

REVIEW

Time should be allocated for regular review of the program, problem solving, and critical reflection. These activities help solve practical problems and also develop a sense of collegiality among staff.

The teaching process

The focus here is on the teaching practices that occur within a program, how these can be characterized, and how quality teaching can be achieved and maintained.

Teaching model and principles

This book has emphasized the curriculum as a network of interacting systems involving teachers, learners, materials, schools, administrators, and curriculum planners, and choices at one level affect other elements in the system. Thus the choice of a particular curriculum philosophy or ideology implies a particular model of teaching. Roberts (1998, 103) compares two teaching models implicit in many language programs: the *operative* model and the *problem-solving* model:

In an "operative" model the teacher is restricted to meeting the requirements of a centralized system, such as the delivery of a textbook as planned, to a set timescale. Such a limited role, limited to that of curriculum transmission, implies training objectives based on mastery of a set of competencies determined by the centralized syllabus. In the case of the "problem solver" model, a decentralized curriculum gives teachers greater autonomy in making educational decisions. A diversified language curriculum, characterized by adaptation to learners' needs, requires teachers to be able to diagnose problems and adapt materials and design original learning activities.

The former can be viewed as a teaching model compatible with a mechanistic model of organization design and the latter to the organic model (discussed earlier in this chapter). In planning the kind of teaching that will characterize a language course, it is necessary to develop a model of teaching that is compatible with the overall assumptions and ideology of the curriculum and of the language program. Different models of teaching make different assumptions about the nature of language and of language learning, the roles of teachers, learners, and instructional materials, and different assumptions about the processes of language learning and teaching.

In language teaching programs, teaching models are often based on particular methods or approaches. For example:

- *The communicative approach:* The focus of teaching is authentic communication; extensive use is made of pair and group activities that involve negotiation of meaning and information sharing. Fluency is a priority.
- *The cooperative learning model:* Students work in cooperative learning situations and are encouraged to work together on common tasks and to coordinate their efforts to complete tasks. Rewards systems are group-oriented rather than individually oriented.
- *The process approach:* In writing classes, students take part in activities that develop their understanding of writing as a process. Different stages in the writing process (planning, generating ideas, drafting, reviewing, revising, editing) form the focus of teaching.

- *The whole-language approach:* Language is taught as a whole and not through its separate components. Students are taught to read and write naturally, with a focus on real communication, authentic texts, and reading and writing for pleasure.

Rather than drawing on a particular approach or method, the teaching model in a program may be based on a coherent set of principles that reflect how teaching and learning should be approached. This is the teaching philosophy of the program and serves as the basis for decisions about classroom methodology. The following statements describe the teaching philosophy supporting a secondary school EFL English program:

- There is a consistent focus throughout on learning English in order to develop practical and functional skills, rather than as an end in itself.
- Students are engaged in practical tasks that relate to real-world uses of English.
- Realistic and communicative uses of language are given priority.
- Maximum use is made of pair and group activities in which students complete tasks collaboratively.
- There is an appropriate balance between accuracy-focused and fluency-focused activities.
- Teachers serve as facilitators of learning rather than as presenters of information.
- Assessment procedures reflect and support a communicative and skill-based orientation to teaching and learning.
- Students develop an awareness of the learning process and their own learning styles, strengths, and weaknesses.
- Students develop the ability to monitor their own learning progress and ways of setting personal goals for language improvement.

These statements were produced through discussion with teacher trainers, curriculum planners, and teachers and served as a reference for materials developers, teacher trainers, and teachers. Articulating a teaching philosophy in this way can help clarify decisions relating to choice of classroom activities, materials, and teacher evaluation. In the case of a teaching model that is based on an existing teaching model such as communicative language teaching, the philosophy and principles of the model are accepted as givens: Teachers are expected to be familiar with them and to put the principles into practice.

Unless a teaching model is agreed upon, it is difficult to make decisions about what constitutes acceptable or unacceptable teaching practices. At the same time, teachers should have the opportunity to teach in ways that reflect their own preferred teaching styles. Teachers teach in different ways. Even though two teachers work toward identical goals they may choose different ways of getting there. Teachers bring to teaching their own personal beliefs and principles and these help to account for how they interpret their role in the classroom as well as differences in the way they teach. Teachers' principles are a product of their experience, their training, and their beliefs. Breen (no date, 45) comments:

Any innovation in classroom practice – from the adoption of a new task or textbook to the implementation of a new curriculum – has to be accommodated within a teacher's own pedagogic principles. Greater awareness of what these are on the part of the designer or curriculum planner and, indeed, the teachers themselves, will facilitate harmony between a particular innovation and the teacher's enacted interpretation of it in the classroom. The opportunity for teachers to reflect upon the evolving relationship between their own beliefs and their practices lies at the heart of curriculum change.

Examples of teachers' principles cited by Breen are:

- Selectively focus on the form of the language.
- Selectively focus on vocabulary or meaning.
- Enable the learners to use the language.
- Address learners' mental-processing capacities.
- Make the new language familiar and manageable.
- Make the learners internalize and remember the new language.
- Take account of learners' affective involvement.
- Directly address learners' needs or interests.
- Monitor learner progress and provide feedback.
- Facilitate learner responsibility or autonomy.
- Manage the lesson and the group.

In any group of teachers there are some principles that are shared as well as some that are held by individual teachers. As teachers plan lessons and teach, they draw on a teaching philosophy as well as their personal principles to help them shape and direct their teaching (Bailey 1996; Richards 1998). Opportunities for teachers to clarify their teaching principles can help focus on issues concerning choice of teaching methods, activities and materials, the purposes underlying different teaching strategies, and criteria for evaluating the effectiveness of lessons. Leung and Teasdale (1988, 20) comment: "Clearly there can be effective teaching without teachers making explicit the theories which underlie their practice. However, we would contend that, other things being equal, privileging and developing the intellectual frameworks which inform teaching offers a principled way of conceptualizing teaching as purposeful action."

At a practical level, the following decisions are therefore needed in formulating the teaching approach for a program:

- What teaching model or philosophy of teaching should the program reflect?
- What teaching principles are consistent with this model or philosophy?
- What other kinds of principles do teachers hold?
- What are the expected roles of teachers?
- What are the expected roles of learners?
- What is the role of instructional materials?
- What kinds of classroom activities and practices are recommended?

Maintaining good teaching

Quality teaching cannot simply be assumed to happen. It results from an active, ongoing effort on the part of teachers and administrators to ensure that good teaching practices are being maintained. This involves the establishment of shared commitment to quality teaching and the selection of appropriate measures to bring it about. The following are strategies that address this issue.

MONITORING

Information needs to be collected regularly on all aspects of the program to find out how teachers are teaching the course, what is working well or proving difficult, and what issues teachers need to resolve. Monitoring can take place through formal and informal mechanisms such as group meetings, written reports, classroom visits, and student evaluations. (This is also known as "formative evaluation," discussed more fully in Chapter 9.)

On the role of meetings, Davidson and Tesh (1997, 187) observe:

What kinds of meetings are necessary in a language program? Certainly, at a minimum, the entire group of teachers and administrators needs to meet at the beginning of the term, at mid-term, and at the end of the term. Other groups and subgroups need to meet more often and for more specific purposes throughout the term. Meetings need to be run so that maximum participation by all employees is assured and so that communication flows in all directions, both vertically and laterally.

OBSERVATION

Regular observation of teachers by other teachers or supervisors can provide positive feedback on teaching as well as help identify areas that might need attention. Observation may, but need not, involve evaluation. Peer observation can also be used to enable teachers to share approaches and teaching strategies. Or, while observing a colleague, a teacher can collect information the colleague is interested in obtaining. This might include information on how students complete a learning activity or the type and frequency of questions the teacher uses (Richards and Lockhart 1994). Teachers can also make use of self-observation through audio- or video-recording their lessons and reviewing the recording to see what it tells them about their teaching.

IDENTIFICATION AND RESOLUTION OF PROBLEMS

Timely identification of problems in a program is essential to ensure that small problems do not develop into bigger ones. Good communication systems can help ensure that problems are brought to the attention of teachers or supervisors for timely resolution.

SHARED PLANNING

Teachers often work in isolation and do not always have the opportunities to benefit from the collective expertise of their colleagues. One way to avoid this is to build in opportunities for collaborative planning, as when teachers work together in pairs or groups on course planning, materials development, and lesson planning. During the process of planning, potential problems can often be identified and resolved.

DOCUMENTATION AND SHARING OF GOOD PRACTICES

A great deal of excellent teaching goes on in schools, but much of it is known only to individual teachers or supervisors. Teachers should be encouraged to report on their positive teaching experiences. For example, teachers might write short case accounts of a successful course they taught and share them with other teachers or post them on the Internet. They could write short articles for an in-house newsletter or teachers' magazine or present ideas at informal lunch meetings. Classes can be video-recorded to provide input to workshops or teacher-training sessions. Meetings or "mini-conferences" can be arranged in which teachers report on classroom innovations or other activities they wish to share with colleagues. Davidson and Tesh (1997, 190) give the following examples:

1. The teacher has given a presentation at a professional conference and can adapt that presentation for an in-service.

2. The teacher has attended a professional conference or workshop and can share what was learned.
3. The teacher has read a current publication in the field and can tell colleagues about it.
4. The teacher has a practical teaching strategy to share.
5. The teacher has developed audio, video, or written materials relevant to the language program curriculum and can provide a demonstration.
6. The teacher has used the textbooks on the booklist for the coming semester and can share ideas about what works and what does not work.
7. The teacher would like to lead a discussion concerning a particular curricular or program issue.

SELF-STUDY OF THE PROGRAM

Self-study involves a study of a program's practices and values as part of the process of self-evaluation and review. It is part of the process of demonstrating a commitment to quality and to long-term goals and professional development. "By undertaking self-study, a language program declares itself interested in the assessment of its quality and the outcome of its teaching mission, and committed to long-term change and professional growth" (Carkin 1997, 56). A self-study should be undertaken every three to five years and involves teachers, administrators, and students in a process of examining all aspects of a school's operations (Kells 1988). Guidelines for conducting self-study have been published by TESOL and NAFSA (TESOL 1986a, 1986b; Marsh 1994).

Evaluating teaching

If a program seeks to provide quality teaching, it is essential that teachers' performance be regularly reviewed. This involves the development of an appraisal system. An appraisal system may have several different purposes:

- to reward teachers for good performance
- to help identify needs for further training
- to reinforce the need for continuous staff development
- to help improve teaching
- to provide a basis for contract renewal and promotion
- to demonstrate an interest in teachers' performance and development

The purpose of the appraisal will determine the type of appraisal that is carried out.

DEVELOPING THE APPRAISAL SYSTEM

An appraisal system is likely to have greater credibility if it represents both teachers' and administrators' views. It should therefore be produced collaboratively and represent all points of view. However, any appraisal system needs to recognize that there is no single correct way of teaching. Teachers have different styles of teaching, and two teachers may conduct their classes very differently yet both be excellent teachers. Therefore, criteria for the recognition of good teaching have to be developed that recognize the complexity of teaching as well as the fact that it is a uniquely individual activity. In language teaching, there are no universally accepted criteria for assessing teacher effectiveness and several different kinds of appraisal approaches are used. Criteria are generally established on an institutional basis, drawing on general principles for teacher effectiveness and factors specific to the type of program in which the teachers work. For example, candidates taking the UCLES Certificate in English Language Teaching to Adults (UCLES 1998) are assessed during teaching practice on planning and use of materials, classroom teaching skills, and awareness of teaching and learning processes (see Appendix 3). Brown (1994) contains an evaluation checklist that includes the following categories: "preparation," "presentation," "execution/methods," "personal characteristics," "teacher/student interaction" (see Appendix 4). Murdoch (1997) contains a questionnaire designed to identify the perceived qualities and competencies of good English teachers, and is organized according to three areas – ELT Competencies, General Teaching Competencies, and Knowledge and Attitudes (see Appendix 5).

THE FOCUS OF APPRAISAL

Although appraisal usually involves observation of a teacher teaching one or more classes, the focus of appraisal may include a number of other aspects of a teacher's work, such as:

- lesson plans
- teacher-made classroom materials
- course outlines and handouts
- class assignments
- participation in profession development activities

CONDUCTING THE APPRAISAL

A teaching appraisal may be carried out by a supervisor, a colleague, the teacher himself or herself, or students.

- *Appraisal by a supervisor:* Supervisors often assume the role of appraiser, though many teachers find that they prefer appraisal to be carried by someone other than a supervisor. The presence of a supervisor in the classroom may inhibit the teacher from performing to his or her best. Such assessments may also be flavored by subjective factors. In addition, if the supervisor is largely an administrator rather than a classroom teacher, he or she may not have a good understanding of the classroom situation, resulting in misperceptions about different aspects of the lesson. In order to provide some consistency to appraisals, checklists are often used (see Appendix 4).
- *Appraisal by a colleague:* Peer appraisal is generally less threatening for a teacher than appraisal by a colleague and may result in more constructive feedback. A colleague will often have a better understanding of the difficulties a teacher faces and perhaps be able to suggest useful ways of addressing them. Appendix 8 presents an example of a peer appraisal form used in a large English program. The form was developed by teachers in the program and provides an opportunity for the teacher to respond to the appraiser's comments.
- *Self-appraisal:* Teachers themselves are often in a good position to assess their own teaching and self-appraisal is perhaps the least threatening form of teacher assessment. Self-appraisal may take a variety of forms:
- *Lesson reports:* The teacher may use structured descriptions of a lesson with an evaluation of each component. (See Appendix 6 for an example of a self-evaluation form.)
- *Teaching journal:* The teacher may keep a regular journal about his or her class, and describe and reflect on different aspects of planning and teaching the course.
- *Audio/video recording:* The teacher may record a number of lessons of his or her class or arrange to have someone else record them, review the recordings, and comment on the strengths or weaknesses of the lessons.
- *Student appraisal:* Students are in a good position to assess the effectiveness of teaching, although the extent to which they are able to do so depends on the type of feedback instrument they are given. Although students are often critical, they usually have a good sense of whether a teacher prepares his or her lesson, teaches relevant content, provides lessons that are engaging, relevant, and at an appropriate level of difficulty. What students may not be able to recognize is how difficult the course (or a particular group of students) is to teach due to the personal dynamics of the class and its members). Appendix 7 contains an example of a student appraisal form.

The learning process

Learning is not the mirror image of teaching. The extent to which teaching achieves its goals will also dependent on how successfully learners have been considered in the planning and delivery process. The following factors may affect how successfully a course is received by learners.

UNDERSTANDING OF THE COURSE

It is important to ensure that the learners understand the goals of the course, the reason for the way it is organized and taught, and the approaches to learning they will be encouraged to take. It cannot be simply assumed that learners will be positively disposed toward the course, will have the appropriate skills the course demands, or will share the teacher's understanding of what the goals of the course are. Brindley (1984, 95) states:

When learners and teachers meet for the first time, they may bring with them different expectations concerning not only the learning process in general, but also concerning what will be learned in a particular course and how it will be learned. The possibility exists, therefore, for misunderstanding to arise. It is, accordingly, of vital importance that, from the beginning of the course, mechanisms for consultation are set up, in order to ensure that the parties involved in the teaching-learning process are aware of each other's expectations. If learners are to become active participants in decision making regarding their own learning, then it is essential that they know the teacher's position and that they be able to state their own. Teachers, conversely, need to canvass learners' expectations and be able to interpret their statements of need.

VIEWS OF LEARNING

Learners enter a course with their own views of teaching and learning and these may not be identical to those of their teachers. How do they see the roles of teachers and learners? What do they feel about such things as memorization, group work, the importance of grammar, and pronunciation? Alcorso and Kalantzis (1985) found that teachers rated the usefulness of communicative activities highly, whereas their learners tended to favor more traditional activities such as grammar exercises, copying written materials, memorizing, and drill work. What roles are learners expected to play during the course? Courses may assume a variety of different learner roles, such as:

- manager of his or her own learning
- independent learner

- needs analyst
- collaborator and team member
- peer tutor

How happy are learners with the roles expected of them? Will they need any special orientation or training in order to carry out these roles effectively?

LEARNING STYLES

Learners' learning styles may be an important factor in the success of teaching and may not necessarily reflect those that teachers recommend. In a study of the learning style of adult ESL students, Willing (1985, cited in Nunan 1988, 93) found four different learner types in the population he studied:

Concrete learners: These learners preferred learning by games, pictures, films and video, talking in pairs, learning through the use of cassettes, and going on excursions.

Analytical learners: These learners liked studying grammar, studying English books, studying alone, finding their own mistakes, having problems to work on, learning through reading newspapers.

Communicative learners: This group liked to learn by observing and listening to native speakers, talking to friends in English, watching TV in English, using English in shops, and so on, learning English words by hearing them and learning by conversations.

Authority-oriented learners: These students liked the teacher to explain everything, writing everything in a notebook, having their own textbook, learning to read, studying grammar, and learning English words by seeing them.

A questionnaire on preferred learning styles, classroom activities, and teaching approaches can be used to identify learners' learning style preferences. Where discrepancies are identified between views of teaching and learning on the part of teachers and learners, these may have to be addressed through learner training, discussion, and orientation to the course.

MOTIVATION

It is also important to find out what the learners' motivations are for taking the course. Why are the learners in the course and how will it affect their lives? What do they want from it? Which aspects of it are they most interested in? It may be that learners have very different priorities. For example, Brindley (1984, 119) cites the following preferences for three learners in an adult ESL class in Australia to show how individual learner choices may differ markedly. In such cases, counseling and individualized instruction may be needed.

In this course I want to:

	Ranked Priorities for 3 learners		
Understand English grammar better	2	3	3
Write English more fluently and correctly	1	7	5
Understand radio and TV better	5	6	6
Know more about Australian culture	3	2	4
Understand Australians better when they speak to me	6	1	1
Read and understand newspapers better	4	4	2
Communicate better with my workmates	10	5	9
Learn more vocabulary	8	10	9
Learn how to spell better	9	8	8
Learn how to pronounce English better	7	9	7

SUPPORT

Support mechanisms provided for learners are another component of course delivery. These include the kinds of feedback learners will get about their learning and opportunities that are provided for faster or slower learners. Self-access components might be provided to allow learners to address specific learning needs and interests.

One resource from among the many that have been considered in this and earlier chapters plays a key role in influencing the nature and quality of course organization and teaching in a language program: the instructional materials and resources that teachers use in the classroom. These are the focus of Chapter 8.

Discussion questions and activities

1. How would you characterize the organizational culture and structure of a language teaching institution you are familiar with? To what extent is the organizational culture a positive one, in your opinion?
2. Consider a teaching context that you are familiar with. What factors in the school or institution create positive support for good teaching? What factors do not? Suggest three changes that you think would improve the quality of the teaching.
3. To what extent is a concern for quality reflected in the practices of your

school or an institution you are familiar with? What quality measures are or should be in place?

4. Examine the mission statement in Appendix 1. Prepare a mission statement for your program or institution. Then reflect on the process of developing a mission statement and the role such a statement could play in creating a quality culture in the institution.

5. Use the guidelines for Best Practice in Appendix 2 to examine a language teaching institution you are familiar with. To what extent do the guidelines provide a framework for identifying good practice in the institution? Are additional criteria needed?

6. What opportunities are available for teacher development in your institution or an institution you are familiar with? Suggest three approaches to teacher development that could be implemented and what each would seek to accomplish.

7. Prepare a statement of the teaching philosophy that supports a program you teach in or that you are familiar with.

8. What provisions are made to assist inexperienced teachers in your school or language program? What incentives and rewards exist to provide continued motivation for excellent and experienced teachers?

9. Use one of the teaching evaluation forms in Appendixes 3 or 4 to evaluate a teacher's class. How useful was the form? Would you wish to revise the form on the basis of your experience?

10. Complete the questionnaire on the qualities of a good teacher in Appendix 5, then compare your ratings in groups. How useful do you think such an approach is to determining the qualities of a good teacher?

11. Do you think teachers can provide reliable self-appraisals of their own lessons? Why or why not? Examine the self-appraisal form in Appendix 6 and try it out, if possible (or ask a teacher to try it out). How adequate was it as a basis for self-appraisal?

12. Examine the student appraisal form in Appendix 7. Would you be able to use this form or a modified version of it in your own teaching?

Appendix 1 Institutional mission statement

An example of an institutional mission statement (from Department of English, City University of Hong Kong).

The goals of the department

The Department of English has developed the following mission statement to represent its commitments and goals:

The goals of the Department of English are to promote the effective learning and teaching of English and the learning and practice of professional communication skills in the City University and in the community, and to provide leadership in language and communication education in Hong Kong and the region.

To achieve this, the Department of English:

- offers degree courses in Teaching English as a Second Language and in Professional Communication
- delivers instruction in English for students in the City University to meet their communicative, academic and professional needs
- supports a technology-based learning environment for teaching professional communication skills
- seeks to provide staff with the opportunity for continued professional development
- conducts research and development activities which support the Department's goals
- provides resources and expertise in language education through seminars, conferences, workshops and consultancies
- encourages collaboration with other institutions

Appendix 2   Best practice in English language teaching*

1. Institution

PHYSICAL FACILITIES

A quality language centre is characterised by:

- clean and safe premises;
- classrooms and offices which are not overcrowded;
- adequate ventilation, heating, cooling and lighting; and
- adequate precautions in case of fire.

The physical facilities contribute to an atmosphere conducive to learning.

MANAGEMENT AND ADMINISTRATION

A quality language centre:

- is under the direction of an appropriately-trained and experienced management and administration team which is knowledgeable about the design, implementation, and evaluation of ELT programs;
- seeks to attract and retain a staff of trained, dedicated, professional ELT practitioners;
- recognises the importance of appropriate salary and benefits as well as the importance of staff development. The centre has clearly stated policies concerning these issues;
- reviews its employment conditions and procedures periodically in light of generally accepted ELT standards and local market conditions; and
- takes account of input from teachers, support staff and students in making decisions regarding personnel practices, management of resources and program evaluation.

The management strives to engender a positive teaching and learning environment.

* Document prepared by EL centers in Indonesia (IALF), Thailand (ELCA), Laos (VUC), and Cambodia (ACE), for establishing quality standards for language training centers in Southeast Asia. Reprinted with permission.

2. Staff

TEACHING STAFF

A quality language centre:

- employs teachers who have internationally recognised qualifications in language teaching;
- recognises that the number of contact hours, preparation hours and office presence of teachers directly influence teacher effectiveness;
- ensures equal opportunity regarding all aspects of employment, including the possibility of job security of employment; and
- provides support in the form of administrative systems, office space, telephones, duplicating facilities (with clear guidelines about copyright laws), and space for professional development seminars and workshops.

SUPPORT STAFF

A quality language centre recognises the vital role that non-teaching staff play in supporting training activities and contributing to the quality of the service provided to clients.

STAFF DEVELOPMENT

A quality language centre:

- actively supports and engages in continuing staff development for all employees. There is continuous, ongoing in-service training, using a range of learning modes conducted by members of staff as well as by invited trainers from outside;
- keeps to a minimum the number of under-trained teaching staff and support staff. There is a plan in place to ensure that staff development opportunities are made available as appropriate;
- supports membership in professional organisations, attendance at workshops and conferences, and participation in professional activities outside the workplace; and
- engages in and/or encourages research on various aspects of ELT by staff.

3. Program management

CURRICULUM

A quality language centre:

- designs and implements curricula that are informed by an analysis of learner needs and the assessment of the learners' levels of proficiency;

- documents curricula, and such documentation includes details of program goals and objectives, expected learner outcomes, teaching materials, methodology, assessment criteria, and evaluation procedures;
- assesses student progress on a regular basis. The instruments for assessment are selected or developed according to principles generally recognised in the field of ELT and are culturally appropriate. They relate directly to the stated goals and objectives of the training program. Students are regularly informed of their progress;
- acknowledges that factors such as class size, course length and course intensity are often beyond the control of the training provider. However, curricula are developed with these considerations in mind;
- engages in regular evaluation of its curriculum and courses in response to changing student needs, new trends in ELT and the changing global context. Teachers and students are involved in this evaluation which leads to program re-design, with the development of new approaches, new components, and/or new courses; and
- seeks periodic external evaluation through consultation with experienced, recognised professionals in appropriate fields, such as applied linguistics and ELT management. These individuals work with staff to share expertise and to provide objective appraisals of the program's effectiveness.

4. Resources

A quality language centre:

- provides instructional materials to facilitate successful language learning. These resources are up-to-date and accessible to all teachers and include print materials, video tape recorders and cassettes, audio tape recorders and cassettes, as well as a range of realia;
- recognises the contribution that computerised language instruction and self-access resources make to effective language learning and wherever possible aims to provide such resources;
- maintains a resource collection of relevant books, journals and other materials which is easily accessible to teachers and students; and
- documents procedures for the selection, evaluation, purchase and upkeep of equipment and materials and ensures that all concerned are actively involved in decision-making related to these matters.

Appendix 3 Assessment criteria for teaching practice

Assessment criteria for teaching practice in the Certificate in English Language Teaching to Adults (UCLES 1998).

Scope
By the end of the 6 hours' teaching practice successful candidates, at pass level, should show convincingly and consistently that they can:

Plan for the effective teaching of adult learners by:

- identifying appropriate learning outcomes;
- selecting and/or designing tasks and activities appropriate for the learners, for the stage of the less and overall lesson objectives;
- selecting and making appropriate use of a range of materials and resources;
- adapting materials for use with a particular group;
- presenting materials for classroom use with a professional appearance and with regard to copyright requirements;
- anticipating potential difficulties with language and tasks

Demonstrate classroom teaching skills by:

- establishing rapport and developing motivation;
- adjusting their own language to meet the level and needs of the learners;
- giving clear instructions;
- providing accurate and appropriate models of language;
- focusing on appropriate specific language and/or skills;
- conveying the meaning of new language with clear and appropriate context;
- checking students' understanding of the new language;
- clarifying forms of language;
- identifying errors and sensitively correcting students' oral language;
- identifying errors and sensitively correcting students' written language;
- monitoring and evaluating students' progress.

Demonstrate an awareness of teaching and learning processes by:

- teaching a class with sensitivity to the needs, interests, and background of the group;
- organising the classroom to suit the learners and/or the activity;
- setting up and managing pair, group, individual, and plenary work;
- adopting a teacher role appropriate to the stage of the lesson and the teaching context;

- teaching in a way which helps to develop learner self-awareness and autonomy.

Focus

The syllabus focus to include:

Language awareness
  (Syllabus Topic 1)
The learner, the teacher and the teaching/learning context
  (Syllabus Topic 2)
Planning for effective teaching of adult learners of English
  (Syllabus Topic 3)
Classroom management and teaching skills for teaching English to adults
  (Syllabus Topic 4)
Resources and materials for teaching English to adults
  (Syllabus Topic 5)
Professional development for teachers of English to adults
  (Syllabus Topic 6)

Appendix 4   Checklist for evaluating a teacher's lesson (from Brown 1994)

Teacher observation form A: Observing other teachers

Please try to keep in mind the following criteria when observing a teacher. Circle or check each item in the column that most clearly represents your evaluation: 4 excellent, 3 above average, 2 average, 1 unsatisfactory, N/A not applicable. *In addition* or *in lieu of* checking a column, you may write comments in the space provided.

I. PREPARATION

Degree to which . . .

1. The teacher was well-prepared and well-organized in class.
   Comment: N/A 4 3 2 1

2. The lesson reviewed material and looked ahead to new material.
   Comment: N/A 4 3 2 1

3. The prepared goals/objectives were apparent.
   Comment: N/A 4 3 2 1

II. PRESENTATION

Degree to which . . .

4. The class material was explained in an understandable way.
   Comment: N/A 4 3 2 1

5. The lesson was smooth, sequenced, and logical.
   Comment: N/A 4 3 2 1

6. The lesson was well-paced.
   Comment: N/A 4 3 2 1

7. Directions were clear and concise and students were
   able to carry them out.
   Comment: N/A 4 3 2 1

8. Material was presented at the student's level of
   comprehension.
   Comment: N/A 4 3 2 1

9. An appropriate percentage of the class was student
   production of the language.
   Comment: N/A 4 3 2 1

10. The teacher answered questions carefully and
    satisfactorily.
    Comment: N/A 4 3 2 1

11. The method/s was/were appropriate to the age and
    ability of students.
    Comment: N/A 4 3 2 1

12. The teacher knew when the students were having
    trouble understanding.
    Comment: N/A 4 3 2 1

13. The teacher showed an interest in, and enthusiasm for,
    the subject taught.
    Comment: N/A 4 3 2 1

III. EXECUTION/METHODS

14. There were balance and variety in activities during
    the lesson.
    Comment: N/A 4 3 2 1

15. The teacher was able to adapt to the unanticipated
    situations.
    Comment: N/A 4 3 2 1

16. The material was reinforced.
    Comment: N/A 4 3 2 1

17. The teacher moved around the class and made eye contact
    with students.
    Comment: N/A 4 3 2 1

18. The teacher knew students' names.
    Comment: N/A 4 3 2 1

19. The teacher positively reinforced the students.
    Comment: N/A 4 3 2 1

20. Student responses were effectively elicited (i.e., the order
    in which the students were called on).
    Comment: N/A 4 3 2 1

21. Examples and illustrations were used effectively.
    Comment: N/A 4 3 2 1

22. Instructional aids or resource material was used effectively.
    Comment: N/A 4 3 2 1

23. Drills were used and presented effectively.
    Comment: N/A 4 3 2 1

24. Structures were taken out of artificial drill contexts and
    applied to the real contexts of the students' culture
    and personal experiences.
    Comment: N/A 4 3 2 1

25. Error perception.
    Comment: N/A 4 3 2 1

26. Appropriate error correction.
    Comment: N/A 4 3 2 1

IV. PERSONAL CHARACTERISTICS

27. Patience in eliciting responses.
    Comment: N/A 4 3 2 1

28. Clarity, tone, and audibility of voice.
    Comment: N/A 4 3 2 1

29. Personal appearance.
    Comment: N/A 4 3 2 1

30. Initiative, resourcefulness, and creativity.
    Comment: N/A 4 3 2 1

31. Pronunciation, intonation, fluency, and appropriate
    and acceptable use of language.
    Comment: N/A 4 3 2 1

V. TEACHER/STUDENT INTERACTION

Degree to which . . .

32. Teacher encouraged and assured full student participation
    in class.
    Comment: N/A 4 3 2 1

33. The class felt free to ask questions, to disagree, or to
    express their own ideas.
    Comment: N/A 4 3 2 1

34. The teacher was able to control and direct the class.
    Comment: N/A 4 3 2 1

35. The students were attentive and involved.
    Comment: N/A 4 3 2 1

36. The students were comfortable and relaxed, even during
    intense intellectual activity.
    Comment: N/A 4 3 2 1

37. The students were treated fairly, impartially, and with
    respect.
    Comment: N/A 4 3 2 1

38. The students were encouraged to do their best.
    Comment: N/A 4 3 2 1

39. The teacher was relaxed and matter-of-fact in voice
    and manner.
    Comment: N/A 4 3 2 1

40. The teacher was aware of individual and group needs.
    Comment: N/A 4 3 2 1

41. Digressions were used positively and not over-used.
    Comment: N/A 4 3 2 1

Appendix 5   Qualities and competencies of a good English teacher

Questionnaire designed to elicit views on qualities and competencies of a good English teacher (from Murdoch 1997).

Questionnaire: What makes a good English language teacher?

Read each statement below concerning the qualities of an excellent EFL teacher. Then send the number below corresponding to the rating and most closely reflects your own reaction to each statement.

1 = totally irrelevant; 2 = of minor importance; 3 = important;
4 = very important; 5= absolutely essential. If, for any reason,
you do not choose to react to a statement, circle NS (not sure).

If you feel there are other desirable teacher qualities which are not covered by the statements in this questionnaire, please mention them in the Comments section at the end of the form. Please indicate which Part of the questionnaire your contribution relates to. Thank you.

PART A: ELT COMPETENCIES

1. The teacher presents language points in clear and
   interesting ways.   1 2 3 4 5 NS

2. The teacher employs a range of techniques to teach
   new vocabulary.   1 2 3 4 5 NS

3. The teacher tries to relate language forms, functions
   and vocabulary to contexts relevant to students' interests.   1 2 3 4 5 NS

4. The teacher employs a range of techniques for practising
   grammatical forms.   1 2 3 4 5 NS

5. The teacher sets up interactive pair/group activities
   appropriately.   1 2 3 4 5 NS

6. The teacher employs a variety of activities for developing
   speaking/listening/reading/writing skills.   1 2 3 4 5 NS

7. The teacher achieves a good balance between accuracy-
   focused, and integrative, content-focused activities.   1 2 3 4 5 NS

8. The teacher uses games and puzzles effectively and
   appropriately.   1 2 3 4 5 NS

9. The teacher gives students sufficient time to respond to
   questions.   1 2 3 4 5 NS

10. The teacher encourages students to ask questions.   1 2 3 4 5 NS

11. The teacher elicits language and background knowledge from students appropriately.   1 2 3 4 5 NS

12. The teacher does not impede student learning via over-use of the mother tongue, or attempts to learn the students' mother tongue.   1 2 3 4 5 NS

13. The teacher is a good language model for the students.   1 2 3 4 5 NS

14. Teacher talk time is appropriate for the language level of the class.   1 2 3 4 5 NS

15. The teacher uses, and gets students to use, correct classroom language.   1 2 3 4 5 NS

16. The teacher deals with errors systematically and effectively.   1 2 3 4 5 NS

17. The teacher gets students to self-correct minor mistakes.   1 2 3 4 5 NS

18. The teacher gets students to correct/comment on each other's written work.   1 2 3 4 5 NS

19. The teacher makes students aware of the strategies they can use to learn English more effectively.   1 2 3 4 5 NS

20. The teacher uses/develops appropriate quizzes and tests to evaluate students' progress and increase motivation.   1 2 3 4 5 NS

21. The teacher gives students some say in the selection of classroom activities.   1 2 3 4 5 NS

22. The teacher maintains a dialogue with students to gauge their reaction to the materials and his/her teaching methods.   1 2 3 4 5 NS

23. The teacher makes students aware of the pedagogic purposes of classroom activities.   1 2 3 4 5 NS

24. The teacher takes into account students' different style of language learning.   1 2 3 4 5 NS

PART B: GENERAL TEACHING COMPETENCIES

1. The teacher has a good classroom presence and personality.   1 2 3 4 5 NS

2. The teacher is patient, polite and enjoys helping students acquire new skills/knowledge.   1 2 3 4 5 NS

3. The teacher positions himself/herself well at different stages of the class.   1 2 3 4 5 NS

4. The teacher's style of dressing is an asset in the classroom.   1 2 3 4 5 NS

  5. The teacher communicates an enthusiasm for the subject.   1 2 3 4 5 NS

  6. The teacher establishes a good rapport with students.   1 2 3 4 5 NS

  7. The teacher has good strategies for dealing with inappro-
     priate student behaviour.   1 2 3 4 5 NS

  8. The teacher does not intimidate shy students in the class.   1 2 3 4 5 NS

  9. The teacher recognises student achievement and develops
     students' interest in learning.   1 2 3 4 5 NS

 10. The teacher attends to the learning needs of the various
     ability levels in the class.   1 2 3 4 5 NS

 11. The teacher gives appropriate feedback to students about
     their progress.   1 2 3 4 5 NS

 12. The teacher is able to adapt his/her teaching plan to
     respond to students' immediate needs and reactions to
     planned activities.   1 2 3 4 5 NS

 13. The teacher's lessons have sufficient variety and change
     of pace to sustain students' interest.   1 2 3 4 5 NS

 14. The teacher prepares classes adequately and has clear
     aims and objectives.   1 2 3 4 5 NS

 15. The teacher uses a variety of techniques to ask questions
     and elicit responses from students.   1 2 3 4 5 NS

 16. The teacher gives clear and sufficient instructions,
     examples or demonstrations before students begin activities.   1 2 3 4 5 NS

 17. The teacher organises students well.   1 2 3 4 5 NS

 18. The teacher makes good use of the whiteboard.   1 2 3 4 5 NS

 19. The teacher makes good use of visuals and other media.   1 2 3 4 5 NS

 20. The teacher constantly checks to find out if students have
     understood teaching points or benefitted from activities.   1 2 3 4 5 NS

PART C: KNOWLEDGE AND ATTITUDES

  1. The teacher believes that learning English is vitally
     important for students' future success.   1 2 3 4 5 NS

  2. The teacher sees language learning as part of a larger
     process of promoting international contacts and interest
     in other cultures.   1 2 3 4 5 NS

3. The teacher believes that education has a vital role in
   determining the future nature of societies.   1 2 3 4 5 NS

4. The teacher is knowledgeable concerning the use of
   different varieties and styles of English in different
   societies/cultures.   1 2 3 4 5 NS

5. The teacher considers students' cultural background to be
   of great importance when preparing an ELT course.   1 2 3 4 5 NS

6. The teacher believes that he/she should empower students
   to become increasingly more responsible for their own
   progress in learning.   1 2 3 4 5 NS

7. The teacher is prepared to experiment and carry out classroom research in order to further improve his/her teaching
   competence.   1 2 3 4 5 NS

8. The teacher makes constant efforts to maintain/develop
   his/her own English communication skills.   1 2 3 4 5 NS

9. The teacher is aware of the value of professional development activities and makes full use of available professional
   support.   1 2 3 4 5 NS

10. The teacher is enthusiastic about working with colleagues
    to raise the quality of ELT programmes.   1 2 3 4 5 NS

Appendix 6   Self-evaluation of a teacher's lesson (from Britten and O'Dwyer 1995)

Class: _____   Date: _____

Domain		Imp = Improvable NA = Not Applicable	OK	Imp	NA
Language content	1	Were you teaching any specific language items in this lesson? If so, did you find out how many students grasped the meanings?			
	2	Did enough students get the chance to re-use the target language items?			
	3	Did they use these items to say anything meaningful?			
	4	Do they have a written record of the new learning?			
Skills practice	5	Were you trying to practise one specific skill or a mixture? Were some tasks, or parts of tasks, appropriate for weak students and some for the better ones?			
	6	Did they find the activities motivating?			
	7	Did most of the students get some practice in the target skills?			
Correction	8	Did you concentrate on relevant points and avoid overkill in correcting mistakes? Did you at certain points concentrate only on the content of the students' contributions and ignore errors of form?			
	9	Was there a satisfactory level of accuracy in language practice? If not, did you locate and solve the problem?			
	10	Did you give scope for self-correction and peer correction?			

Domain		Imp = Improvable NA = Not Applicable	OK	Imp	NA
Stages in lesson	11	Did you try to do too much, or too little?			
	12	Could the activities have been better sequenced?			
Class management	13	Did you generally keep control of who spoke, and when (not too much calling out)?			
	14	Did you make sure some reluctant students participated (non-volunteers)?			
	15	Was there as much student talk as teacher talk?			
	16	Did they use English to each other?			
	17	Did you do anything to leave them with a feeling of achievement (evaluate, summarise, look ahead)?			
Other					

Two things you'd like to do better next time you teach this class.	What can you do about it in planning the lesson?	What can you do while teaching the lesson?

	1*	2	3	E	NA
Lesson structure					
1.1 Varieties of activities					
1.2 Sequencing of activities					
1.3 Clarity of tasks, instructions					
1.4 Visuals, realia					
1.5 Students' experience, knowledge, own lives					
(other)					
New language items					
2.1 Presentation					
2.2 Comprehension check					
2.3 Re-use					
2.4 Record in notebooks					
(other)					
Skills practice					
3.1 Participation of weak students					
3.2 Level of task difficulty					
3.3 Repetition and mechanical practice					
3.4 Meaningful practice					
3.5 Student-to-student work					
(other)					
Class management					
4.1 Hands up, nominating students to speak					
4.2 Non-volunteers					
4.3 Students' names					
4.4 Teacher talking time					
(other)					

*1 needs improvement   2 satisfactory   3 good   E excessive   NA Not applicable in this lesson

	1	2	3	E	NA
Feedback to students					
5.1 Encouraging, praising, motivating students					
5.2 Standard of correctness in accuracy work					
5.3 Self-correction by students, peer-correction					
5.4 Avoidance of correction during fluency work (communication)					
(other)					

Points to improve before next self-evaluation	1.	2.

Appendix 7   Student appraisal form

Example of a student appraisal form, Department of English, City University of Hong Kong.

Department of English: Teaching feedback questionnaire

Explanation: The purpose of this questionnaire is to provide the nominated teacher with feedback on his/her teaching performance. Your feedback is an important element in the ongoing process of assessing and improving teaching within the institution. Please think carefully before making your judgements.

Directions: *Student comments should apply ONLY to the identified teacher and to his/her performance.*

Staff Member: _____

Course Title: _____

Year: 19___ – ___   Semester: _____

NOTE: This is a general questionnaire. Please indicate the teaching context (lecture and/or tutorial) to which your comments refer.

TEACHING

In general, I have found that this teacher:

	Strongly disagree					Strongly agree
1. has communicated class materials clearly.	1	2	3	4	5	6	7
2. has been well prepared for classes.	1	2	3	4	5	6	7
3. has organized class time effectively.	1	2	3	4	5	6	7
4. ha stimulated my interest in the subject.	1	2	3	4	5	6	7
5. has been responsive to student problems.	1	2	3	4	5	6	7

6. Having considered various aspects of the performance of the nominated teacher, how would you rate the teaching overall?
(Circle one grade. Do not circle the descriptions.)

1	2	3	4	5	6	7
Very poor	Poor	Acceptable	Very good			Excellent

7. Which aspects of the teaching were most useful?

_____

_____

8. Which aspects of the teaching were least useful?

_____

_____

COURSE

9. How do you rate the content (topics, skills, etc.) of this course?

1   2   3   4   5   6   7
Not useful   Very useful

10. How do you rate the course materials (textbook, readings, etc.) in this course?

1   2   3   4   5   6   7
Not useful   Very useful

11. Which aspects of the course were most useful?

_____

_____

_____

_____

12. Which aspects of the course were least useful?

_____

_____

_____

_____

13. Any suggestions about how the course could be improved?

_____

_____

_____

_____

Appendix 8   Peer appraisal form

Example of a peer appraisal form, Department of English, City University of Hong Kong.

Department of English Peer Review Report

(use additional paper as required)

Teacher's Name: _____

Observer: _____

Module No.: _____

Date: _____   Class Time: _____

Nature and goals of the lesson: _____

1. **Aims and objectives**

   Were the aims and objectives for the lessons clearly explained?
   Did the lesson have a clear focus?

   Comments:

2. **Appropriacy of materials**

   How appropriate were the classroom activities to achieve the aims and objectives?
   How effectively was the content presented?
   Was the material/content too much or too little for the lesson?

   Comments:

3. **Organization of the lesson**

How appropriate was the organization of the lesson?

Comments:

4. **Stimulating learner interest**

To what extent was the teacher able to stimulate and sustain student interest for the duration of the class?

Comments:

5. **Opportunities for learner participation**

Did the students have enough opportunities to participate in the learning activities?
Did all the students get enough opportunities to participate in the learning activities?

Comments:

6. **Use of teaching aids**

To what extent were the teaching aids (handouts, OHP, whiteboard, etc.) used in the lesson effective?

Comments:

7. **Explaining difficult concepts**

To what extent was the teacher able to explain difficult concepts to the learners?

Comments:

8. **Effectiveness**

Was the lesson effective? Why or why not?

Comments:

9. **Any other general observations**

Self-appraisal report and response

(Space provided for teacher to respond.)

References

Alcorso, C., and M. Kalantzis. 1985. *The learning process and being a learner in the AMEP.* Report to the committee of review of the adult migrant education program. Canberra, Australia: Department of Immigration and Ethnic Affairs.

Bailey, K. M. 1996. The best-laid plans: teachers' in-class decisions to depart from their lesson plans. In K. Bailey and D. Nunan (eds.), *Voices from the language classroom.* New York: Cambridge University Press. 15–40.

Breen, M. No date. A pragmatics of language teaching: From practice to principles. Unpublished manuscript.

Brindley, G. 1984. *Needs analysis and objective setting in the adult migrant education program.* Sydney: N.S.W. Adult Migrant Education Service.

Britten, D., and J. O'Dwyer. 1995. Self-evaluation in in-service teacher training. In P. Rea-Dickins and A. Lwaitama (eds.), *Evaluation for development in English language teaching.* London: Macmillan 87–106.

Brown, H. D. 1994. *Teaching by principles.* Englewood Cliffs, NJ: Prentice Hall.

Carkin, S. 1997. Language program leadership as intercultural management. In Christison and Stoller 1997. 49–60.

Christison, M. A., and F. Stoller (eds.). 1997. *A Handbook for Language Program Administrators.* Burlingame, CA: Alta Books.

Davidson, J., and J. Tesh. 1997. Theory and practice in language program organization design. In Christison and Stoller 1997. 177–198.

Eskey, D. 1997. The IEP as a non-traditional entity. In Christison and Stoller 1997. 21–30.

Henry, A. R. 1997. The decision-maker and negotiator. In Christison and Stoller 1997. 77–90.

Kells, H. R. 1988. *Self-study processes: A guide for postsecondary and similar service-oriented institutions and programs.* 3d ed. New York: Macmillan.

Klinghammer, S. 1997. The strategic planner. In Christison and Stoller 1997. 61–76.

Leung, C., and A. Teasdale. 1998. ESL teacher competence: Professionalism in a social market. *Prospect* 13(1): 4–24.

Lortie, D. 1975. *Schoolteacher: A sociological study.* Chicago: University of Chicago Press.

Marsh, H. L. 1994. *NAFSA's self-study guide: Assessment of programs and services for international education exchange at postsecondary institutions.* Washington, DC: NAFSA: Association of International Educators.

Morris, P. 1994. *The Hong Kong school curriculum.* Hong Kong: Hong Kong University Press.

Murdoch, G. 1997. What makes a good English language teacher? In *TESOL Arabia 1997 Third International Conference,* vol 11. Conference Proceedings Selected Papers, March. 96–108.

Nunan, D. 1988. *The learner-centred curriculum.* New York: Cambridge University Press.

Roberts, J. 1998. *Language teacher education.* London: Arnold.

Richards, J. C. 1998. *Beyond training.* New York: Cambridge University Press.

Richards, J. C., and C. Lockhart. 1994. *Reflective teaching in second language classrooms.* New York: Cambridge University Press.

Stoller, F. 1997. The catalyst for change and innovation. In Christison and Stoller 1997. 33–48.

TESOL. 1986a. *TESOL's manual for self study.* Washington, DC: TESOL.

TESOL. 1986b. *The TESOL core standards for language and professional preparation programs.* Washington, DC: TESOL.

University of Cambridge Local Examinations Syndicate (UCLES). 1996. *Cambridge integrated language teaching schemes: Certificate in English language teaching to adults.* Cambridge: Cambridge University Press.

University of Cambridge Local Examinations Syndicate (UCLES). 1998. *Syllabus and assessment guidelines for course tutors and assessors.* Cambridge: Cambridge University Press.

8 The role and design of instructional materials

Teaching materials are a key component in most language programs. Whether the teacher uses a textbook, institutionally prepared materials, or his or her own materials, instructional materials generally serve as the basis for much of the language input learners receive and the language practice that occurs in the classroom. In the case of inexperienced teachers, materials may also serve as a form of teacher training – they provide ideas on how to plan and teach lessons as well as formats that teachers can use. Much of the language teaching that occurs throughout the world today could not take place without the extensive use of commercial materials. These may take the form of (a) printed materials such as books, workbooks, worksheets, or readers; (b) nonprint materials such as cassette or audio materials, videos, or computer-based materials; (c) materials that comprise both print and nonprint sources such as self-access materials and materials on the Internet. In addition, materials not designed for instructional use such as magazines, newspapers, and TV materials may also play a role in the curriculum.

Cunningsworth (1995, 7) summarizes the role of materials (particularly course books) in language teaching as:

- a resource for presentation materials (spoken and written)
- a source of activities for learner practice and communicative interaction
- a reference source for learners on grammar, vocabulary, pronunciation, and so on
- a source of stimulation and ideas for classroom activities
- a syllabus (where they reflect learning objectives that have already been determined)
- a support for less experienced teachers who have yet to gain in confidence

Dudley-Evans and St. John (1998, 170–171) suggest that for teachers of ESP courses, materials serve the following functions:

- as a source of language
- as a learning support

- for motivation and stimulation
- for reference

ESP materials may therefore seek to provide exposure to the specialized genres and registers of ESP, to support learning through stimulating cognitive processes and providing a structure and progression for learners to follow, to motivate learners through providing achievable challenges and interesting content, and to provide a resource for self-study outside of the classroom.

Some teachers use instructional materials as their primary teaching resource. The materials provide the basis for the content of lessons, the balance of skills taught, and the kinds of language practice students take part in. In other situations, materials serve primarily to supplement the teacher's instruction. For learners, materials may provide the major source of contact they have with the language apart from the teacher. Hence the role and uses of materials in a language program are a significant aspect of language curriculum development. In this chapter, we will examine the role, design, and use of materials in language teaching, with particular focus on print materials and textbooks.

Authentic versus created materials

When plans regarding the role of materials in a language program are made, an initial decision concerns the use of authentic materials versus created materials. *Authentic materials* refers to the use in teaching of texts, photographs, video selections, and other teaching resources that were not specially prepared for pedagogical purposes. *Created materials* refers to textbooks and other specially developed instructional resources. Some have argued that authentic materials are preferred over created materials, because they contain authentic language and reflect real-world uses of language compared with the contrived content of much created material. Allwright (1981, 173) thus describes a language course for foreign students at a British university in which one of the guiding principles was "Use no materials, published or unpublished, actually conceived or designed as materials for language teaching." Such an imperative seems to reflect a very low opinion of the abilities of materials writers to create pedagogically useful language learning resources! Advantages claimed for authentic materials are (Phillips and Shettlesworth 1978; Clarke 1989; Peacock 1997):

They have a positive effect on learner motivation because they are intrinsically more interesting and motivating than created materials. There is a huge supply of interesting sources for language learning in the media and on the Web and these relate closely to the interests of many language learners.

They provide authentic cultural information about the target culture. Materials can be selected to illustrate many aspects of the target culture, including culturally based practices and beliefs and both linguistic and non-linguistic behavior.

They provide exposure to real language rather than the artificial texts found in created materials that have been specially written to illustrate particular grammatical rules or discourse types.

They relate more closely to learners' needs and hence provide a link between the classroom and students' needs in the real world.

They support a more creative approach to teaching. In using authentic materials as a source for teaching activities, teachers can develop their full potential as teachers, developing activities and tasks that better match their teaching styles and the learning styles of their students.

However, critics of the use of authentic materials point out:

Created materials can also be motivating for learners. Published materials are often designed to look like teenage magazines and other kinds of real-world materials and may be just as interesting and motivating for learners.

Authentic materials often contain difficult language and unneeded vocabulary items, which can be an unnecessary distraction for teachers and learners. Since they have not been simplified or written to any lexical or linguistic guidelines, they often contain language that may be beyond the learners' abilities.

Created materials may be superior to authentic materials because they are generally built around a graded syllabus and hence provide a systematic coverage of teaching items.

Using authentic materials is a burden for teachers. In order to develop learning resources around authentic materials, teachers have to be prepared to spend a considerable amount of time locating suitable sources for materials and developing activities and exercises to accompany the materials.

In many language programs, teachers thus use a mixture of created and authentic materials because both have their advantages as well as limitations. Furthermore, the distinction between authentic and created materials is becoming increasingly blurred, because many published materials incorporate authentic texts and other real-world sources. Clarke (1989, 79) comments:

Such books [begin to] take on the aura, if not the actuality, of authenticity, containing considerable amounts of photographically reproduced 'realia', in the form of newspaper articles, maps, diagrams, memo pads, menus, application forms, advertisements, instructional leaflets and all the rest. Some books, indeed, almost entirely consist of authentic material, including illustrations, extracted from newspapers, or magazines.

Textbooks

Commercial textbooks together with ancillaries such as workbooks, cassettes, and teachers' guides are perhaps the commonest form of teaching materials in language teaching. Haines (1996, 27) characterizes differences between past and current trends in English language textbooks.

Then	*Now*
author and academic centered	market led
uncertain global market	specific fragmented markets
European focus	Pacific Rim/Latin American focus
sell what is published	international or local culture
culture and methodology of origin	indigenous learning situations
English for its own sake	English for specific purposes
UK/US publisher dominance	rise in local publishing
native speaker expertise	nonnative speaker competence
culturally insensitive	culturally sensitive
low risk/competition	high risk/competition
little design	design rich
artificial texts and tasks	authenticity
single-volume titles	multicomponent/multimedia

Textbooks are used in different ways in language programs. For example, a reading textbook might be the basis for a course on reading skills, providing both a set of reading texts and exercises for skills practice. A writing textbook might provide model compositions and a list of topics for students to write about. A grammar textbook might serve as a reference book and provide examples as well as exercises to develop grammatical knowledge. A speaking text might provide passages for students to read and discuss. A listening text together with audiocassettes or CDs might serve as the primary listening input in a listening course.

The use of commercial textbooks in teaching has both advantages and disadvantages, depending on how they are used and the contexts for their use. Among the principal advantages are:

They provide structure and a syllabus for a program. Without textbooks a program may have no central core and learners may not receive a syllabus that has been systematically planned and developed.

They help standardize instruction. The use of a textbook in a program can ensure that the students in different classes receive similar content and therefore can be tested in the same way.

They maintain quality. If a well-developed textbook is used, students are exposed to materials that have been tried and tested, that are based on sound learning principles, and that are paced appropriately.

They provide a variety of learning resources. Textbooks are often accompanied by workbooks, CDs and cassettes, videos, CD-ROMs, and comprehensive teaching guides, providing a rich and varied resource for teachers and learners.

They are efficient. They save teachers' time, enabling teachers to devote time to teaching rather than materials production.

They can provide effective language models and input. Textbooks can provide support for teachers whose first language is not English and who may not be able to generate accurate language input on their own.

They can train teachers. If teachers have limited teaching experience, a textbook together with the teacher's manual can serve as a medium of initial teacher training.

They are visually appealing. Commercial textbooks usually have high standards of design and production and hence are appealing to learners and teachers.

As with all examples of created materials, however, there are also potential negative effects of commercial textbooks. For example:

They may contain inauthentic language. Textbooks sometimes present inauthentic language because texts, dialogues, and other aspects of content tend to be specially written to incorporate teaching points and are often not representative of real language use.

They may distort content. Textbooks often present an idealized view of the world or fail to represent real issues. In order to make textbooks acceptable in many different contexts, controversial topics are avoided and instead an idealized white middle-class view of the world is portrayed as the norm.

They may not reflect students' needs. Because textbooks are often written for global markets, they may not reflect the interests and needs of students and hence may require adaptation.

They can deskill teachers. If teachers use textbooks as the primary source of their teaching, leaving the textbook and teacher's manual to make the major instructional decisions for them, the teacher's role can become reduced to that of a technician whose primary function is to present materials prepared by others.

They are expensive. Commercial textbooks represent a financial burden for students in many parts of the world.

In making decisions about the role of commercial textbooks in a program, the impact of textbooks on the program, on teachers, and on learners has to be carefully assessed.

Evaluating textbooks

With such an array of commercial textbooks and other kinds of instructional materials to choose from, teachers and others responsible for choosing materials need to be able to make informed judgments about textbooks and teaching materials. Evaluation, however, can only be done by considering something in relation to its purpose. A book may be ideal in one situation because it matches the needs of that situation perfectly. It has just the right amount of material for the program, it is easy to teach, it can be used with little preparation by inexperienced teachers, and it has an equal coverage of grammar and the four skills. The same book in a different situation, however, may turn out to be quite unsuitable. It contains too little material, it is not sufficiently challenging for teacher and students, and has elements in it (such as a grammar syllabus) that are not needed in the program. Before one can evaluate a textbook, therefore, information is needed on the following issues:

The role of the textbook in the program
- Is there a well-developed curriculum that describes the objectives syllabus and content of the program or will this be determined by the textbook?
- Will the book or textbook series provide the core of the program, or is it one of several different books that will be used?
- Will it be used with small classes or large ones?
- Will learners be expected to buy a workbook as well or should the textbook provide all the practice students need?

The teachers in the program
- How experienced are the teachers in the program and what is their level of training?
- Are they native speakers of English? If not, how well do they speak English?
- Do teachers tend to follow the textbook closely or do they use the book simply as a resource?

- Do teachers play a part in selecting the books they teach from?
- Are teachers free to adapt and supplement the book?

The learners in the program
- Is each student required to buy a book?
- What do learners typically expect in a textbook?
- Will they use the book in class and at home?
- How will they use the book in class? Is it the primary source of classroom activities?
- How much are they prepared to pay for a book?

It is also necessary to realize that no commercial textbook will ever be a perfect fit for a language program. Two factors are involved in the development of commercial textbooks: those representing the interests of the author, and those representing the interests of the publisher (Byrd 1995; Werner, et al. 1995). The author is generally concerned to produce a text that teachers will find innovative, creative, relevant to their learners' needs, and that they will enjoy teaching from. The author is generally hopeful that the book will be successful and make a financial profit because a large investment of the author's personal time and effort is involved. The publisher is primarily motivated by financial success. However, in order to achieve a profit publishers generally recognize that a book must have qualities of excellence that will distinguish it from its competitors. Ariew describes the compromises authors and publishers often have to make in order to achieve their sometimes conflicting goals:

A truly innovative approach may be unfamiliar with teachers and so meet with their resistance: it may be threatening to the people responsible for text adoptions, and it may create public controversy. A publisher's success is based on the ability to satisfy the majority of the public; thus, the preference to aim for the mainstream, to sterilize situations and vocabulary and arouse as little controversy as possible. These products of compromise may be as boring as the innovative materials are threatening. Falling too close to either end of the spectrum can have a catastrophic impact on a text's marketability. (Ariew 1982, 12)

In an attempt to make an author's manuscript usable in as large a market as possible, the publisher often has to change it substantially. Some of these changes are necessitated by the fact that teachers with very different levels of experience, training, and teaching skill might be using the book. Exercises should have explicit goals, procedures for using activities should be obvious and uncomplicated, and teachers should not have to spend much time working out how to use the material. In addition, content that would not be welcome in particular markets may have to be removed. As a consequence, much of the "flavor" and creativity of the author's original manuscript may disappear.

At the same time, the publisher will try to satisfy teachers' expectations as to what a textbook at a certain level should contain. For example, if an introductory ESL textbook does not include the present continuous in the first level of the book, teachers may feel that it is defective and not wish to use it. Ariew describes the process of making the textbook usable in the widest possible market as "homogenization."

Many publishers systematically delete all (or all but traditional consideration of) topics believed to be controversial or taboo. This tendency has several significant consequences. Besides making texts look alike, these biases affect the treatment of target cultures and may result in inaccurate descriptions or characterizations. The text becomes an ethnocentric clone of the most conservative expression of our own culture. (Ariew 1982, 12–13)

Criteria for textbook evaluation

Cunningsworth (1995) proposes four criteria for evaluating textbooks, particularly course books:

1. They should correspond to learners' needs. They should match the aims and objectives of the language learning program.
2. They should reflect the uses (present or future) that learners will make of the language. Textbooks should be chosen that will help equip students to use language effectively for their own purposes.
3. They should take account of students' needs as learners and should facilitate their learning processes, without dogmatically imposing a rigid "method."
4. They should have a clear role as a support for learning. Like teachers, they mediate between the target language and the learner.

Cunningsworth (1995) presents a checklist for textbook evaluation and selection (see Appendix 2) organized under the following categories:

- aims and approaches
- design and organization
- language content
- skills
- topic
- methodology

- teachers' books
- practical considerations

Dudley-Evans and St. John (1998, 173) suggest that operating with so many categories is often not very practical and it is easier to use two or three key criteria in the first instance and then apply others if or when needed. They propose the following questions to ask when selecting ESP materials:

1. Will the materials stimulate and motivate?
2. To what extent does the material match the stated learning objectives and your learning objectives? (It is rare for a single set of published material to match the exact learning needs of any one ESP learner group, and activities do not always meet the stated objectives.)
3. To what extent will the materials support the learning process?

The type of evaluation a textbook receives will also reflect the concerns of the evaluator. One teacher may look at a book in terms of its usability. The teacher is primarily interested in whether the book works easily in her class, can be used flexibly, and could easily be adapted. Another teacher may look at a book much more critically in terms of its theoretical orientation and approach. If it is a book that teaches conversation skills, what theory of conversation is it based on? What kind of syllabus is it based on and what is the validity of the activities it makes use of? Two teachers evaluating a writing text may likewise look at it from very different perspectives. One may subscribe to a process-oriented view of writing and look for activities that practice such processes as generating ideas, drafting, reviewing, revising, and editing. Another may be more concerned to see that adequate treatment is given to different conventions for organizing different kinds of texts, such as narrative writing, expository writing, and descriptive writing. In any language program, therefore, it is unlikely that a published checklist can be used without adaptation as a basis for evaluating and choosing textbooks. Based on the factors in each situation, questions specific to that situation need to be generated around the main issues involved in textbook evaluation and selection:

- program factors – questions relating to concerns of the program
- teacher factors – questions relating to teacher concerns
- learner factors – questions relating to learner concerns
- content factors – questions relating to the content and organization of the material in the book
- pedagogical factors – questions relating to the principles underlying the materials and the pedagogical design of the materials, including choice of activities and exercise types

Adapting textbooks

Most teachers are not creators of teaching materials but providers of good materials. Dudley-Evans and St. John (1998, 173) suggest that a good provider of materials will be able to:

1. select appropriately from what is available
2. be creative with what is available
3. modify activities to suit learners' needs
4. supplement by providing extra activities (and extra input)

Commercial textbooks can seldom be used without some form of adaptation to make them more suitable for the particular context in which they will be used. This adaptation may take a variety of forms.

Modifying content. Content may need to be changed because it does not suit the target learners, perhaps because of factors related to the learners' age, gender, social class, occupation, religion or cultural background.

Adding or deleting content. The book may contain too much or too little for the program. Whole units may have to be dropped, or perhaps sections of units throughout the book omitted. For example, a course may focus primarily on listening and speaking skills and hence writing activities in the book will be omitted.

Reorganizing content. A teacher may decide to reorganize the syllabus of the book, and arrange the units in what she considers a more suitable order. Or within a unit the teacher may decide not to follow the sequence of activities in the unit but to reorder them for a particular reason.

Addressing omissions. The text may omit items that the teacher feels are important. For example a teacher may add vocabulary activities or grammar activities to a unit.

Modifying tasks. Exercises and activities may need to be changed to give them an additional focus. For example, a listening activity may focus only on listening for information, so it is adapted so that students listen a second or third time for a different purpose. Or an activity may be extended to provide opportunities for more personalized practice.

Extending tasks. Exercises may contain insufficient practice and additional practice tasks may need to be added.

The ability to be able to adapt commercial textbooks in these ways is an essential skill for teachers to develop. Through the process of adaptation the teacher personalizes the text, making it a better teaching resource, and individualizes it for a particular group of learners. Normally this process takes place gradually as the teacher becomes more familiar with the book, because the dimensions of the text that need adaptation may not be apparent until the book is tried out in the classroom. When a number of teachers in a program are teaching from the same textbook, it is useful to build in opportunities for teachers to share information about the forms of adaptation they are making.

Preparing materials for a program

In cases where institutionally developed materials are being considered for a language program, both the advantages and the disadvantages of setting up a materials development project need to be carefully considered at the outset.

Advantages

Advantages of building a materials development component into a program include:

Relevance: Materials can be produced that are directly relevant to students' and institutional needs and that reflect local content, issues, and concerns.

Develop expertise: Developing materials can help develop expertise among staff, giving them a greater understanding of the characteristics of effective materials.

Reputation: Institutionally developed materials may enhance the reputation of the institution by demonstrating its commitment to providing materials developed specifically for its students.

Flexibility: Materials produced within the institution can be revised or adapted as needed, giving them greater flexibility than a commercial course book.

Disadvantages

Disadvantages also need to be considered before embarking on materials development.

Cost: Quality materials take time to produce and adequate staff time as well as resources need to be allocated to such a project.

Quality: Teacher-made materials will not normally have the same standard of design and production as commercial materials and hence may not present the same image as commercial materials.

Training: To prepare teachers for materials writing projects, adequate training should be provided. Materials writing is a specialized skill and potential materials writers need the opportunity to develop the necessary skills. Workshops can be developed for this purpose, as well as the creation of writing teams that contain a balance of relevant expertise.

The nature of materials development

It is also important to understand the nature of materials development and the processes that are typically involved if quality materials are to be created. Dudley-Evans and St. John (1998, 173) observe that "only a small proportion of good teachers are also good designers of course materials." Many teachers underestimate how commercial teaching materials are developed and the developmental processes that are normally involved. Preparing effective teaching materials is similar to the processes involved in planning and teaching a lesson. The goal is to create materials that can serve as resources for effective learning. The writer starts with a learning goal in mind and then seeks to create a set of activities that enable that goal to be reached. Shulman's (1987, 15) description of the central acts of teaching also apply to the processes of materials development. He sees it as a process of transformation:

The key to understanding the knowledge base of teaching lies at the intersection of content and pedagogy, in the capacity of a teacher to transform the content knowledge he or she possesses into forms that are pedagogically powerful and yet adaptive to the variations in ability and background presented by students.

Shulman goes on to describe the transformation phase of this process as consisting of:

- *preparation:* critical interpretation and analysis of texts, structuring and segmentation, development of a curricular repertoire, and clarification of purposes
- *representation:* use of a representational repertoire that includes analogies, metaphors, examples, demonstrations, explanations, and so forth
- *selection:* choice from among an instructional repertoire that includes modes of teaching, organizing, managing, and arranging
- *adapting and tailoring to student characteristics:* consideration of conceptions, preconceptions, misconceptions, and difficulties; language, culture, and motivations; and social class, gender, age, ability, aptitude, interests, self-concepts, attention

In both materials development and classroom teaching the goal is to develop a sequence of activities that leads teachers and learners through a learning route that is at an appropriate level of difficulty, is engaging, that provides both motivating and useful practice. Good materials do many of the things that a teacher would normally do as part of his or her teaching. They should:

- arouse the learners' interest
- remind them of earlier learning
- tell them what they will be learning next
- explain new learning content to them
- relate these ideas to learners' previous learning
- get learners to think about new content
- help them get feedback on their learning
- encourage them to practice
- make sure they know what they are supposed to be doing
- enable them to check their progress
- help them to do better

(Rowntree 1997, 92)

Tomlinson (1998) suggests that good language teaching materials have the following characteristics:

- Materials should achieve impact.
- Materials should help learners feel at ease.
- Materials should help learners to develop confidence.
- What is being taught should be perceived by learners as relevant and useful.
- Materials should require and facilitate learner self-investment.
- Learners must be ready to acquire the points being taught.
- Materials should expose the learners to language in authentic use.
- The learners' attention should be drawn to linguistic features of the input.
- Materials should provide the learners with opportunities to use the target language to achieve communicative purposes.
- Materials should take into account that the positive effects of instruction are usually delayed.
- Materials should take into account that learners have different learning styles.
- Materials should take into account that learners differ in affective attitudes.
- Materials should permit a silent period at the beginning of instruction.
- Materials should maximize learning potential by encouraging intellectual, aesthetic, and emotional involvement that stimulates both right and left brain activities.
- Materials should not rely too much on controlled practice.
- Materials should provide opportunities for outcome feedback.

This may seem a somewhat cumbersome list to apply in actual practice. Any developer of teaching materials will have to develop his or her own set of working principles that can be referred to in planning and assessing materials as they are written. For example, I used the following checklist in developing a set of low-level speaking materials. The list identifies the qualities each unit in the materials should reflect:

• Gives learners something they can take away from the lesson
• Teaches something learners feel they can use
• Gives learners a sense of achievement
• Practices learning items in an interesting and novel way
• Provides a pleasurable learning experience
• Provides opportunities for success
• Provides opportunities for individual practice
• Provides opportunities for personalization
• Provides opportunities for self-assessment of learning

Each draft of the materials was then examined to assess the extent to which these principles were reflected. Achieving these goals through the design of instructional materials depends on the art, experience, skills, and craft of the materials developer.

Decisions in materials design

In Chapters 5 and 6, the following processes of program design and materials design were discussed:

• developing aims
• developing objectives
• developing a syllabus
• organizing the course into units
• developing a structure for units
• sequencing units

When the process of writing begins, further decisions need to be made. These concern:

• choosing input and sources
• selecting exercise types

CHOOSING INPUT AND SOURCES

No matter what type of materials are being prepared decisions concerning input are involved. Input refers to anything that initiates the learning process and that students respond to in some way in using the materials. The following are examples of input questions in the design of different kinds of materials:

Grammar materials: Will the new grammar items be presented through the medium of texts, conversational extracts, or a corpus of utterances? How will these be selected?

Listening materials: Will the source of listenings be authentic recordings taken from real-world sources, scripted materials on different topics, or a mixture of both?

Reading materials: What kinds of texts will students read (such as magazine articles, newspaper articles, extracts from books), and how will these be chosen?

Writing materials: Will students be shown examples of different types of compositions? Will these be examples of real texts or will they be specially written? Will examples of student writing also be included? If so, how will these be chosen? For example, Raimes (1988) sees the primary texts in a writing course as:

the students' texts: that is, the writing students do
the teacher's texts: that is, the comments teachers write on their papers
other authentic texts: supplementary readings for writing stimulus and close
   analysis

Speaking materials: What will the source of speaking activities be? Will dialogues, recordings, texts, topics, pictures, situations, and so on be used, and how will these be selected?

Often writers start with resources taken from magazines, books, the Internet, television, or radio. (A large amount of material is available on the World Wide Web, including articles, photographs, audio and video materials, and much of it can be used free.) It is important, however, to realize that many of the sources for teaching materials that exist in the real world have been created by someone and that copyright permission may be required in order to use it as a source of teaching materials in an institution or textbook, even if they are adapted or modified in some way. It is normally not possible, for example, to use the following without permission from the copyright holder:

- segments taken from commercially broadcast materials (radio, video, musical recordings)
- magazine articles, newspaper articles, chapters from books

However, if materials are being used for legitimate educational purposes and not being sold to make a profit it is often possible to obtain permission without payment of a fee. A letter is written to the copyright holder (such as a publisher) outlining the wish to use the materials and describing how they will be used and in what quantities. (Rowntree, 1997)

SELECTING EXERCISE TYPES

One of the most difficult decisions in writing is deciding on the types of exercises that will be used. The issue is how to create exercises that engage learners in the use of skills and processes related to specific language teaching objectives. A review of the exercise types used in current commercial textbooks is a good starting point. In Richards (1990), for example, exercise types related to different types of listening skills are presented as follows:

Exercises that develop "top-down" listening
- Listen to part of a conversation and infer the topic of a conversation.
- Look at pictures and then listen to conversations about the pictures and match them with the pictures.
- Listen to conversations and identify the setting.
- Read a list of key points to be covered in a talk and then number them in sequence while listening to the talk.
- Read information about a topic, then listen to a talk on the topic and check whether the information was mentioned or not.
- Read one side of a telephone conversation and guess the speaker's responses: then listen to the conversation.
- Look at pictures of people speaking and guess what they might be saying or doing; then listen to their actual conversations.
- Complete a story, then listen to how the story really ended.
- Guess what news headlines might refer to, then listen to news broadcasts about the events referred to.

Exercises that involve listening for interactional purposes
- Distinguish between conversations that have an interactional and a transactional purpose.
- Listen to conversations and select suitable polite comments and other phatic responses.
- Listen to utterances containing complements or praise and choose suitable responses.
- Listen to conversations containing small talk and indicate when the speaker is preparing to introduce a real topic.
- Listen to conversations and rate them according to the degree of familiarity of the speakers.

- Listen to conversations and check whether the speaker is issuing a real invitation or using a pseudoinvitation to close a conversation.

Grellet (1981) contains an extensive taxonomy of exercises for teaching reading skills. Under the category "understanding meaning," she illustrates exercises of the following types:

Involving a nonlinguistic response to the text
- ordering a sequence of pictures
- comparing texts and pictures
- matching
- using illustrations
- completing a document
- mapping it out
- using the information in a text
- jigsaw reading

Involving a linguistic response to the text
- reorganizing the information: reordering events
- reorganizing the information: using grids
- comparing several texts
- completing a document
- question types
- study skills: summarizing
- study skills: note taking

Crandall (1995) gives further useful suggestions for the design of exercises in reading materials (see Appendix 1). Candlin (1981) contains an exercise typology for the design of communicative exercises. Reviewing published materials for information of this kind is a good way to get a sense of the range of possible exercise types that can be used in materials.

Managing a materials writing project

Materials writing projects are of different scope and dimensions. Some may be the responsibility of an individual teacher; others may be assigned to a team of writers. The management of a team-based writing project involves addressing the following issues:

Selecting the project team: How many people will take part in the project and what will their roles and responsibilities be? In a small in-house project there may be two or three writers sharing responsibilities for all aspects of the project. In a large-scale project, however, the following people might be involved:

- *project director:* responsible for overall management of the project, for setting goals and ensuring that targets are met, and for liaising with all parties involved
- *writers:* those responsible for writing all components of the course
- *media specialist:* a person who can help with such aspects as use of audiovisual materials and computer software
- *editor:* a person who reviews everything the writers have produced and prepares the final version of the materials for publication or duplication
- *illustrator:* someone responsible for preparing and selecting art and illustrations
- *designer:* the person who is responsible for the layout, type style, graphics, and the overall format of the materials

Planning the number of stages involved: A materials project always goes through several different stages of development. Typical stages might include:

- first draft
- comments on first draft
- second draft
- further comments
- tryout of the materials
- final revisions of materials

These processes are not necessarily linear. Carey and Briggs (1977, 286) comment: "Many activities occur simultaneously, and one often works one part of a product through a phase of design and then cycles back and begins the same phase again with another part of the product."

Identifying reviewers: A crucial source of input to the developmental process is critical feedback on materials as they are written. A key person is someone who can cast a critical eye over the materials as they are drafted and provide constructive feedback on them. People involved in a materials writing project should be open to feedback and suggestions and be prepared to undertake extensive revisions of materials if necessary. Things that seem perfectly obvious to the writer may not strike another person in the same way. In commercial projects, this role is undertaken by editors and reviewers. In institutional projects, this responsibility needs to be assigned to a member of the project team. It is also useful to involve the participation of classroom teachers in the process to review materials as they are written. Focus groups can also be set up consisting of five or six experienced teachers who meet to discuss materials in progress and give suggestions for improving them.

Planning the writing schedule: A writing schedule can now be developed with dates assigned for the different stages in the process. Even though aspects of the writing process are often cyclical, as noted, for practical planning purposes the different stages in the writing process need to be represented within a tentative time frame.

Piloting the materials: Piloting involves trying out materials with a representative group of learners and teachers before they are made available for wider use in order to identify problems or faults in them that can be identified before they are used more widely. Piloting seeks to find answers to question such as these:

- Are the materials comprehensible and the instructions clear?
- Do they contain any editorial or content errors?
- Is the pacing of the materials appropriate?
- Do the materials do what they are supposed to do?
- Do they address learners' needs?
- Is there sufficient quantity of practice material?
- Are the materials sufficiently interesting and engaging?

Davison (1998, 184) comments:

In general, piloting provides a feel for whether the material actually "works" or not; whether the aims of the material are fulfilled; whether it is appropriate in level, content, and approach; whether it relates well to teachers' expectations and stages of development, and whether it successfully promotes learning.

The intention is to have a group of teachers and students work through the materials in conditions as close as possible to those under which the final version of the materials will be used. However, it is often not possible to pilot materials in a near-final form, because art and design may await finalization of the manuscript. A practical solution is to have sections of the materials piloted by different teachers rather than have a few teachers try out all of the materials. This can speed up the piloting process and enable more teachers to participate. Following the piloting, both students and teachers complete a review sheet or questionnaire and may also be interviewed to find out what they think about the materials. Any problems identified can be addressed at this stage. In some cases, this may involve a substantial rewriting of the materials.

Design and production: Design issues refer to the layout of text and art on each page. An effective design is a major factor in the reception and usability of materials. Will art and illustrations be added to the manuscript and who will be responsible for these? Production issues relate to the printing of the materials. Will the materials be printed from the writers' files, reset, photocopied, laser printed, or sent to a commercial printer?

An example of how some of these issues were addressed in a materials development project is given in Appendix 3.

Monitoring the use of materials

No matter what form of materials teachers make use of, whether they teach from textbooks, institutional materials, or teacher-prepared materials, the materials represent *plans* for teaching. They do not represent the process of teaching itself. As teachers use materials they adapt and transform them to suit the needs of particular groups of learners and their own teaching styles. These processes of transformation are at the heart of teaching and enable good teachers to create effective lessons out of the resources they make use of. It is useful, therefore, to collect information on how teachers use course books and other teaching materials in their teaching. The information collected can serve the following purposes:

- to document effective ways of using materials
- to provide feedback on how materials work
- to keep a record of additions, deletions, and supplementary materials teachers may have used with the materials
- to assist other teachers in using the materials

Monitoring may take the following forms:

- *Observation:* classroom visits to see how teachers use materials and to find out how materials influence the quality of teaching and interaction that occurs in a lesson
- *Feedback sessions:* group meetings in which teachers discuss their experience with materials
- *Written reports:* the use of reflection sheets or other forms of written feedback in which teachers make brief notes about what worked well and what did not work well, or give suggestions on using the materials
- *Reviews:* written reviews by a teacher or group of teachers on their experiences with a set of materials and what they liked or disliked about them
- *Students' reviews:* comments from students on their experience with the materials

Having considered the different processes and elements that constitute the development and implementation of a language curriculum and the dynamics of the curriculum in action, we can now consider the curriculum as a whole and how it can be monitored, reviewed, and evaluated. This is the focus of the final chapter.

Discussion questions and activities

1. What roles do instructional materials play in your language program or one you are familiar with? What mechanisms are in place for the following procedures?

   selecting materials
   adapting materials
   monitoring teachers' use of materials
   developing original materials

2. Have you any experience with using authentic materials in teaching? What problems do they pose for teachers? Do you think they are preferable to created materials?

3. What do you think is an appropriate role for commercial materials in a language program? How can mechanisms be set in place to ensure that materials facilitate creative teaching rather than dominate teachers' decision making?

4. Examine a commercial textbook and its suitability for a specific teaching context. What criteria would you use to evaluate it? In what way do you think the book would need to be adapted to suit the needs of the program?

5. Use the checklist in Appendix 2 to evaluate a course book. How useful is the checklist for this purpose?

6. Take a chapter from a commercial textbook and discuss how you would adapt it to match your teaching style or the needs of a particular group of learners.

7. Choose some authentic materials (e.g., a magazine article, a section of a TV schedule) and use them to plan teaching materials for a specific teaching context you are familiar with. Decide what the goals of the materials will be and what exercise types you will use with the materials.

8. Examine a set of teaching materials for a specific skill area (e.g., reading, speaking, listening). What exercise types are used in the materials? How appropriate are these exercise types? What other exercise types could have been used in the materials?

9. Observe a teacher using teaching materials or a textbook and document how the teacher uses the materials. In what ways does the teacher adapt and extend the materials?

Appendix 1   Guidelines for developing reading activities (from Crandall, 1995)*

General guidelines for reading activities

In developing reading materials, it is helpful to consider the following general guidelines. The reading text should:

1. Encourage appropriate use of both top-down and bottom-up strategies.
2. Offer opportunities for developing speed/fluency as well as deliberateness/accuracy.
3. Include different text types, rhetorical genres, and topics.
4. Incorporate different types of reading tasks with different purposes (reading to learn, reading to do, reading to evaluate, reading for enjoyment).
5. Offer sufficient interaction with a topic or text to develop content and related vocabulary knowledge.
6. Encourage students to examine their own reading strategies and try out different strategies for dealing with different types of texts or for reading for different purposes.
7. Introduce students to different types of directions encountered in texts and tests.
8. Assist in identifying and building culturally variable information needed for text interpretation, while treating positively the students' primary language and culture.

Prereading activities

1. Discussion questions and prewriting activities that help relate the reading to a student's prior experiences, activating and expanding the student's content and formal schemata, building vocabulary, and helping to identify cultural influences that may affect reading comprehension or interpretation. Brainstorming, semantic mapping, and free writing might all be used.
2. Prediction activities that draw attention to the organization of the text and to identification of potential themes and directions the author may take.
3. Skimming activities that provide students with a general idea of the text themes and the organization and development of ideas.

* From *Material Writer's Guide, 1st edition,* by P. Byrd ©1995. Reprinted with permission of Heinle & Heinle, an imprint of the Wadsworth Group, a division of Thomson Learning. Fax 800 730-2215.

4. Questions and other activities that focus on graphic cues such as titles, chapter headings, indentations, and white space, as well as any visuals and other text displays that highlight the organization and relative importance of various themes in the text.
5. Scanning activities that highlight key (including technical) vocabulary, as well as names, dates, places, and other important facts.
6. Questions that can serve to focus a student's attention during reading as well as engage a student sufficiently to motivate doing the reading.

Activities for use during reading

1. Filling out a graphic while reading: completing a Venn diagram (for comparisons), a flow chart (for processes), a table (for classifications or definitions), or other organizers that reflect the logical relations between ideas in the text and highlight for the student what is important enough to be noted and remembered (Crandal 1993). A variety of forms can also be used in this manner.
2. Guided or controlled writing assignments or discussion questions that encourage students to react to and reflect upon what they are reading at key stages in the process and to note confusion or questions they hope to have answered before the end of the reading.
3. Underlining, highlighting, or note-taking activities that help students develop more effective study skills.
4. Vocabulary building activities that help students find clues for meaning within the text.
5. Periodic paraphrasing and summarizing activities, which encourage students to see how an idea is developed and a text is structured, to draw inferences, and to effectively tie new ideas to prior topics.
6. Timed activities that encourage rapid reading, perhaps combined with questions that require skimming for general answers or scanning for key information.

Postreading activities

1. Vocabulary activities, helping students to expand their vocabulary by applying affixes and roots drawn from the key vocabulary in the reading, using charts and tables to illustrate the relationships between words.
2. Questions to encourage critical analysis and evaluation of the reading.
3. Activities that help students to summarize the text, beginning with partially completed summaries.
4. Cloze activities and sentence strip activities for developing vocabulary, grammar, and discourse knowledge.

5. Journal writing, either monologic or dialogic, to encourage students to reflect on, synthesize, or evaluate what they have read.
6. Application activities, which encourage students to apply what they have read to some task or activity.

Appendix 2   Checklist for evaluation and selection of course books (from Cunningsworth 1995)

Aims and approaches
❏ Do the aims of the course book correspond closely with the aims of the teaching programme and with the needs of the learners?
❏ Is the course book suited to the learning/teaching situation?
❏ How comprehensive is the course book? Does it cover most or all of what is needed? Is it a good resource for students and teachers?
❏ Is the course book flexible? Does it allow different teaching and learning styles?

Design and organization
❏ What components make up the total course package (e.g., students' books, teachers' books, workbooks, cassettes)?
❏ How is the content organized (e.g., according to structures, functions, topics, skills, etc.)?
❏ How is the content sequenced (e.g., on the basis of complexity, "learnability," usefulness, etc.)?
❏ Is the grading and progression suitable for the learners? Does it allow them to complete the work needed to meet any external syllabus requirements?
❏ Are there reference sections for grammar, etc.? Is some of the material suitable for individual study?
❏ Is it easy to find your way around the course book? Is the layout clear?

Language content
❏ Does the course book cover the main grammar items appropriate to each level, taking learners' needs into account?
❏ Is material for vocabulary teaching adequate in terms of quantity and range of vocabulary, emphasis placed on vocabulary development, strategies for individual learning?
❏ Does the course book include material for pronunciation work? If so, what is covered: individual sounds, word stress, sentence, stress, intonation?

❑ Does the course book deal with the structuring and conventions of language use above sentence level, for example, how to take part in conversations, how to structure a piece of extended writing, how to identify the main points in a reading passage? (More relevant at intermediate and advanced levels.)

❑ Are style and appropriacy dealt with? If so, is language style matched to social situation?

Skills

❑ Are all four skills adequately covered, bearing in mind your course aims and syllabus requirements?

❑ Is there material for integrated skills work?

❑ Are reading passages and associated activities suitable for your students' levels, interests, etc.? Is there sufficient reading material?

❑ Is listening material well recorded, as authentic as possible, accompanied by background information, questions, and activities which help comprehension?

❑ Is material for spoken English (dialogues, roleplays, etc.) well designed to equip learners for real-life interactions?

❑ Are writing activities suitable in terms of amount of guidance/control, degree of accuracy, organization of longer pieces of writing (e.g., paragraphing) and use of appropriate styles?

Topic

❑ Is there sufficient material of genuine interest to learners?

❑ Is there enough variety and range of topic?

❑ Will the topics help expand students' awareness and enrich their experience?

❑ Are the topics sophisticated enough in content, yet within the learners' language level?

❑ Will your students be able to relate to the social and cultural contexts presented in the course book?

❑ Are women portrayed and represented equally with men?

❑ Are other groups represented, with reference to ethnic origin, occupation, disability, etc.?

Methodology

❑ What approach/approaches to language learning are taken by the course book? Is this appropriate to the learning/teaching situation?

❑ What level of active learner involvement can be expected? Does this match your students' learning styles and expectations?

❑ What techniques are used for presenting/practising new language items? Are they suitable for your learners?

❑ How are the different skills taught?

❑ How are communicative abilities developed?

❑ Does the material include any advice/help to students on study skills and learning strategies?

❑ Are students expected to take a degree of responsibility for their own learning (e.g., by setting their own individual learning targets)?

Teachers' books

❑ Is there adequate guidance for the teachers who will be using the course book and its supporting materials?

❑ Are the teachers' books comprehensive and supportive?

❑ Do they adequately cover teaching techniques, language items such as grammar rules and culture-specific information?

❑ Do the writers set out and justify the basic premises and principles underlying the material?

❑ Are keys to exercises given?

Practical considerations

❑ What does the whole package cost? Does this represent good value for money?

❑ Are the books strong and long-lasting? Are they attractive in appearance?

❑ Are they easy to obtain? Can further supplies be obtained at short notice?

❑ Do any parts of the package require particular equipment, such as a language laboratory, listening centre, or video player? If so, do you have the equipment available for use and is it reliable?

Appendix 3   Case study of materials development project (adapted from Richards 1995)

Background

Target: To write a two-level conversation course intended primarily for Japan, Korea, and Taiwan, to be used as a text to support conversation classes in universities, junior colleges, and private language schools.

Researching the need for a new series

In planning the course it was necessary to determine what potential users of the course might be looking for. Information was obtained from the following sources:

1. The project editor's interviews with classroom teachers in Japan, Taiwan, and Korea.
2. The publisher's marketing representatives (some twenty people) who are responsible for selling the publisher's existing books and who would also be responsible for sales of the new series. The marketing staff were a key source of information since they are in daily contact with schools and teachers. They know which courses are popular and why, and what kinds of materials teachers are looking for.
3. Consultants. A group of consultants was identified to provide input to the project. These were experienced teachers in the kinds of institutions where the course would likely be used.
4. Students. Through the consultants, information was also sought from students on their views on textbooks and on the materials they were studying from.

Key features of the course

The goal of gathering information from consultants and the publisher's marketing representatives was to develop a preliminary profile of the project, which produced the following specifications of the project:

PROJECT SPECIFICATIONS

Market:	50% Universities
	30% Private language schools and vocational colleges
	20% Junior colleges
Levels:	2
Extent:	96 pp.
Colors:	4
Trim:	8.5 × 11
Starting point:	false beginner
Ending point:	intermediate
Components:	text
	CDs
	audiocassettes
	placement and achievement tests; unit quizzes;
	video (tentative)
Distinguishing features:	learner-centered syllabus based on student questionnaires; student questionnaires within the text; student-centered activities with extensive cognitive skill development; conversation management strategies
Other features:	task-based; extensive graphic organizers; easy to use
Art:	mix of illustrations and photos; sophisticated look for universities
Balance of skills:	75% speaking; 25% listening
Syllabus:	topical
Length of units:	4 pp.; two 2-pp. lessons
Activities per page:	2
Listenings per unit:	2
Number of units:	20
Time per lesson:	50 minutes
Teacher profile:	80% foreign with varied levels of training
Piloting:	Yes

It was decided to involve students in the development of the project to the maximum degree possible. Information was gathered from students through the teachers who were consultants to the project. In order to obtain information about the life and interests of students in the age and social group the course was planned for, a questionnaire was developed which sought information about how students spent their leisure time, what they were interested in learning about American culture, the kinds of books they enjoyed studying from in class, what they found difficult about learning English, what foreign countries they would like to learn more about, and what they thought an ideal conversation text would contain. Over 200 students in 14 institutions completed the questionnaire. Students and teachers were also surveyed to find out the kinds of topics they felt they would like to see in a conversation course. A questionnaire with a list of 50 possible topics for inclusion in the series was developed and sent to a sample of teachers and students.

Developing a syllabus

We decided to work on Book 1 first, and with the help of the editors and the consultants the following topics were selected for Book 1.

1. music	11. health and fitness
2. work	12. the family
3. shopping	13. house and neighborhood
4. making friends	14. school life
5. clothes	15. social English
6. food and eating	16. leisure and entertainment
7. cities and places	17. places and directions
8. special days	18. movies
9. on vacation	19. useful things
10. sports and hobbies	20. television

The unit titles were simply working titles at this stage, and the sequence of units was also provisional, because until the materials were written and field-tested it would be difficult to determine which units were judged to be simple or difficult.

The unit format

After experimenting with half a dozen different proposals, it was decided that each unit would contain five pages and that those five pages would divide into four separate one-page lessons plus a one-page extension activity. Within a lesson there would be two to three exercises that accomplished the presentation, practice, and free production phase of a lesson. There would be at least one listening activity per unit.

Sample unit

Next, one of the topics for Book 1 was used as the basis of a sample unit. This draft itself went through at least six revisions before it was ready for classroom testing. These revisions addressed exercise design, unit flow, and interest level. The plan was to have the sample unit taught by several different teachers in Japan and to conduct focus groups (group meetings in which participants gave feedback on the materials) with teachers and students. The publishers had copies of the unit prepared, with rough black-and-white art and a simple cassette recording of the listening passages.

Piloting the sample unit

The next step in the process was to have the sample lesson taught to see if it worked, to find out whether teachers and students liked it, and to identify what its strengths and weaknesses were. For the piloting the publishers secured the cooperation of a private university in Tokyo, which agreed to pilot the unit. Both the editor and I visited the university, explained the project to the program director, and watched two teachers teach the sample unit to two different classes of young Japanese students. Following the piloting of the unit, the editor and I met with the teachers to discuss the unit, spoke to the students about the material, and also met with a focus group of teachers from the same institution to get their reactions to the unit.

The general reaction to the sample unit was quite positive, although some activities worked better than others and my overall impression of the unit was that the idea of using four single-page lessons was not very successful. The teachers were able to get through two pages in a 90-minute lesson, so it would make sense to have two two-page lessons per unit rather than four one-page lessons. The idea of having a topic-based unit with a variety of short student-centered activities, which contained both language control and language support, seemed to work well. I now had all the information I needed to do a first draft of the whole of Book 1.

Writing the first draft of book 1

I now began writing a first draft of the complete manuscript of Book 1. This included 20 five-page units, each consisting of two two-page lessons and an extra page devoted to a project-based activity. This was sent to seven reviewers. These reviewers were identified by the publisher, and chosen on the basis of their teaching background and their ability to write useful reviews. They were asked to examine the manuscript and to respond to five questions:

1. How much variety and balance is there in the material?
2. How original and distinctive is it, compared to other books available?

3. How would you rate the interest level of the material?
4. What is the overall appeal of the material?
5. If you were the editor, what advice would you give to the author?

A few weeks later the reviewers' comments were received. Their reactions are summarized as follows:

1. *Variety and balance.* Most of the reviewers felt that the book had a good balance and variety of activities. They felt that there were a good number of activities that got away from the mundane, predictable kind of activities seen in many textbooks.
2. *Originality.* Reviewers thought that the most original features of the book were the projects and the surveys, especially the thought-provoking questions in some of the surveys. However, too many exercises were rated as unoriginal, boring, and flat.
3. *Interest level.* The reviewers evaluated each unit in terms of interest level. Most were rated as being of moderate interest, some were of high interest, and others achieved a low rating.
4. *Appeal.* The overall appeal of the book was thought to be high, because of the topics, projects, and survey.
5. *Suggestions.* The reviewers' suggestions can be summarized as follows:

   - Develop and highlight the projects.
   - Provide more language support for the projects.
   - Weed out dull, flat exercises.
   - Consistently maintain thought-provoking questions, puzzles, and highly engaging activities.
   - Focus on "asking for clarification" as a strategy.
   - Build in ways of carrying on a conversation, so that a conversation will not die out because there are no helps or hints as to how to continue it.

The editor also offered his own interpretation of the progress made so far.

Overall, we're off to a good start. There's a nice progression of activities in each lesson; a good focus on conversational language samples; the interviews at the end of each unit are a very good feature; overall, the project work is excellent; and there's a nice predictable structure and progression to the lessons.

What we need to do now is to get more personality and originality into a number of units. The Japanese market is flooded with books based on a functional syllabus, and after all these years it's really hard to do something new and fresh using that approach. The units in this manuscript that are functionally organized (e.g., *Places and Directions, Cities and Places, Leisure and Entertainment*) for me were the least interesting. The units that are based on topics that are really interesting to students *(Music, Movies, Television, On*

Vacation) are by far the most interesting and the most in line with where the market is right now.

The direction the manuscript needs to go in is clear: *more topic-based units, more real-world content and more focus on the world of the students.* As far as the projects are concerned, this is an excellent section that will really add to the appeal of the course, although too many of them involve poster work; we need some more variety here. There are several key topics that are missing: dating, travel, customs, careers, environmental issues, campus life, student lifestyles, dos and don'ts in other countries. Some of these are more appropriate for Level 2. Others can be the focus of existing units.

The editor and I then met to go through the reviews and to look closely at each unit of the draft manuscript to determine what features could be incorporated into the next draft of the manuscript. The main decisions we reached at that meeting were:

- Each book would be reduced from 20 units to 15 units.
- We were undecided about the fifth page in each unit, the project page. For version 2 of the manuscript I would just develop four-page units, while we sought further advice on the feasibility of doing project work with students of very limited oral proficiency.
- More language support should be provided for activities. Fuller lists of words and expressions which students could use for each exercise should be included.
- Each page of the book had to be challenging enough to provide enough material for about 30 minutes of classroom time.
- Each unit should contain one exercise that practices conversation management strategies.
- Every exercise should have some novel or special feature, that is, some special twist to make it more appealing and original.
- Each unit should contain at least one activity that presents real-world content, that is, genuine information about lifestyles in the United States or other countries, to provide something to interest students.

A second version of Book 1 was then written. This contained substantial revisions of the first draft, as well as some entirely new units. Probably 60 percent of the material in the second version of the manuscript was new. This formed the basis of a pilot version of the book.

Piloting the course

The manuscript was now prepared for pilot testing. Rather than have teachers pilot the whole book, the manuscript was divided into three sections and individual teachers were asked to try out different sections in their classes. After they had taught each unit they were asked to complete a questionnaire in which they commented on the unit as a whole and on each exercise in the unit. Some thirty teachers took part in the pilot.

Preparing the final manuscript

From the piloters' comments a further round of suggestions was obtained that formed the basis for the final revisions of the manuscript. During the revision process, exercises were replaced, fine-tuned, and clarified, tape-scripts and art specifications revised, and the manuscript moved forward unit by unit to final content editing, design, and publication. The same process was followed for Book 2. The course was published with the title *Springboard* (New York: Oxford University Press, 1998).

References

Allright, R. 1981. Language learning through communication practice. In C. J. Brumfit and K. Johnson (eds.), *The communicative approach to language teaching.* Oxford: Oxford University Press. 167–182.

Ariew, R. 1982. The textbook as curriculum. In T. Higgs (ed.), *Curriculum, competence and the foreign language teacher.* Lincolnwood, IL: National Textbook Company. 11–34.

Briggs, L. (ed.). 1977. *Instructional design: Principles and applications.* Englewood Cliffs, NJ: Educational Technology Publications.

Byrd, P. 1995. *Material writer's guide.* New York: Heinle and Heinle.

Candlin, C. 1981. *The communicative teaching of English: Principles and an exercise typology.* London: Longman.

Carey, J., and L. Briggs. 1977. Teams as designers. In Briggs 1977. 261–310.

Clarke, D. F. 1989. Communicative theory and its influence on materials production. *Language Teaching* 22(2): 73–86.

Crandall, J. A. 1993. Content-centered learning in the United States. *Annual Review of Applied Linguistics* 13: 111–126.

Crandall, J. 1995. The why, what, and how of ESL reading instruction: Some guidelines for writers of ESL reading textbooks. In Byrd 1995. 79–94.

Cunningsworth, A. 1995. *Choosing your coursebook.* Oxford: Heinemann.

Davison, P. 1998. Piloting – a publisher's view. In Tomlinson 1998. 149–189.

Dudley-Evans, T., and M. St. John. 1998. *Developments in English for specific purposes.* New York: Cambridge University Press.

Grellet, F. 1981. *Developing reading skills.* Cambridge: Cambridge University Press.

Haines, D. 1996. Survival of the fittest. *The Bookseller* (February): 26–34.

Peacock, M. 1997. The effect of authentic materials on the motivation of EFL learners. *ELT Journal* 51(2): 144–153.

Phillips, M. K., and C. Shettlesworth. 1978. How to arm your students: A consideration of two approaches to providing materials for ESP. In *English for Specific Purposes. ELT Documents 101.* London: ETIC Publications, British Council. 23–35.

Raimes, A. 1988. The texts for teaching writing. In B. Das (ed.). *Materials for language teaching and learning.* Singapore: SEAMEO RELC. 41–58.

Richards, J. C. 1995. Easier said than done: An insider's account of a textbook project. In A. Hidalgo, D. Hall, and G. Jacobs (eds.), *Getting started: Materials writers on materials writing.* Singapore: SEAMEO RELC. 95–135.

Richards, J. C. 1990. *The language teaching matrix.* New York: Cambridge University Press.

Rowntree, D. 1997. *Making materials-based learning work.* London: Kogan Page.

Shulman, L. 1987. Knowledge and teaching: Foundations of the new reform. *Harvard Educational Review* 57(1): 1–22.
Tomlinson, B. (ed.). 1998. *Materials development in language teaching.* New York: Cambridge University Press.
Werner, P., M. Church, M. Gill, K. Hyzer, M. Knezevic, A. Niedermeier, and B. Wegmann. 1995. Working with publishers. In Byrd 1995. 173–214.

9 *Approaches to evaluation*

A recurring theme throughout this book has been reflective analysis of the practices that are involved in planning and teaching a language course. This has involved an examination of the context in which the program occurs, of the goals, syllabus, and structure of a course, and how these can be planned and developed, as well as analysis of the teaching and learning that takes place during the course. The focus throughout has been analysis of the different factors that determine the successful design and implementation of language programs and language teaching materials. This overall and interlinked system of elements (i.e., needs, goals, teachers, learners, syllabuses, materials, and teaching) is known as the second language curriculum. However, once a curriculum is in place, a number of important questions still need to be answered. These include:

- Is the curriculum achieving its goals?
- What is happening in classrooms and schools where it is being implemented?
- Are those affected by the curriculum (e.g., teachers, administrators, students, parents, employers) satisfied with the curriculum?
- Have those involved in developing and teaching a language course done a satisfactory job?
- Does the curriculum compare favorably with others of its kind?

Curriculum evaluation is concerned with answering questions such as these. It focuses on collecting information about different aspects of a language program in order to understand how the program works, and how successfully it works, enabling different kinds of decisions to be made about the program, such as whether the program responds to learners' needs, whether further teacher training is required for teachers working in the program, or whether students are learning sufficiently from it.

Evaluation may focus on many different aspects of a language program, such as:

- *curriculum design:* to provide insights about the quality of program planning and organization

- *the syllabus and program content:* for example, how relevant and engaging it was, how easy or difficult, how successful tests and assessment procedures were
- *classroom processes:* to provide insights about the extent to which a program is being implemented appropriately
- *materials of instruction:* to provide insights about whether specific materials are aiding student learning
- *the teachers:* for example, how they conducted their teaching, what their perceptions were of the program, what they taught
- *teacher training:* to assess whether training teachers have received is adequate
- *the students:* for example, what they learned from the program, their perceptions of it, and how they participated in it
- *monitoring of pupil progress:* to conduct formative (in-progress) evaluations of student learning
- *learner motivation:* to provide insights about the effectiveness of teachers in aiding students to achieve goals and objectives of the school
- *the institution:* for example, what administrative support was provided, what resources were used, what communication networks were employed
- *learning environment:* to provide insights about the extent to which students are provided with a responsive environment in terms of their educational needs
- *staff development:* to provide insights about the extent to which the school system provides the staff opportunities to increase their effectiveness
- *decision making:* to provide insights about how well the school staff – principals, teachers, and others – make decisions that result in learner benefits

(Sanders 1992; Weir and Roberts 1994)

Since the 1960s, curriculum evaluation has become of increasing interest to educators and curriculum planners. Funding for national curriculum projects in many parts of the world was often linked to a requirement to provide evaluation reports that demonstrated accountability, that helped guide improvement of ongoing projects, and that documented what happened in curriculum projects. Increasingly since then, schools, program administrators, and teachers have had to be accountable for the funds they received or for the programs they have been responsible for, and this has created the need for an understanding of the nature of curriculum evaluation. The scope of evaluation has moved from a concern with test results to the need to collect information and make judgments about all aspects of the curriculum, from planning to implementation (Hewings and Dudley-Evans 1996).

Purposes of evaluation

Weir and Roberts (1994) distinguish between two major purposes for language program evaluation, program accountability, and program development. Accountability refers to the extent to which those involved in a program are answerable for the quality of their work. Accountability-oriented evaluation usually examines the effects of a program or project at significant end points of an educational cycle and is usually conducted for the benefit of an external audience or decision maker. Development-oriented evaluation, by contrast, is designed to improve the quality of a program as it is being implemented. It may involve staff who are involved in the program as well as others who are not and may have a teacher-development focus (Weir and Roberts 1994, 5). The different purposes for evaluation are referred to as *formative, illuminative,* and *summative* evaluation.

Formative evaluation

Evaluation may be carried out as part of the process of program development in order to find out what is working well, and what is not, and what problems need to be addressed. This type of evaluation is generally known as *formative evaluation.* It focuses on ongoing development and improvement of the program. Typical questions that relate to formative evaluation are:

• Has enough time been spent on particular objectives?
• Have the placement tests placed students at the right level in the program?
• How well is the textbook being received?
• Is the methodology teachers are using appropriate?
• Are teachers or students having difficulties with any aspect of the course?
• Are students enjoying the program? If not, what can be done to improve their motivation?
• Are students getting sufficient practice work? Should the workload be increased or decreased?
• Is the pacing of the material adequate?

   Information collected during formative evaluation is used to address problems that have been identified and to improve the delivery of the program.

Example 1: During the implementation of a new primary course in an EFL context it is found that rather than using the task-oriented communicative methodology that provides the framework for the course, a number of teachers are resorting to a teacher-dominated drill and practice mode of teaching that is not in harmony with the course philosophy. In order to address this problem a series of Saturday morning workshops are held to identify the kinds of problems teachers are having with the materials. Videos are used to model more appropriate teaching strategies and teachers agree to attempt to implement in their classrooms some of the techniques they have seen demonstrated and to report back on their experiences at subsequent workshops.

Example 2: A few weeks after a course on integrated skills has started, it is found that there are different perceptions of what the priorities in the course are. Teachers are spending very different amounts of time on different components of the course and are emphasizing different things. A series of meetings are held to review teachers' understanding of the course objectives and to further clarify the weighting that should be given to different course components. Peer observation is then suggested as a way for teachers to compare teaching styles and priorities and to enable them to achieve a consensus concerning teaching practices.

Example 3: A 10-week course on conversation skills has been started for a group of low-level learners. Pronunciation is not a major element of the course because it is assumed that most pronunciation problems will sort themselves out after a few weeks. However, four weeks after the course has commenced, teachers report that a number of students have persistent and major pronunciation problems that the course is not addressing. It is decided to refocus one section of the course to include a pronunciation component. Individual diagnostic sessions are held with students who have the most serious pronunciation problems, and laboratory work as well as classroom time is allotted to systematic pronunciation work for the remainder of the course.

Illuminative evaluation

Another type of evaluation can be described as *illuminative evaluation*. This refers to evaluation that seeks to find out how different aspects of the program work or are being implemented. It seeks to provide a deeper understanding of the processes of teaching and learning that occur in the program, without necessarily seeking to change the course in any way as a result. Questions that might be asked within this framework are:

- How do students carry out group-work tasks? Do all students participate equally in them?
- What type of error-correction strategies do teachers use?

- What kinds of decisions do teachers employ while teaching?
- How do teachers use lesson plans when teaching?
- What type of teacher-student interaction patterns typically occur in classes?
- What reading strategies do students use with different kinds of texts?
- How do students understand the teacher's intentions during a lesson?
- Which students in a class are most or least active?

Example 1: A teacher is teaching a course on reading skills and has developed a course which focuses on a wide variety of reading skills, such as skimming, scanning, reading for details, surveying a text, critical reading, and vocabulary development. All of the skills receive regular focus throughout the course. The teacher is interested in finding out what the students perceive to be the main point of the course. Students complete a short questionnaire at different times during the course in order to describe their perceptions of what the course is seeking to achieve. At times there is a different perception on the part of students as to the purpose of different activities, or even of whole lessons. After reflecting on this phenomenon, the teacher comes to understand that learners' perceptions of a course may reflect what they are most interested in or what they feel they need most help with at a particular point in time.

Example 2: A teacher is interested in learning more about teacher–student interaction in her own classroom. She invites a colleague to visit her class and to carry out a series of classroom observations. The observer is given the task of noting how often the teacher interacts with different students in the class and the kind of interaction that occurs. This involves noting the kinds of questions the teacher asks and the extent to which she acknowledges and follows up on students' questions. From the data collected by the observer, the teacher is able to assess the extent to which she or the students control classroom interaction and gets a better understanding of how she uses questions to "scaffold" lesson content.

Example 3: A teacher wants to find out more about how students carry out group work and whether he is sufficiently preparing students for group-work tasks. He arranges to record different groups of students carrying out a group-work task and reviews the recordings to find out the extent to which students participate in group discussions and the kind of language they use. On reviewing the recordings, the teacher is pleased to note that the strategy of assigning each member of a group a different role during group tasks –

such as coordinator, language monitor, or summarizer – is proving effective in ensuring that group members participate actively in tasks.

Much classroom action research or teacher inquiry can be regarded as a type of illuminative evaluation. Block (1998) discusses the importance of this type of evaluation in understanding learners' interpretations of the language courses they attend and how learners make sense of their lessons. He suggests that teachers interview learners regularly to find out how they interpret what is going on in a course. Richards and Lockhart (1994) describe a piece of classroom action research of this kind carried out by two primary school teachers who sought to understand the following questions about their classes:

- What learning strategies were used by successful learners in their classes?
- Do the learners use English outside of the classroom?
- Do they feel good about learning English?

The teachers collected information on two learners over a term, using classroom observation, learner journals, and interviews. They found that the successful learners had identified a number of helpful learning strategies that they applied in different ways; for example, in helping to remember things they had studied, the children gave these examples:

It is easy to remember when you listen.
I do it over and over again.
I practice with friends and family.
I stick sentences on my wall in my room.
I spend lots of time going over with my book because I like it and I learn. I
   would still study it if my teacher didn't see it or mark it.

From their classroom research the teachers concluded:

Even though we didn't learn anything particularly surprising from our investigation, it was useful to confirm and make explicit some things which we knew intuitively. We have learned a useful strategy to use in order to more effectively facilitate our students' learning. The strategy involves asking the following questions:

How did you go about doing this?
Which way of doing this works best for you?

Summative evaluation

A third approach to evaluation is the type of evaluation with which most teachers and program administrators are familiar and which seeks to make decisions about the worth or value of different aspects of the curriculum. This is known as *summative evaluation.* Summative evaluation is concerned with determining the effectiveness of a program, its efficiency, and to some extent with its acceptability. It takes place after a program has been implemented and seeks to answer questions such as these:

- How effective was the course? Did it achieve its aims?
- What did the students learn?
- How well was the course received by students and teachers?
- Did the materials work well?
- Were the objectives adequate or do they need to be revised?
- Were the placement and achievement tests adequate?
- Was the amount of time spent on each unit sufficient?
- How appropriate were the teaching methods?
- What problems were encountered during the course?

In order to decide if a course is effective, criteria for effectiveness need to be identified. There are many different measures of a course's effectiveness and each measure can be used for different purposes. For example:

Mastery of objectives: One way of measuring the effectiveness of a course is to ask "How far have the objectives been achieved?" Each objective in the course is examined and criteria for successful achievement of each objective are chosen. In a course on speaking skills, for example, an objective might be: *In group discussions students will listen to and respond to the opinions of others in their group.* The extent to which the students have mastered this objective at the end of the course can be assessed by the teacher's observing students during group discussions and recording on a scale the extent to which they listen and respond to opinions. If students' performance on this objective is poor, reasons would have to be identified. Perhaps, for example, insufficient opportunities were provided in the course for students to practice this task, perhaps the materials relating to this objective were too difficult or not sufficiently interesting.

However, mastery of objectives does not provide a full picture of the effectiveness of a course. Objectives can be achieved despite defects in a course. Students may have realized that the teaching or materials were poor or insufficient and so spent a lot of extra time in private study to compensate for it. Or perhaps mastery of an objective was achieved but the same objective could have been covered in half the amount of time devoted to it. Or the program might have achieved its objectives but students have a very negative perception of it because it was not stimulating or the pacing was inappropriate.

Performance on tests: Apart from the relatively informal way of assessing mastery of objectives, formal tests are probably the commonest means used to measure achievement. Such tests might be unit tests given at the end of each unit of teaching materials, class tests or quizzes devised by teachers and administered at various stages throughout the course, or as formal exit tests designed to measure the extent to which objectives have been achieved. Weir (1995) points out that achievement tests can have an important washback effect on teaching and learning. They can help in the making of decisions about needed changes to a program, such as which objectives need more attention or revision. Brindley (1989) reports, however, that in programs he studied in Australia, teachers preferred to rely on informal methods of ongoing assessment rather than formal exit tests. About the use of informal methods, he comments:

This does not seem to be sufficiently explicit to meet the expectations and requirements of either administrators or learners for more formal information on learners' achievement of a course or a unit. . . . The informal methods of ongoing assessment provided by teachers do not provide the kind of explicit information on achievement required by learners and administrators. (Brindley 1989, 43)

Weir (1995) argues for the need for better measures of summative evaluation and for the development of progress-sensitive performance tests for use during courses.

Measures of acceptability: A course might lead to satisfactory achievement of its objectives and good levels of performance on exit tests yet still be rated negatively by teachers or students. Alternatively, if everyone liked a course and spoke enthusiastically of it, could this be more important than the fact that half the students failed to reach the objectives? Acceptability can be determined by assessments of teachers and students. Reasons for a course being considered acceptable or unacceptable might relate to such factors as time-tabling, class size, choice of materials, or teachers' teaching styles.

Retention rate or reenrollment rate: A measure of a course's effectiveness that may be important from an institution's point of view is the extent to which students continue in the course throughout its duration and the percentage of students who reenroll for another course at the end. If there is a significant dropout rate, is this true of other courses in the institution and the community or is it a factor of a given course only?

Efficiency of the course: Another measure of the success of a course is how straightforward the course was to develop and implement. This may be a reflection of the number of problems that occurred during the course, the time spent on planning and course development, the need for specialized materials and teacher training, and the amount of time needed for consultations and meetings.

Examples of different approaches to determine program effectiveness are given in the appendix.

Issues in program evaluation

Weir and Roberts (1994, 42) propose a broad view of evaluation that is characterized by:

- a need for both insider and outsider commitment and involvement to ensure adequate evaluation
- a central interest in improvement, as well as the demonstration of the "product value" of a program or project or their components
- an associated commitment to a deeper professional understanding of the processes of educational change, as well as the results of that change
- systematic documentation for evaluation purposes both during implementation and at the beginning and end of a program or project's life
- a willingness to embrace both qualitative and quantitative methodology appropriate to the purpose of the evaluation and the context under review

These principles raise the following issues in the evaluation process.

The audience for evaluation

There are many different levels of involvement in language teaching programs and this creates different kinds of audiences for evaluation. In planning an evaluation it is important to identify who the different audiences are and what kind of information they are most interested in (Elley 1989). For example, in developing a new textbook series for public schools funded by the ministry of education, officers in the ministry (who might not be specialists in language teaching) might be primarily interested in how the money provided for the project is spent and whether all components of the project (student books, teacher guides, and workbook) are available in schools by a specific date. Teachers teaching the materials might be primarily concerned that the books provide sufficient material for all the classes on the school timetable. An outside consultant might be interested in the design of the materials and the kind of classroom interaction and language practice they provide for. Vocational training centers might be interested in whether the course prepares school leavers for vocational training programs conducted in English. Therefore, evaluation has to satisfy all interested parties. Questions different audiences might be interested in are:

Students
What did I learn?
How well did I do compare to others?
How well will I rate this course?
How will this help me in the future?
Do I need another course?

Teachers
How well did I teach?
What did my students learn?
Were my students satisfied with the course?
How useful were the materials and course work?
How effective was the course organization?

Curriculum developers
Is the design of the course and materials appropriate?
What aspects of the course need replacing or revising?
Do teachers and students respond favorably to the course?
Do teachers need additional support with the course?

Administrators
Was the time frame of the course appropriate?
Were the management and monitoring of the course successful in identifying and rectifying problems?
Were clients' expectations met?
Were testing and assessment procedures adequate?
Were resources made use of?

Sponsors
Was the cost of the course justified?
Did the course deliver what was promised?
Was the course well managed?
Is the reporting of the course adequate?

Shaw and Dowsett (1986, 66) suggest that three audiences are identifiable for all summative evaluation of language courses:

- *other teachers in the program,* for course design and planning purposes (the main audience)
- *managers of the institution or program,* for the purpose of determining course offerings and placement
- *the curriculum support or development unit,* for the purpose of monitoring the curriculum

In planning an evaluation, these different kinds of audiences need to be carefully identified and the results of the evaluation presented in a way that is appropriate for each audience.

Participants in the evaluation process

Two types of participants are typically involved in evaluation – insiders and outsiders. Insiders refers to teachers, students, and anyone else closely involved in the development and implementation of the program. Formative evaluation, for example, is often carried out by teachers who can monitor a course as it develops to check the extent to which it is working, what difficulties are encountered, how effective the materials are, and what modifications would ensure the smooth running of the program. Students are often key participants in the summative evaluation of the program, providing evidence of their gains in language proficiency and completing evaluations on the way the program was taught and the relevance of what they have learned to their needs. An important factor in successful program evaluations is often the involvement of key insiders in the process of designing and carrying out the evaluation, because as a consequence, they will have a greater degree of commitment to acting on its results. Outsiders are others who are not involved in the program and who may be asked to give an objective view of aspects of the program. They may be consultants, inspectors, or administrators whose job it is to supplement the teachers' perceptions of what happened in a course with independent observation and opinion.

Quantitative and qualitative evaluation

Quantitative measurement refers to the measurement of something that can be expressed numerically. Many tests are designed to collect information that can be readily counted and presented in terms of frequencies, rankings, or percentages. Other sources of quantitative information are checklists, surveys, and self-ratings. Quantitative data seek to collect information from a large number of people on specific topics and can generally be analyzed statistically so that certain patterns and tendencies emerge. The information collected can be analyzed fairly simply because subjective decisions are not usually involved. Traditionally, quantitative data are regarded as "rigorous" or conforming to scientific principles of data collection, though the limitations of quantitative information are also recognized, hence the need to complement such information with qualitative information.

Qualitative measurement refers to measurement of something that cannot be expressed numerically and that depends more on subjective judgment or observation. Information obtained from classroom observation, interviews, journals, logs, and case studies is generally qualitative. Qualitative approaches are more holistic and naturalistic than quantitative approaches and seek to collect information in natural settings for language use and on authentic tasks rather than in test situations. They are normally more exploratory and seek to collect a large amount of information from a fairly small number of cases. The information obtained is more difficult to analyze because it is often open-ended and must be coded or interpreted. Qualitative data are sometimes regarded as "soft" or less rigorous than quantitative data, but such information is essential in many stages of program evaluation.

In language program evaluation both quantitative and qualitative approaches to collecting information are needed, because they serve different purposes and can be used to complement each other. For example, in assessing students' achievement at the end of a course on spoken English, the following procedures might be used:

- performance on an oral proficiency test (quantitative)
- observation of students' performance on classroom tasks with evaluation using a holistic rating scale (qualitative)
- students' self-assessment of improvement in their speaking skills (qualitative)

The importance of documentation

The more documentation that is available about a course, the easier it is to arrive at decisions about it. Relevant documentation includes:

Course statistics: information on why students chose the course, student numbers, attendance, class size, drop outs, use of facilities such as library or self-access center. This kind of information provides an overview of the nature of the course and its mode of operation and may reveal certain patterns or problems.

Relevant course documents: compilation of all relevant documentation about the course, such as descriptions, publicity materials, statements of aims, objectives and syllabus, course materials, teaching guides, newsletters, newspaper articles, reports of planning meetings.

Course work: examples of tests, class assignments, examples of students' work.

Written comments: anything that has been written about the course by external assessors, teachers, learners, managers.

Institutional documents: anything that is available about the school or institution, hiring policy, job descriptions, needs analyses that have been conducted, reports of previous courses.

Course reviews: a written account of a course, prepared by the teacher or teachers who taught the course. This should be both descriptive and reflective. It should be an account of how the course progressed, what problems occurred, the perceived strengths and weaknesses of the course, and suggestions for the future. A well-written review is a useful resource for others who will teach the course and also provides a record of the course. Weir and Roberts (1994, 12) comment: "One shudders to think how many times the wheel has been reinvented in ELT programs and projects around the world. Where is the collective memory of decades of projects? Where does one go to learn from the mistakes and successes of similar projects in the past?"

Implementation

The purpose of evaluation is to promote review, reflection, and revision of the curriculum based on careful compilation of information from a variety of different sources. In order to make decisions based on the evaluation, it is first necessary to review the process of evaluation to ensure that the evaluation was adequately designed. Questions that help determine this are:

Scope: Does the range of information collected include all the significant aspects of the program being evaluated?

Audience: Does the information collected adequately serve the needs of all the intended audiences?

Reliability: Has the information been collected in such a way that the same findings would be obtained by others?

Objectivity: Have attempts been made to make sure that there is no bias in the collecting and processing of information?

Representativeness: Does the information collected accurately describe the program?

Timeliness: Is the information provided timely enough to be of use to the audiences for the evaluation?

Ethical considerations: Does the evaluation follow accepted ethical standards, e.g., such that confidentiality of information is guaranteed and information obtained in a professional and acceptable manner? (Stufflebeam, McCormick, Brinkerhoff, and Nelson 1985)

Once it has been determined that the evaluation meets acceptable standards of adequacy, it is necessary to decide how to make use of the information obtained. The following processes are normally involved:

- Review all information that was collected.
- Disseminate findings to relevant parties.
- Decide on what changes may need to be made.
- Identify costs and benefits of proposed changes.
- Develop a plan for implementation of changes.
- Identify those responsible for taking follow-up action.
- Establish procedures for review of the effectiveness of changes.

Examples of the kinds of changes that might be needed are:

- revision or replacement of some of the course objectives
- preparation of supplementary materials to complement the textbook
- selection of a new textbook to replace the book currently being used
- reorganization of the sequence of skills taught within a course
- organization of in-service training for teachers
- development of a peer review process for teachers
- development of a materials writing project
- setting up of brown-bag seminars for staff to share teaching experiences

Procedures used in conducting evaluations

Many of the procedures used in conducting evaluation are similar to those described elsewhere in this book, though their purposes may be different. Chapter 3 on needs analysis, for example, discusses a number of the procedures mentioned here from the perspective of needs analysis. Here we will consider their role in evaluation and possible advantages or limitations of each procedure.

Tests

Different types of tests can be used to measure changes in learning at the end (or at intermediate stages) of a course. These tests may be:

- institutionally prepared tests such as exit tests designed to measure what students have learned in the course
- international tests, such as TOEFL, IELTS, or a Cambridge proficiency test if these are related to the course aims and content
- textbook tests such as those provided in teachers' manuals or as part of a commercial course
- student records, such as information collected throughout the course based

on course work or continuous assessment. This information may be used to arrive at a final score or grade for a student without using a final test.

Advantages: Tests can provide a direct measure of achievement, particularly if they are based on student performance, that is, they are criterion-referenced.

Disadvantages: It is not always easy to be sure that changes in learning as measured by tests are a direct result of teaching or are linked to other factors. And if there is poor performance on achievement tests, this does not identify the cause of the problem. Is it the teacher, the materials, the students, or the course? Further investigation is normally needed. Student evaluation should not be confused with course evaluation. In addition, sound tests – tests that reflect principles of reliability and validity – are difficult to construct.

Comparison of two approaches to a course

Two different versions of a course might be taught and the results as measured by student achievement compared. The comparative approach seeks to compare the effects of two or more different teaching conditions. It measures the efficiency of the curriculum by comparing the relative effectiveness of two different ways of teaching it.

Advantages: The comparative approach seeks to control all relevant factors and to investigate factors rigorously.

Disadvantages: This approach usually imposes artificial constraints on the teacher. One teacher, for example, might be required always to give explicit error correction and another to give only indirect error correction. But because of human factors, it is very difficult to maintain these kinds of differences. It is usually impossible to control all relevant variables and the results are therefore usually inconclusive.

Interviews

Interviews with teachers and students can be used to get their views on any aspect of the course. Normally, structured interviews provide more useful information than unstructured interviews.

Advantages: In-depth information can be obtained on specific questions.

Disadvantages: Interviews are very time-consuming and only a sample of teachers or students can normally be interviewed in depth; hence the representativeness of their views may be questionable.

Questionnaires

These can be used to elicit teachers' and students' comments on a wide range of issues.

Advantages: Questionnaires are easy to administer and information can be obtained from large numbers of respondents.

Disadvantages: Questionnaires need to be carefully designed if they are to elicit unbiased answers, and information may be difficult to interpret. For example, if students indicate that they found a particular unit in a course difficult, follow-up investigation may be needed to determine exactly why they perceived it to be difficult. Was it the unit itself or was it badly taught?

Teachers' written evaluation

Teachers can complete a course evaluation using a structured feedback form that elicits comments on all aspects of the course.

Advantages: Teachers are in a good position to report on a course and a well-designed evaluation form provides information quickly in a way that is easy to summarize.

Disadvantages: The information obtained may be impressionistic and biased, because it presents only the teacher's point of view.

Diaries and journals

Teachers can keep an ongoing record of their impressions and experiences of a course. Diaries provide a narrative record of things the teacher does, problems encountered, critical incidents, time allocation, and other issues.

Advantages: Diaries and journals provide relatively detailed and open-ended information and can capture information that may be missed by other means.

Disadvantages: It is difficult to decide how to use the information obtained. Diaries are impressionistic and unsystematic. They also require cooperation and a time commitment on the part of the teacher.

Teachers' records

Use can be made of available written records of courses, such as reports of lessons taught, material covered, attendance, students' grades, and time allocation.

Advantages: Records can provide a detailed account of some aspects of the course.

Disadvantages: Not all of the information collected may be relevant. Some information may be impressionistic and represent only the teacher's point of view.

Student logs

Students might be asked to keep an account of what happened during a course, how much time they spent on different assignments, how much time they allocated to homework and other out-of-class activities.

Advantages: Provides the students' perspective on the course and gives insights that the teacher may not be aware of.

Disadvantages: Requires the cooperation of students and time commitment. Students may not see the benefit of such an activity.

Case study

A teacher may conduct a case study of a course or some aspect of a course. For example, the teacher might document how he or she made use of lesson plans throughout a course, or trace the progress of a particular learner.

Advantages: Case studies provide detailed information about aspects of a course, and over time the accumulated information from case studies can provide a rich picture of different dimensions of a course.

Disadvantages: The information collected may not be typical or representative, and case studies are time-consuming to prepare.

Student evaluations

Students can provide written or oral feedback on a course both during the course and after it has been taught, commenting on features such as the teacher's approach, the materials used, and their relevance to the students' needs.

Advantages: Student evaluations are easy to obtain, provide feedback on a wide range of topics, and enable large numbers of learners to be involved.

Disadvantages: Information obtained may be subjective and impressionistic and is sometimes difficult to interpret or generalize.

Audio- or video-recording

Lessons can be recorded to provide examples of different teaching styles and lesson formats.

Advantages: Recordings can provide a rich account of teaching in real time and record information that is difficult to document in other ways.

Disadvantages: The presence of the recording instrument or person making the recording can be disruptive and can bias the data. Good recordings are difficult to set up.

Observation

Regular observation of classes may be made by other teachers or a supervisor. Observation is usually more useful if it is structured in some way, such as by giving a specific task to the observer and by providing procedures for the observer to use (e.g., checklists or rating scales).

Advantages: Observers can focus on any observable aspect of the lesson and can provide an objective eye, identifying things that may not be apparent to the teacher. If teachers observe each other's classes, it also provides a basis for follow-up discussion and reflection.

Disadvantages: The observer's presence may be intrusive. As noted earlier, observation is a specialized skill and requires preparation and explicit guidance if it is to be useful.

Weir and Roberts (1994, 134) summarize the focus and procedures available in program evaluation:

Focus	*Procedures*
Teacher beliefs	Pre/Post: questionnaires interviews observations review of lesson plans
Teacher abilities	Observations/videotapes Self-assessment quizzes Pre/Post: questionnaires interviews observations review of lesson plans
Teacher practices	Record of activities Lesson plan reviews Observations/videotapes Interviews Questionnaires
Student behaviors	Student interviews Student questionnaires Teacher logs

Student behaviors	Observation
(cont.)	Teacher interviews
Student learnings	Chapter/unit tests
	Standardized test
	Teacher logs
	Student assignments
	Comparison of present term grades to previous grades (or grades of another group of students)
	Student interviews
	Teacher questionnaires
	Student questionnaires
	Teacher interviews

Discussion questions and activities

1. What procedures can be used to carry out a formative evaluation of a new program as it is being implemented? Identify the goals of such an evaluation for a program you are familiar with and suggest procedures that could be used to achieve these goals.
2. How useful do you think illuminative evaluation is in program evaluation? Discuss a program you are familiar with and suggest information that could be collected as part of the process of illuminative evaluation. What use could be made of the information collected?
3. What do you think are the best ways to measure the effectiveness of a language program? Discuss a program you are familiar with and compare different options for determining its effectiveness.
4. Imagine that you have been asked to visit a school or institution and to conduct an evaluation of its language programs. List some of the questions you would want to ask the school's directors in planning how you will carry out the evaluation.
5. As part of a program evaluation, you want to assess the adequacy of teacher-training provision for teachers in the program. Discuss how you would approach this issue and procedures you could use.
6. Review the two examples given in the appendix. Evaluate the evaluation design and suggest how the evaluation might have been improved or done differently.

Appendix   Examples of program evaluations

Example 1: Evaluation of a primary English course in an EFL country

A new primary English program is developed for an EFL context. English has not been taught previously at this level and will now be taught from year 2 of primary school. Three years are budgeted for the development of materials for the program and for training of teachers. The new course is introduced on a progressive basis over 4 years, beginning with 16 schools in year 1, 32 schools in year 2, and so on. An evaluation is required after the program has been in place for 3 years. The evaluation addresses formative, illuminative, and summative issues. Because not all schools can be examined in depth, the following evaluation plan is developed:

- a questionnaire to all schools and teachers involved in the new program
- an in-depth study of eight representative schools

Time frame: 4 weeks

Audiences for the evaluation:

- curriculum development unit in ministry of education
- ministry of education officials
- schools (teachers and principals)
- teacher trainers in teacher-training colleges

The eight targeted schools were studied in the following way:

- classroom observation
- interviews with teachers and principals
- interviews with students
- tests to determine levels of achievement
- documentation (minutes of teachers' meetings, teachers' reports, teachers' teaching logs)

Three reports are prepared:

- a report for the curriculum development unit
- a report for schools and teachers
- a report for teacher trainers

The first report was an overview and summary of all the information collected and the strengths and weaknesses of the program that were identified, with recommendations for modifications in different aspects of the program as well as more school-based support for some aspects of the program.

The second reports focused on the things students appeared to be learning and problems teachers had reported as well as suggestions from teachers and schools on how aspects of the program could be fine-tuned. Comments on the appropriateness of the teachers' methodology were also included.

The third report commented on the extent to which the teachers were reflecting principles and practices that had been emphasized in the teacher training that all teachers had received. Problems teachers identified were summarized as input to future teacher-training sessions.

Example 2: Evaluation of courses in a private language institute

A large private language institute with up to five hundred students in courses at any given time and offering a range of general English courses as well as company courses wants to develop an evaluation system for its courses and to gather information that will be useful in strategic planning. The emphasis is primarily summative. Other aspects of evaluation (formative and illuminative) are dealt with incidentally by teachers and coordinators.

Audiences for the evaluation:

- the owners and board of directors of the school
- the school director
- coordinators and teachers

Both qualitative and quantitative measures needed to determine the following:

- client satisfaction
- teacher competence
- teacher satisfaction
- adequacy of placement and achievement tests
- adequacy of course curriculum and materials
- adequacy of teaching methods
- efficiency of course development and delivery
- adequacy of administrative structures and support
- course marketing and financial matters

Time frame for the evaluation: 3 weeks

Evaluation data was collected in the following ways:

- *Expert review.* A consultant was hired to review existing curriculum and tests; a marketing consultant was hired to review course marketing and business management practices in the school.
- *Focus groups.* Meetings were held with representative groups of teachers, students, and coordinators to identify strengths and weaknesses of existing practices and to recommend changes.
- *Student evaluations of courses and teaching.* A detailed evaluation form was developed to gather student feedback on different aspects of the courses and the teaching.
- *Observation.* Coordinators were asked to conduct at least two observations of each teacher, to identify teachers' strengths and weaknesses, and to make recommendations for in-service training.
- *Test analysis.* A review team was established to review placement and achievement tests.
- *Test results.* Test scores are reviewed for all classes to determine the percentage of students in each class who achieve a passing grade. If less than 10 percent of students achieve the grade the course is targeted for, closer scrutiny is undertaken to determine the cause.
- *Administrative review.* A management group reviewed all administrative procedures and systems and asked teachers to complete a questionnaire on the adequacy of existing administrative systems.
- *Self-reports.* Teachers provided reports on how much time they spent on course preparation, individual student consultation, reading, professional development and administrative matters.
- *Interviews.* Interviews were held with student representatives to determine students' perceptions of the institute, its teachers, and its programs, and to compare it with other institutions.

Several documents resulted from the evaluation:

- An overall summary of the evaluation and its findings for the principal and to serve as a public document for any interested persons.
- A report for the owners and board of directors of the school that briefly described how and why the evaluation was conducted, an analysis of the strengths and weaknesses that were identified, and recommendations for follow-up action.
- A report for coordinators and teachers with curriculum development responsibilities outlining findings in relation to course offerings, tests, materials, and teaching.

- A report for classroom teachers on the main findings in relation to teachers, teaching, and students. This report served as the focus of working groups who were given the task of recommending changes in course delivery and other areas.
- A copy of all the reports for senior management. This information was to be used to formulate a strategic plan for the next 5 years' operation of the institute.

References

Block, D. 1998. Tale of a language learner. *Language Teaching Research* 2(2): 148–176.

Brindley, G. 1989. *Assessing achievement in the learner-centred curriculum.* Sydney: National Centre for English Language Teaching and Research.

Brown, J. D. 1995. The elements of language curriculum. Boston: Heinle and Heinle.

Elley, W. 1989. Tailoring the evaluation to fit the context. In R. K. Johnson (ed.), *The second language curriculum.* New York: Cambridge University Press. 270–285.

Hewings, M., and T. Dudley-Evans. 1996. *Evaluation and course design in EAP.* Hertfordshire, UK: Prentice Hall Macmillan.

Richards, J. C., and C. Lockhart. 1994. *Reflective teaching in second language classrooms.* New York: Cambridge University Press.

Sanders, J. R. 1992. *Evaluating school programs: An educator's guide.* Newbury Park, CA: Corwin Press.

Shaw, J. M., and G. W. Dowsett. 1986. *The evaluation process in the adult migrant education program.* Adelaide: Adult Migrant Education Program.

Stufflebeam, D., C. McCormick, R. Brinkerhoff, and C. Nelson. 1985. *Conducting educational needs assessment.* Hingham, MA: Kluwer-Nijhoff.

Weir, C. 1995. *Understanding and developing language tests.* Hertfordshire, UK: Prentice Hall Macmillan.

Weir, C., and J. Roberts. 1994. *Evaluation in ELT.* Oxford: Blackwell.

Author index

Subject index

314